To my father Jack Hedges

Career Minister US Information Agency

For the peripatetic life which allowed me to sample

the best of France and the USA

To Jack Richards of Phillips Academy Andover

a true scholar athlete

who imbued me with a love of European history

To Briton C. Busch of Colgate University

law student turned historian

who introduced me to military history and the

history of the British Empire

The Frenchmen
who won the American War of
Independence
Their Contribution and Subsequent Careers

JEFFREY HEDGES

2023

Cover Art: "*The Ranger* and *Drake* in the Chenal du Four, 1778," watercolor by Mark Myers RSMA, F/ASMA

John Paul Jones captained the USS Ranger when it captured HMS Drake in the Irish Sea on April 24, 1778. This watercolor depicts the two ships sailing to Brest using the Chenal du Four channel.

ISBN 979-8-989443-0-1

Éditions Les Haies, Chapel Hill, North Carolina

Table of Contents

Glossary   ix

Chapter One: Special Topics   3

Chapter Two: Expanded Biographies   44

Chapter Three: Sources & Methodology   76

Chapter Four: Naval Biographies   81

Chapter Five: Army Biographies   202

Chapter Six: The Cutting Room Floor   374

Postscript   423

Appendix   447

Bibliography   449

Index   454

Foreword

The purpose of this book is to bring to an English-speaking audience the substantial French historical research and analysis done by French experts on their country's participation in the American War of Independence. The focus is on the naval and army participants serving with French or American forces in a professional or volunteer capacity. Spain's contribution is also addressed.

Firstly, the American War of Independence was an extension of the Seven Years' War for the French and as such was fought on a global scale in India, the West Indies, Cape Verde, the Cape of Good Hope, Minorca, and in the Atlantic. Given the wealth of the Caribbean colonies, protecting them and ensuring unimpeded trade was the prime mission of the French Navy. Some 8000 to 10,500 French soldiers were at Yorktown. The French army at the time had over 60,000 officers and 217,000 men,[1] and France

---

[1]Tom Schachtman, *How the French saved America: Soldiers, Sailors, Diplomats, Louis XVI and the success of*

and Spain together had a 40,000-man army and naval force besieging Gibraltar in 1782–83.

Looking back, the fighting on land and sea was infrequent and often a defeat, such as the siege of Savannah and the bungled relief of Charleston. The French expeditionary corps was engaged in one major battle at Yorktown/Gloucester. French soldiers at Charleston, Newport, Savannah, and Pensacola were deployed directly from the fleet, as was the case with Saint-Simon's troops at Yorktown.

I keep referring to the "French" army but war in the 18th century was an international business. 20 percent of Louis XVI's regiments were foreign, down from 28 percent in 1757. Three foreign legions were raised during the war, one of which served at Yorktown as the Lauzun Legion. It is considered the forerunner of today's Foreign Legion. Several foreign officers served in America with the French fleet and expeditionary corps.

When peace came in 1783, a number of our 'Americains' were at the end of their careers while others

---

the American Revolution (New York, 2017), 27. Hereafter cited at Schactman.

were just starting in their profession. The Revolution, Consulate, and Empire brought years of turmoil and opportunity in various spheres. Some of our 'Americains' reached top governmental and political positions. Others became marshals and admirals, and not only in the French forces. Two of them are buried in the Pantheon—France's top civic honor.

This book is structured to address topics that have been neglected and are relevant to the American War of Independence in its greater scope, provide expanded biographies of the key players, and snapshot biographies of the 244 sailors and soldiers who achieved the rank of *contre amiral* or *general de brigade* before, during, or after the war. More detail is given in the source and methodology section.

vi

Acknowledgements

I want to thank *The Napoleonic Quarterly* podcast created by Alexander Stevenson, which introduced me to Professor Alexander Mikaberidze, who in turn gave me the idea and supported my decision to go forward with this project.

I make no claim to original research as this was done and synthesized particularly well by Lt. Col. (er.) Gilbert Bodinier for the army and Christian de la Jonquieres for the navy. I have cross-checked their work with those of George Six, M. et Mme Quintin, and Etienne Taillemite. *C'est grâce à vos efforts et dedication à votre art que ce livre a été concu et vue le grand jour.*

Thanks also go to the staff of the Davis Library at UNC–Chapel Hill for putting up with my many requests and frequent library card losses.

Un grand merci to David Ferrabee, a self-published author and top PR professional for steering me in the right direction in getting this book out into the world.

The staff at McIntyre Books at Fearrington Village, NC, gave me valuable tips on the art of self-publishing.

The team at Tanager Wealth Management, whose success allowed me to retire to write this book.

Applause for Mollie Madden for her great editing and to Oliver Nash for his cover.

Ben Sweezy, who fixed my database so it could be shared with other students of this period, deserves a special shout-out.

Finally, my heartfelt thanks and appreciation go to Kate, who keeps us all on the straight and narrow. She has supported her husband's and children's crazy ideas for over forty-six years.

Glossary

Aide-de-camp: personal assistant to a general or senior officer. Louis XVI mandated that Count Rochambeau could have six at one time during the American campaign.

Adjutant General: a designated staff officer and was followed by his actual rank, such as colonel.

Brigadier des Armées Navales: title awarded to the most senior *capitaines de vaisseau*. It was supplanted by *chef de division* in 1786.

Brigadier: In the Royal Army this was the intermediary step between colonel and *maréchal de camp*.

Cadet-gentilhomme: Each infantry regiment was allocated two per company. It was the entry level position for a nobleman. The cadet was considered an ordinary soldier but lived with the officers.

Cape Henry: a naval battle between a small French squadron deployed from Newport in March 1781 to interdict the resupply of Benedict Arnold's forces in Virginia.

Capitaine de Vaisseau: the senior non-flag rank. It took most officers twenty years to achieve this rank.

Chef de Division: formerly Brigadier des Armées Navales.

Chef d'Escadre: under the Ancien Regime, first step in flag rank. The title was changed to *contre amiral* under the Revolution.

Enseigne de Vaisseau: the lowest commissioned *officier rouge*, whose next promotion would be to *lieutenant de vaisseau* and then *capitaine de vaisseau.*

Expedition Particuliere: This was the code name for Rochambeau's corps, as the French tried to disguise their intentions.

Flutte: the smallest ship in the French navy, followed by a brulot.

General de Division: the rank that replaced lieutenant general after the Revolution.

Gloucester: a town on the other side of the river above Yorktown, which was a possible escape route for Cornwallis's forces. British troops commanded by lieutenant colonel Tarleton were besieged in the town by a force commanded by the Duc de Choisy.

Garde de Marine: equivalent to a midshipman in the US Navy.

Lieutenant General des Armées Navales: the highest flag rank held on active service under the Ancien Regime.

Maréchal de Camp: under the Ancien Regime, the first step in general rank. It became *chef de brigade* and then *general de brigade* under the Revolution.

Maréchal d'Empire: a personal title awarded by Napoleon to senior generals. It was equivalent to *maréchal de France* under the monarchy and later regimes.

Merite Militaire: It was introduced to reward the mainly Protestant foreign born officers who were not eligible for the Order of Saint Louis in 1759. It was merged with that order at the start of the Revolution but then abolished in 1793.

Mestre de camp: Under the Ancien Regime this rank was the equivalent to an army colonel.

Officier Rouge: noble naval officers distinguished by the color of their coats. The others wore blue coats.

Order of Saint Louis: Created by Louis XIV in 1693, it was awarded for bravery or for at least twenty years' service. It was sought after, as it carried a pension, and the award resulted in the sons of the recipient being able to serve as officers regardless of their social background. Its lowest level was chevalier. The next level was commandeur, limited to eighty holders, and then *grand croix,* limited to forty holders after 1779.

Ouessant: French for Ushant, where the indecisive opening naval battle of the war took place in July 1778 off the coast of Brittany in the western most part of France.

Quiberon Bay: a failed landing of emigrés from a British fleet on the Quiberon Peninsula in Brittany. The aim was to link up with the Vendean insurgents and establish royalist control in western France. The fighting lasted from June 23 to July 22, 1795. Most emigrés taken prisoner were executed as traitors.

Savannah: a joint American and French operation besieging Savannah in September/October 1779. The French fleet was commanded by admiral d'Estaing, who was wounded in one of the assaults. Despite having numerical superiority, the Franco-American forces withdrew without taking the town as d'Estaing needed to get his ships back to the West Indies before hurricane season.

Vice Amiral: under the Ancien Regime there were three of these positions. A fourth was added in March 1784 to recognize Suffren's achievements in the Indian

Ocean. It was stipulated that this position would be eliminated after Suffren's death.

Volunteer: a nobleman who could not obtain an appointment as a *cadet-gentilhomme* in the army or *garde de marine* in the navy.

Chapter 1: Special Topics

French Land Forces in North America

French Army historian Lt. Col. Gilbert Bodinier undertook a compilation of the 1050 army officers and volunteers who served in the American War of Independence for the Ministere de la Guerre historical section in the 1980s.[1]

The participants consisted of:

- 87 Volunteers who joined the Continental Army either of their own volition or on the instructions of the French government. Bodinier raised his estimate to 100 in his second book. These volunteers came from France, Canada, and the West Indies.[2]

---

[1]Gilbert Bodinier, *Dictionnaire des Officiers de l'Armée Royale qui ont combattu aux Etats-Unis pendant la guerre d'independence*, Memoire & Documents 5th edition (Versailles, 2010), 8–9. Hereafter cited as Bod.

[2]Gilbert Bodinier, *Les Officiers de l'Armée royale combattants de la guerre d'independence des États-Unis de Yorktown à l'An II* (ArméeVincennes, 1983), 264, 268. Hereafter cited as Bod. 2. Four of these men served under John Paul Jones in the nascent American navy.

- The d'Estaing Expeditionary Corps to Savannah in October 1779. 285 officers served in this campaign.[3] It consisted of detachments of the Agenois (73 officers and men), Armagnac (277), Auxerrois (191), Cambresis (182), Champagne (67), Dillon (350), Gatinais (80), Walsh (26), Belsunce-Dragon and Condé-Dragons (73), Foix (286), Martinique (88), Guadeloupe, Le Cap (97), and Port-au-Prince (134) regiments, as well as 640 *volontaires de Saint Dominique*, a unit of Black slaves and freemen led by French officers and four independent companies totaling 240 officers and men.

  A detachment of the"Metz artillery was also present at the siege. The main commanders were Jules Bethisy, Arthur Dillon,and Baron Stedingk. The Vicomte de Noailles commanded the reserves (4pprox.. 1040) whose main components were the Saint-Domingue volunteers, and de Sablieres oversaw the entrenchments.[4] Some 4557 officers and

---

[3]Bod., 7.
[4]Scott Martin and Bernard Harris, *Savannah 1779–The British Turn South* (Oxford, 2017), 24. Hereafter cited as Martin. Sablieres is mentioned as a senior officer in this

men served at Savannah along with 28 cannon and 9 mortars.[5]

- Rochambeau's expeditionary corps, which served in America between July 1780 and December 1782 when it was repatriated to France. 496 officers served in the corps.[6]

At Yorktown Rochambeau had the 4800 troops he brought down from Newport,[7] as well as the force transported by de Grasse from the West Indies under the Marquis de Saint-Simon. The French formed the left wing. The Chevalier de Chastellux acted as second in command. There were

---

work while Bodinier refers to a non-commissioned officer serving with the *volontaires de Saint Domingue* named Gleyzal de Sabliere (Bod., 221–22).

[5]Martin, 24.

[6]Bod, 7–8.

[7]Jerome A. Greene, The Guns of Independence: The Siege of Yorktown 1781 (Beatie Ca 2013), page 17. Hereafter cited as Greene. Jean-Christian Petitfils, *Louis XVI* (Paris, 2021), 475, claims there were 10,500 French troops at Yorktown. Hereafter cited as Petitfils. Brendan Morrisey, *Yorktown 1781: The world turned upside down* (Oxford, 1997), 35, provides a list of the French forces at Yorktown of 8670 men, including the 670 artillerymen under Aboville. Hereafter cited as Morrisey.

three brigades plus the Touraine regiment, engineers, and artillery, including those from the Metz Artillerie.[8]

The Bourbonnais brigade commande by Baron de Viomenil consisted of the Bourbonnais regiment under the Marquis de Laval and the Deux-Ponts regiment under the Comte Forbach. The Comte de Viomenil commanded the Soisonnais brigade made up of the Soissonais regiment led by Colonel d'Ollieres and the Saintonge Regiment commanded by the Comte de Custine.

- The reinforcement provided by de Grasse's fleet from the West Indies to support Rochambeau in September–October 1781 at Yorktown. The Marquis de Saint-Simon's brigade consisted of the Agenais, Gatinais and Touraine regiments. These units were commanded by Colonel d'Autichamp, the Marquis

---

[8]Greene, 105. The French whether serving in the Continental or French armies provided all the engineers at Yorktown.

de Rostaing, and the Vicomte de Poudeux, respectively.[9] This force consisted of 214 officers.[10]

- Officers from various regiments on board Grasse's fleet besieging Gloucester. The Duc de Choisy commanded these troops consisting of detachments from the Augoumois, Bourbon, Bresse, Brie, and Colonel General regiments, along with the Lauzun Legion detached from Rochambeau's main force. 27 officers served in this engagement.[11]

Siege of Pensacola, a joint French and Spanish operation March–May 1781, in which detachments of the Agenais, Cambresis, Gatinais, Orleans, and Poitou regiments and Metz Artillerie participated, operating from Admiral Monteil's squadron. 19 officers served in the siege, most of whom later served at Yorktown.[12]

Rochambeau's corps initially consisted of 5000 men drawn from the following regiments: Auxonne artillerie (400 men); Bourbonnais,

---

[9]Greene, 83–86.
[10]Bod., 8.
[11]Bod., 8.
[12]Bod., 8.

Saintonge, Soissonnais, and Royal Deux-Ponts infantry regiments; as well as the Lauzun Legion (600 men), which was a mixed mounted and infantry unit raised by the Duc of Lauzun, as a precursor to the French Foreign Legion.[13] The infantry regiments consisted of two battalions of 500 men each.[14] The expeditionary force was originally to number 8000 and had these additional units were designated to participate: Auvergne, Neustrie, and Rouergue infantry regiments. The navy was unable to provide sufficient transportation, so these regiments were left behind under the command of Wittgenstein and eventually returned to their home depots.[15] Rochambeau never received entire units as

---

[13]Lee Kennett, *The French Forces in America 1780–83* (Westport, CT, 1977), 15. Hereafter cited as Kennett.
[14]Kennett, 23.
[15]George Six, *Dictionnaire Bibliographique des Generaux et Amiraux Français de la Revolution et l'Empire: 1792–1814*, vol, 2 (Paris, 1934, 1971), 430. Born in 1735, Wittgenstein initially served in Germany and then joined the Alsace regiment in 1761. He had a distinguished career in the French army, rising to the rank of lieutenant general during the Revolution. He fought to defend the Tuileries on August 10, 1792, was arrested, and massacred the following month. Hereafter cited as Six.

reinforcements from France during the campaign, but he did receive replacement officers.

Assisting Rochambeau in the command of the corps were the Baron de Viomenil and the Chevalier de Chastellux. Rochambeau was allocated six aides-de-camp (ADC) at the start, but as the war went on the ADCs rotated and numbered a total of 38.[16] The Marquis de Saint-Simon had 8 ADCs.

Rochambeau was supported by several specialist officers. Aboville was the chief artilleryman, Desandrouins was the chief engineer, and Rochambeau's son served as adjutant general. Blanchard served as commissary general and Tarle as Intendant. The corps had a provost marshal and a finance officer, as well as doctors, surgeons, and a chief chaplain. The medical contingent under Coste numbered 100.[17] There were also two dentists and an executioner.

Prior to the arrival of the expedition, Ethis de Corny, who travelled back with Lafayette in March

---

[16]Bod. 2, 247–48.
[17]Kennett, 24.

1780, was assigned to set up a hospital in Providence, RI, and obtain supplies. He was constrained, having been provided with only 60,000 livres in cash and no letters of credit.

The corps was officer heavy: 492 officers served under Rochambeau during the war, and this did not include the volunteers with the Continental Army who were re-integrated into French service. There were 69 artillery,[18] 24 staff,[19] and 18 cavalry officers.[20] The French cavalry played a minor role in the war. There were also 83 foreign officers, including those in the Deux-Ponts and Dillon regiments.[21]

Excluding Yorktown and the fighting on the way down from Newport, the French army was involved in three amphibious operations under naval command at Savannah,

---

[18] Bod. 2, 97.
[19] Bod. 2, 100. A formal general staff was created in June 1783; it consisted of a director and a staff of 24 officers. 8 officers serving in North America were among the first 16 selected.
[20] Bod. 2, 99.
[21] Bod. 2, 91–92.

Gloucester, and Pensacola. The troops involved were either regular or militia units based in the West Indies who were transported by the fleet. As a result, few units fought in more than one major engagement: The Agenais and Gatinais infantry regiments served at both Savannah and Pensacola, while the Metz artillerie served at Savannah. All three units were at Yorktown.

It is estimated that 2112 Frenchmen died in North America in battle, either from their wounds or sickness. 999 of these were soldiers,[22] and the three regiments with the highest losses were the Gatinais, Saintonge, and Soissonnais with over 100 killed each.

French Naval Operations during the War

France's official involvement with the rebellious thirteen colonies began with the signing of the treaty of commerce and amity on February 6, 1778. This was the culmination of many actions over several years, so a fleet of twelve ships of

---

[22]Warrington Dawson, "Les 2112 Français morts aux Etats-Unis de 1777 a 1783 en combatatnt pour l'independence Americaine," *Journal de la société des americanistes* 28, no. 1 (1936): 1–154.

the line and five frigates under Admiral d'Estaing left Toulon in April and arrived off the coast of North America on July 11. There was no opportunity to engage the British in any meaningful fashion, so d'Estaing left for the West Indies on November 4. D'Estaing had two missions: the protection of France's West Indian colonies and their valuable trade of sugar, coffee, cotton, and indigo and cooperating with American forces. On November 17, the British captured Saint Lucia, giving them an excellent location to watch over Martinique and Guadeloupe. D'Estaing tried to dislodge the British but failed miserably.[23]

Meanwhile, back in France the Brest squadron under admiral Orvilliers had fought the British off the coast of

---

[23]Christian de la Jonquieres, *Officiers de Marine aux Cincinnati-Annuaire* (Toulouse, 1988), prreface, 10–15. Hereafter cited as La Jonquiere; Andre Taillemite, one of France's foremost naval historians and president of l'academie de Marine, provided an excellent overview of France's naval contribution in his preface to Christian de La Jonquieres's membership list of the naval officers who became members of the French chapter of the Society of the Cincinnati.

Brittany at Ouessant on July 27. This battle was indecisive but important for French morale.

1779 began with the signing of the Franco-Spanish alliance which aimed to combine the naval forces of both countries to counteract the British fleet. The allies agreed on an invasion of England which would require the Brest squadron to join up with the Spanish fleet out of Cadiz; this occurred on July 26. This combined fleet consisted of forty-five ships of the line and sixteen frigates. Due to sickness among the crews and poor coordination between the forces, the attempt to blockade the English Channel was abandoned, and Orvilliers returned to Brest in mid-November.

In the West Indies, d'Estaing had received reinforcements from France, raising his force to twenty-four ships of the line and ten frigates. He took Grenada on July 4 and fought an indecisive engagement against the British the following day. Summoned to assist the Americans in the Carolinas, he embarked additional militia in Saint-Domingue and sailed to Savannah. The combined Franco-American attack against an inferior force failed in September-October, and the fleet was battered by storms. D'Estaing returned to Europe. On December 18, Admiral

Lamotte-Picquet and his force fended off a British squadron seeking to capture a French convoy.

At Spain's insistence, the French abandoned the project of invading England and instead focused on a joint siege of Gibraltar, which was successfully resupplied by the British in January 1780. In February, Admiral Guichen led a fleet of ships of the line and frigates from Brest to secure the French possessions in the Caribbean and protect the trade routes. Another objective was to capture Jamaica in conjunction with his Spanish allies. Guichen kept the British at bay through three engagements that spring. The link up with the Spanish to invade Jamaica never occurred, and Guichen sailed for France on August 15, successfully escorting a convoy of ninety-five merchantmen.

France had decided to send a military expedition to support the American rebels, and this left Brest under the command of Admiral Ternay in early 1780. It consisted of seven ships of the line and three frigates and transports carrying the 6000-man force commanded by Rochambeau. It arrived in Rhode Island on July 11 where the expedition landed at Newport. The naval minister, Sartine, was replaced by the Duc de Castries on October 14 for not having achieved better results. Castries developed a four-prong strategy: 1) interdict the Channel; 2) continue the siege of Gibraltar; 3) organize a diversion in the Indian Ocean; and 4) deploy sufficient naval forces to America to provoke a decisive battle.

On March 22, 1781, Admiral de Grasse led a powerful fleet including a hundred merchantmen out of Brest and sailed for the West Indies. A week later Suffren and his five-ship squadron peeled off for the Indian Ocean, heading initially for the Cape of Good Hope. Suffren inflicted significant losses on the British in the battle of la Praya off the Cape Verdes islands on April 16.

In late April de Grasse repelled two attacks on Martinique by Admiral Hood. On June 2, he captured Tobago and then sailed to Saint Domingue. Upon arrival he received an urgent request to support the Franco-American force intending to march to Virginia.

In the meantime, Admiral Destouches, who had succeeded Ternay in command at Newport, had sent a small force to intercept supplies intended for the British forces advancing across the Carolinas toward Yorktown. Known as the battle of Cape Henry, it did not prevent the British from landing supplies.

De Grasse embarked 3300 soldiers under the Marquis de Saint-Simon, as well as cash and bullion raised in Havana, to pay the French and American troops. He sailed with twenty-eight ships on August 5 and arrived on the 28 at Cape Henry where he barred access to the British so Cornwallis's forces now at Yorktown could be neither resupplied nor reinforced. Admiral Barras, now in command of the Newport squadron, brought Rochambeau's artillery and ferried troops from Annapolis to Virginia. Yorktown surrendered on October 19.

1781 had been busy elsewhere. On May 2, la Motte Picquet captured the convoy carrying the loot plundered earlier by Admiral Rodney in his sacking of St. Eustacius. A convoy escorted by Guichen was mauled near Brest on December 13. The siege of Gibraltar continued, and Franco-Spanish forces attached Minorca on July 25. The island was eventually captured in February 1782.

1782 was a mixed year for the French. Admiral de Grasse was badly beaten at the battle of the Saintes in April. An attack on Gibraltar failed. Laperouse led a successful expedition in the Hudson Bay, destroying several British fur outposts in May–June. The French were far more successful in the Indian Ocean. Suffren resupplied the Dutch forces at the Cape of Good Hope and then proceeded to Reunion. In December, he successfully supported the forces under Hyder Ali fighting the French in India. Suffren would continue to harass and defeat British naval forces in the region until the end of the war.

The War ended with the signing of the Treaty of Versailles in September. Military operations in the Americas had essentially ceased months earlier when the preliminary agreement was drafted at the start of 1783.

According to Taillemite, the war demonstrated both the progress the French Navy had made since the Seven Years War with accelerated naval construction, the use of annual fleet exercises to develop tactics, and the rapid advancement of talented officers to flag rank. The downside was that the reforms concerning training and officer recruitment were never implemented. France's financial woes also meant that it could not match Britain's spending on new ships.

French & Spanish Support: Key to the Success of the Rebellion

The focus on foreign support for the rebellion has centered on the naval and military forces supplied by the French.

Americans remember Lafayette, d'Estaing, and maybe Kalb but are largely unaware of Spain's role and of the multifaceted support provided by both France and Spain and to a lesser extent Holland.

Back in 1768, Baron Kalb was sent to North America on a fact-finding mission by French foreign minister, Vergennes.[24] To Vergennes's disgust, Kalb reported that the colonists would not approve of foreign interference in their relationship with the mother country. Fast forward seven years and the colonies were in open rebellion and their leaders sought support wherever they could find it.

The colonies had limited financial resources, no arms making capacity, or ability to equip an army or navy. The European powers were initially not ready to support the rebellious colonies openly; however, both France and Spain provided supplies. Gunpowder came from Holland and guns from Liege and Saint-Etienne. In September 1776, Caron de Beaumarchais, author of the *Marriage of Figaro*, provided weapons and supplies through a dummy company

---

[24]Larrie D. Ferreiro, *Brothers at Arms: American Independence and the Men from France and Spain who saved it* (New York, 2016), 25–26. Hereafter cited as Ferreiro.

Roderigue Hortalez et Cie.[25] He was one of twenty-odd French suppliers to the insurgents. Gardoqui acting on behalf of Spain provided 100,000 flints, 45,000 pounds of lead, and blankets.[26] These were shipped from Bilbao to Havana and then onto New Orleans, where the Americans took delivery.

One way for the Americans to generate funds and supplies was by commissioning privateers. It is estimated that 1697 vessels crewed by 58,400 sailors were granted letters of marque or commissions by the Continental Congress.[27] France, Spain, and Holland provided access to their ports in Europe and the Caribbean where American privateers could sell their prizes and resupply themselves. St Eustacius's governor was the first official to recognize the stars and stripes by providing a gun salute on the entrance of an American ship into its harbor on November 16, 1776.[28]

---

[25]Normand Desmarais, *America's First Ally: France in the Revolutionary War* (Philadelphia, 2019), 3–13. Hereafter cited as Desmarais.
[26]Eric Jay Dolin, *Rebels at Sea: Privateering in the American Revolution* (New York, 2022), 61. Hereafter cited as Dolin.
[27]Dolin, throughout.
[28]Barbara W. Tuchman, *The First Salute* (New York, 1988), 5. Hereafter cited as Tuchman.

In 1775 it is estimated that the British annual West Indian sugar trade was worth £3 million, which was twice the amount of the total value of goods exported from the thirteen colonies to the mother country.[29] French disregard for the rules of privateering led to Great Britain's declaration of war. By early 1778, it is estimated that over 559 British merchantmen plying the West Indian trade had been captured by privateers and the Continental Navy for a loss of £2.6 million since the beginning of hostilities. At least 1600 British merchantmen were taken during the war.[30]

The Americans also needed seasoned engineers and artillerymen: France was recognized as having the best of both. Louis XVI gave a two-year leave of absence to four engineers, led by Duportail, to assist the American forces and encouraged Baron Kalb to volunteer as well. His government largely ignored the stream of volunteers—who could be considered as traitors for serving a foreign government—whom Silas Deane recruited while serving as American commissioner in Paris. Deane also recruited Tronson de Coudray as head of both the Artillery and

---

[29]Dolin, 91.
[30]Dolin, 162–63.

Engineers.[31] Over a hundred volunteers from France, Canada, and Louisiana travelled to the colonies, including Lafayette.[32] Not all of them were employed, and many were disappointed by the ranks they were given.

The financial contribution by the French, Spanish, and Dutch was massive. Relying on Wenger's synthesis of several sources, including Ferreiro, the contribution totaled $1.8 billion in 2010 dollars. This included significant cash grants and military supplies provided by France and Spain, the maintenance of French military forces in support of the colonists and loans, including those made by the Dutch.[33] (See Appendix I for details.)

The Haitian Connection

Saint-Domingue,[34] as Haiti was then known, was the jewel in France's colonial empire, especially after the losses of

---

[31]Ferreiro, Chapter 4: The Soldiers.
[32]Bod., 8.
[33]William V. Wenger, *The Key to American Independence: Quantifying Foreign Assistance to the American Revolution* (Self-published, 2018). Hereafter cited as Wenger.
[34]"Six Facts to Remember on the Reparations Owed by Haiti to France," (New York Times May 22 2022). The New York

Canada and large parts of India in 1763. It is estimated that the population of the island was 445,000, with enslaved people representing 95 percent of the total.[35] Much of the fortune of French aristocrats and bourgeois was derived from West Indian sugar colonies.[36] One reason that Bonaparte re-instituted slavery in 1802[37] was that his wife's family had extensive land holdings there,[38] as did several other prominent officials.

Times estimated that the current value of the payments made by Haiti on the loan is $560 million.

[35]François Blancpain, *La colonie Française de saint domingue de l'esclavage à* l'independance (Paris, 2004), 15. Saint Domingue had been annexed to the French crown in 1641. Hereafter cited as Blancpain.

[36]Blancpain, 9. According to the 1788 census there were 27,717 whites, 21,808 free people of mixed race and 405,528 slaves on Saint-Domingue.

[37]Blancpain, 66. In the 1788–89 accounting year, it is estimated that 793 sugar refineries generated 140 million livres worth of sugar for export, or 50% of global production. Total exports from the island that year exceeded 200 million livres. In 1789 95% of all French exports came from Saint Domingue.

[38]It applied only to the sugar producing colonies in the Caribbean and was abolished at the Congress of Vienna in 1815. Ironically it could not be reimposed in Saint-Domingue as the island was in revolt.

Free Blacks and slaves had volunteered to serve in the local militia the Chasseurs-Volontaires de Saint-Domingue raised in March 1779 to defend the colony against British aggression. Ironically, they were embarked in d'Estaing fleet at Cape Francais along with the 156 white grenadiers of their regiment's regular army units for Savannah where they landed in August 1779. Of the 2800 French troops deployed at Savannah, 547 were Volontaires.[39] They served under French officers and were commanded by Rouvray. The Volontaires distinguished themselves in defending the trenches on September 24, losing twelve officers and eighty-eight men.[40] The siege failed with an overall loss of 61 French officers and 760 soldiers killed.[41] Then the fleet and army contingent returned to the Caribbean. In early 1781, 303 men of the

---

[39]Erik Noel, *Les Beauharnais: Une Fortune Antillaise 1756–96* (Paris, 2002).

[40]Martin, 24; Bod. 2, 231.

[41]Clement Lanier, "Les Negres d'Haiti dans la guerre d'independence americaine," *Genese: Journal genealogique et historique Port-au-Prince Haiti* 52 (July 1933): 1–21 (author's own pagination). Hereafter cited as Lanier.

Chasseurs Royaux de Saint-Domingue served at the siege of Pensacola.[42]

The alumni of the Volontaires went on to have distinguished careers in France and Saint Domingue. Henri Christophe,[43] later a general in the Haitian uprising and King of northern Haiti was a 12-year-old volunteer at Savannah. Beauvais, Besse, l'Eveille, Rigaud, and Villatte all reached the rank of brigadier general in the French army.

Louis Jacques Beauvais was a volunteer at Savannah. Having returned to Saint-Domingue, his career is unclear until he was named general de brigade in July 1795. He commanded the Western district of Saint-Domingue (1796). He was transferred back to France in 1799, but he died when his ship capsized.[44]

Jean-Baptiste Belley, along with Joseph Boisson, was elected as one of the two Black representatives to the Convention: The island sent two representatives each from the white, Black, and mulatto communities. The abolition of slavery was voted on the day after he took his seat in the Convention in 1794. He was made a member of the conseil

---

[42]Martin, 87.
[43]Lanier, 12–13.
[44]Martin, 89.

de Cinq-Cents in October 1795 and sat on that body until May 1797. In July 1797, he was promoted to chef de brigade and head of the Saint-Domingue gendarmerie.[45]

Martial Besse was a volunteer at Savannah. Having returned to Saint-Domingue, he was placed on the inactive list in 1783. He was named district commander with the rank of lieutenant colonel by commissioner Santhonax (1793) and then held several other commands. In August 1794 he arrived in France. A year later he was named general de brigade. He returned to Saint-Domingue but did not see much service. Having parlayed with the rebelling slaves he was considered unreliable by the French authorities, and he was transferred back to France in 1802. He was held under house arrest but managed to escape. He eventually returned to Saint-Domingue in 1804.[46]

Jean-Pierre L'Eveille served as a volunteer at Savannah and later commanded the 3rd colonial regiment on the island and was appointed chef de brigade. He was expelled from Saint-Domingue in May 1797 and returned to

---

[45]Six, vol. 1, 70.
[46]Quintin, 90–91.

France. He was part of Leclerc's expedition in 1801 but died shortly thereafter.[47]

Andre Rigaud served in Guadeloupe after Savannah being promoted to lieutenant in 1790 and advanced to lieutenant colonel in 1793. As a result of his capture of Leogane and Tiburon he was promoted to brigadier general. He was betrayed by Toussaint Louverture, who saw him as a competitor and fled to Saint Thomas but was captured by an American privateer on the way. He was brought to France. He then was part of Leclerc's expedition to recapture Saint-Domingue but was sent back to France where he was placed under house arrest.[48]

Jean-Louis Villatte served at Savannah and then at the siege of Pensacola with a detachment of the chasseurs royaux. On his return to the island, he was promoted to major in the militia in Saint-Domingue. He was named lieutenant colonel of an irregular cavalry unit by commissioner Santhonax in October 1793. He was arrested for promoting an insurrection and sent back to France by Toussaint Louverture. He was cleared by a court martial and

---

[47]Six, vol. 1, 93.
[48]Six, vol. 2, 117–18.

remained in France until 1801 when he returned to Saint Domingue with the Leclerc expedition and died the next year.[49]

Laurent Ferou served as a volunteer at Savannah. In 1799 he was named a captain under Rigaud. Pierre Change also served under Rigaud, fought at Leogane and Vertieres. He signed the act of independence and later became a councilor of state.[50]

Jean-Baptiste Chavannes served at Savannah. He joined Vincent Oge in October 1790 when the latter landed at Cap-Français to foment a rebellion. They raised a force of roughly 1000 but were defeated and sought refuge in the Spanish part of the island. They were extradited, tried, and executed by being hammered to death.[51]

On the night of August 22, 1791, the first rebellion broke out in Saint-Domingue. It declared its independence in November. Napoleon sent an expeditionary force in 1801 to recapture Saint-Domingue under his brother-in-law Leclerc and Rochambeau fils. The rebellion continued intermittently until 1803 when Haiti became the second

---

[49]Six, vol. 2, 371–72.
[50]Six, vol. 2, 554–55.
[51]Lanier, 12.

independent country in the Americas.[52] France imposed reparations of 150 million francs for the loss of the planters' land and slaves in 1825: This was finally repaid in 1947.[53]

Army Reforms and Education

A myth of the French Revolution is that the Second Estate or nobility was generally united in its aims and outlook. France had two "classes" of nobles: of the sword and of the pen. This, however, is a simplistic view as the modest traditional nobility and high nobility had little in common besides their pedigree. The bourgeoisie monopolized the administrative positions as nobles of the pen. For the small nobility, service as an officer in the army or navy was the major and only socially acceptable professional outlet.[54] The

---

[52]Nikole Hannah-Jones, *The 1619 Project* (New York, 2021), 106–07. Hereafter cited as Hannah-Jones.

[53]Hannah-Jones, 109.

[54]Guy Chaussinand-Nogaret, *The French Nobility in the Eighteenth Century; From Feudalism to Enlightenment* (Cambridge, 1985), 52–53 Hereafter cited as Nogaret. He estimated that a maximum of 250 families in France, including the courtiers at Versailles, had incomes of over 100,000 livres annually. 3600 families had incomes of 10,000–50,000 livres (representing 13 percent of the nobility). A further 7000 families had incomes between 4000 and 10,000 livres, and they accounted for a quarter of

high or court nobles were either from ancient families or had obtained titles by purchasing government positions. 92 percent of colonels in 1763 were from the high nobility or sons of holders of the order of Saint Louis.[55]

Reforms started in the mid-eighteenth century. In 1750, there was an attempt to broaden access to the officer corps by increasing the number of nobles by granting non-noble generals a title and allowing candidates whose families had served three generations in the army to qualify. Only 200 families were eligible, so this reform had little impact.[56]

In 1751, the king opened a military academy in Vincennes (later moved to near the Champs de Mars in Paris) for eighty students. The program consisted of a four-year course, which included writing, math, drawing, and German. The military arts were only added in the third

---

the total. The largest group representing 41 percent of the nobility were 11,000 families with incomes between 1000 and 4000 livres.

[55]Gilbert Bodinier, *Les Officiers du Consulat et de l'Empire* (Versailles, 2014), 13. Hereafter cited as Bod. 3.

[56]Rafe Blaufarb, *The French Army 1750–1820: Careers, Talent and Merit* (Manchester, 2002), 20. Hereafter cited as Blaufarb.

year.[57] A second one was opened at La Fleche in 1764 as a preparatory school for the academy. Entry was limited to poorer nobles, and they were awarded bursaries to attend.[58] The Paris academy was closed, but twelve provincial academies were opened in 1776, including Brienne where Napoleon would study.

A specialist artillery school was established in 1756 at Baupaume, followed by a further seven specialist schools. Mezieres, the engineering school, was founded in 1747. Students were at least 15 years old and had to prove they were either members of the nobility or the sons of senior non-noble officers or of holders of the order of Saint Louis. Upon entry the student became a brevet 2nd lieutenant and received pay. They served two years with artillery, engineering, and infantry units and at the end were examined by senior officers before being commissioned into the corps.[59]

---

[57]Leon Mention, *L'Armée de l'Ancient Regime: De louis XIV a la Revolution* (n.p., 2022), 78–80. Hereafter cited as Mention.

[58]Blaufarb, 20.

[59]Mention, 208.

France was ahead of its time establishing army medical schools in the 1770s at Lille, Metz, and Strasbourg. Students came from civilian schools or had been apprentices. Graduates followed an established career path. The position of inspector general for medical services was created, reporting directly to the Minister of War.[60]

After the disaster of the Seven Years' War when France lost Canada and most of its Indian possessions to the Great Britain, there was a root and branch reform of the army. The impetus was not only to restore French military power and prestige but also to handle the social pressures within the aristocracy, whose main professional outlet was serving in the armed forces.

Under War Minister Saint-Germain there were significant changes. The main one was that companies were no longer the property of their captains,[61] and administrative matters were now dealt with by the army administration at the regimental level. All personnel records were centralized. Thousands of officers including Lafayette were reformed or let go as being surplus to requirements. The king's

---

[60]Mention, 277–78.
[61]Blaufarb, 23.

household troops were reduced by 750 soldiers, and the musketeers and grenadiers disbanded. These units consisted of nobles who bought their positions and rarely served in the field.

The career of an engineer was well defined: two years of instruction at the Mezieres school, followed by a two-year stint with either an infantry or artillery regiment and then a practical assignment under an engineer at a fort or army facility. The training ended with an exam whose successful result led to an appointment as a lieutenant.

Saint-Germain strove to reduce the king's household troops, which were filled even at the soldier level with rich aristocrats and totaled 10,000.[62] These units were bloated and not ready for war. He succeeded in abolishing the musketeers of d'Artagnan fame and downsizing the Gardes du Corps, eliminating 3450 posts. His associate Guibert proposed a more radical solution: reducing the guards regiments and cutting over 1200 senior and junior officer posts. Significant cuts were approved by the Army Council, but implementation did not reduce the budget. Quite to the

---

[62]Blaufarb, 32.

contrary, the army had to repurchase the commissions which yielded a standard 5 percent income.[63]

Saint-Germain was succeeded by Segur in 1777. The aim of the Segur reforms was to limit the influence of the high nobility and of the rich bourgeoisie who could purchase ranks and regiments and therefore circumvent the promotion system.[64] Most nobles retired after 20–25 years of service with a pension.[65]

Segur wanted to regularize what had become a two-tier career track allowing high nobility to continue to play its part but only serve on active service for four months of the year.[66] The king controlled the promotions for these officers. The lower nobility would advance through seniority and

---

[63]Blaufarb, 38–39.

[64]Blaufarb, 35.

[65]Bod. 2, 156. Officers were entitled to a pension based on years of service: 35 years of service resulted in a pension of half one's pay; 30 years a third; and 25 years a quarter equivalent. The Order of Saint Louis carried an additional pension which varied on the grade of the holder.

[66]Bod. 2, 139. This also reduced the costs to the state. A colonel was entitled to a salary of 12,000 livres a year but would only be paid a third of that for his active service.

receive improved pay. Segur failed to get his reforms approved.[67]

These reforms, whether enacted or not, laid the basis for the later achievement of the Revolutionary and Napoleonic armies.[68]

Social Background & Career Progression

Social status was the main driver of career success in the French military under the Ancien Regime. In his groundbreaking follow up work on the 1150 army officers who served as either volunteers or with their units in the American War of Independence, Bodinier found a close correlation between social background and career progression.[69]

---

[67]Blaufarb, 34–35.

[68]Guibert has been called the Father of the Grande Armée. See Jonathan Abel, *Guibert, Father of Napoleon's Grande Armée* (Norman, OK, 2016), 197. In his *essai general de tactique* (1772) Guibert called for mobility, flexibility, and professionalism. He envisaged meshing the best of French and Prussian military practices. His work on the war council resulted in the Reglement of 1791, which remained the basic manual until the 1830s.

[69]Bod., 8–9.

In both the army and the navy there were distinctions made based on social class, but significant divisions also existed within the aristocracy itself. This was also true of officers of foreign origin. At the start of the French Revolution, 75 percent of all army officers were either nobles or the sons of officers awarded the Order of Saint Louis.[70] Eighty-two officers serving in North America could trace their noble lineage back to the Middle Ages.[71]

Being an officer was the preferred career route for most nobles; however, there were far more applicants than positions. Nobles often served as volunteers or in the ranks to get a foot in the door.

For the high nobility, usually recognized by the number of times their families had received the *honneurs de la cour* or official presentation to the monarch at Versailles, there was a fast-track career path plus the opportunity to serve in the *maison du roi* or household troops. Positions in the *maison du roi* were purchased in return for an annual income. Colonels owned their regiments until 1791. Forty-two out of the fifty-seven most senior army officers serving

---

[70]Bod. 3, 13.
[71]Bod. 2, 78.

in North America came from families that had received the *honneurs de la cour* at least once.[72]

Members of the high nobility entered the army young, as officer positions were sometimes obtained for them at birth. A lieutenant from the high nobility was barely fifteen years old,[73] a captain nineteen, and a colonel could be as young as twenty on appointment and no older than thirty-five,[74] skipping several ranks which applied to everyone else.[75] Lafayette was appointed young as captain, commanding a company which was kept for him until he reached 18.[76]

Officers from the lower nobility reached the rank of lieutenant colonel in their mid-forties.[77] Most officers retired with the rank of captain. It should be noted that high nobility did not mean ancient nobility. Being at court required

---

[72]Bod. 2, 109.
[73]Bod. 2, 54.
[74]Bod. 2, 58.
[75]Bod. 2, 72. High nobles skipped the ranks of cadet, 2nd lieutenant, and lieutenant colonel, reaching colonel after serving as lieutenant and captain. Promotion to colonel, however, was not a guarantee one would command a regiment, unless one owned it.
[76]Bod. 2, 56.
[77]Bod. 2, 73.

immense resources, and these were often replenished from the dowry of a well-heeled bourgeois family or the purchase of an office carrying a noble title.

Overseas based regiments had the rank of major and lieutenant colonel.[78] It was often easier to obtain an officer position abroad and then transfer to a metropolitan based one.

For all nobles, finding employment was easier with the sponsorship of the colonel or other regimental officer or with family in the regiment. Another way to advance one's career was to serve on the staff of a general as either an aide or in a specialist role, such as an engineer.

There were eighty-three foreign officers in North America, mostly German and Irish concentrated in the Dillon (Irish) and Deux-Ponts (German) regiments. A number of these officers had been received at court and were treated on the same basis as their counterparts in terms of advancement.

Specialists such as engineers and artillerymen were a mix of noble and non-noble and were required to have an extensive professional education. Only in the infantry was it

---

[78]Bod. 2, 62.

required to be noble to become a colonel. Among the officers serving in America, there were fifty-four non nobles.[79]

The final group of officers was known as roturiers or soldiers of fortune. They had specific positions in infantry regiments, including treasurer, two standard bearers, and junior officers in the grenadier company. They had similar positions reserved for them in the cavalry and artillery. Their positions were unaffected by the increasing restrictions on non-noble officers, perhaps in recognition of their professional skills and experience.

A few words on the navy. Entry into its officer corps had been restricted to nobles since 1689, and higher command was reserved for the 'red' or noble officers. The 'reds', however, could not fill the demand for officers needed to command small ships or in time of war. The 'blue' or auxiliary officers came from the lower deck, merchant

---

[79]Bod. 2, 83–84. This was despite the increasing restrictions on non-noble officers. Between 1718 and 1758 the requirements for proving nobility were made more stringent. After 1761, non-nobles could no longer enter the artillery and engineering arms. Admission to military academies was also denied to non-nobles (1766–81).

marine, or privateering fleet. During the American War of Independence, many officers were drafted from the last two sources and had successful naval careers.

With a few exceptions, a naval officer's career followed a specific path, starting from *garde de marine* to *capitaine de vaisseau.* They were trained onboard ships and at the main naval bases. Junior officers were often detached to temporarily command prizes taken in battle or smaller ships.

In contrast to line officers, many admirals had not served at sea for decades. They were replaced or shunted off into retirement. The navy promoted its best officers, and they were given opportunities to demonstrate their abilities in three fleet exercises in the 1770s. Most of the senior commanders in the war demonstrated their abilities on these occasions.

The Franco-American Impact on Russian Forces

Several "Americains" served in the Russian forces, including John Paul Jones who was appointed as a rear admiral in their navy. After service in Denmark (1761–69), François Angely enlisted in the Russian army and rose to the rank of colonel. He was accused of treating the French prisoners, captured fighting with the Poles against Russia. too generously and left the Russian army prior to his service in America. He was unemployed until named ADC to Baron de Viomenil in the French expeditionary force to America.

Louis Andrault, Marquis de Langeron, was born in 1763 and appointed as an officer of the Gardes Françaises at age 14. He was promoted to second lieutenant in the Bourbonnais regiment and sailed as a replacement on *l'Aigle* to join Rochambeau's corps in September 1782. He rose quickly to colonel while serving with the Armagnac regiment (1788). He killed the bishop of Nevers in a duel and decided to go abroad. He entered Russian service as colonel of the Siberia Grenadier regiment (1790), and he fought against the Swedes and the Turks. He served as an observer with the Austrian army in Northern France and the Netherlands (1793–94). He was promoted to lieutenant general in 1798 and made a count. Andrault was a senior commander at Austerlitz but severely criticized for his actions there. He redeemed himself and held a corps command in the battles in Germany in 1813 and led his corps in the invasion of France the following year. He held several senior administrative posts and fought in the Russo-Turkish

War of 1828–29. He died of cholera in St Petersburg in 1831.[80]

    Jean Prevost de Sansac, Marquis of Traversay, was born on the island of Martinique in 1754. He was commissioned as an *enseigne de vaisseau* in 1773 and spent three years on convoy escort duty between France and the Caribbean. He served at the Battle of Ushant aboard the *Vengeur*. He became captain of HMS *Ceres* which he had helped capture and was at the siege of Savannah. Commanding *Aigrette*, he participated at the battle of the Chesapeake. He was appointed *capitaine de vaisseau* at age 32. At the outbreak of the French Revolution, he commanded *Active* in Martinique. He was recruited to join the Russian Navy as a rear admiral in 1791 and accepted with Louis XVI's permission. Due to anti-French feeling, he resigned and went as Empress Catherine's liaison with the emigré army under Condé based at Koblenz. He returned to Russia in July 1793 and later commanded the Black Sea fleet. In 1809 he was recalled to St Petersburg and appointed Navy Minister. He served in this position until 1828. During

---

[80]Alexander Mikaberidze, *The Russian Officer Corps in the Revolutionary and Napoleonic Wars* (New York, 2005), 218–19. Hereafter cited as Mikaberidze.

his tenure he sponsored several exploratory expeditions to Artic and Antarctic waters, as well as in the Pacific. He died in 1831.[81]

Capellis Marquis du Fort, then a *capitaine de vaisseau*, emigrated after the Revolution and entered Russia's navy. He served in the Black Sea Fleet and as naval commander of Kronstadt and then St. Petersburg. He was promoted to *contre amiral* in the Russian Navy in 1799 and returned to France in 1801.[82]

Segond de Sederon served in the Russian army after the American War of Independence, as did the Comte de Vauban. Apparently, the Duc de Montmorency Laval and the Marquis du Houx de Viomenil were both lieutenant generals in the Russian army after emigrating, but this has been difficult to confirm. The marquis became a Marshall of France upon the Restoration—one of five "Americains" to reach that rank or the equivalent in the navy.

---

[81]Etienne Taillemite, *Dictionnaire des Marins Français*, 2nd ed. (Paris, 2002), 509–10. Hereafter cited as Taillemite.
[82]Christian de la Jonquiere, *Officiers de Marine aux Cincinnati Annuaire* (Brassac, 1988), 55. Hereafter cited as la Jonquiere.

The most famous émigré in Russia, Armand Plessis, Duc de Richelieu, did not serve in America but rose to major general, commanding the Lifeguards regiment in the Russian army and served as governor of Odessa and New Russia. The duke ended up as prime minister of France under the Restoration, reprising the role played by his famous ancestor, Cardinal Richelieu. His friendship with the czar may be a reason why the Russians agreed to withdraw their occupation forces from France under the Treaty of Aix La-Chapelle, which restored France as a great power guaranteeing European security.[83]

Several "Americains" fought against Russia, including Stedingk, who served in senior positions in the Finnish army. Nauckhoff returned to Swedish service after serving in America and participated in the battles of Hogland (1788) and Oland (1789) against the Russian navy. He was later captured by the Russians. He was promoted to colonel in 1793 and to rear admiral in 1797. The chevalier du Houx de Viomenil and his cousin, Baron Antoine fought on the side of the Poles against the Russians in the early 1770s, including at Krakow.

---

[83]Mikaberidze, 328–29.

Chapter 2: Expanded Biographies

Count Axel Fersen: Knight Errant

Count Axel Fersen was born on September 4, 1755, into the high Swedish nobility in Stockholm.[1] His father, Frederik Axel, was the recognized leader of the Hat party, which was the pro-French element at court and had been a distinguished soldier in France. His mother was a lady-in-waiting to Queen Lovisa Ulrika. At age 15, Fersen and his tutor began a four-and-a-half year Grand Tour, which interspersed visiting sites with practical training at various academies en route. They stopped in Paris in November 1773 where Fersen was presented at court and became a favorite of the Dauphine, Marie-Antoinette. He returned to Sweden in late 1774.

In 1780 he obtained a position as aide-de-camp to General Rochambeau, who had been appointed as commanding general of the French expeditionary corps sent

---

[1] H. Arnold Barton, *Count Hans Axel Fersen: Aristocrat in the Age of Revolution* (Woodbridge, CT, 1976).

to America to support the insurrectionists. Fersen was appointed at the suggestion of the Swedish ambassador in Paris. He was more motivated by military glory then any attachment to republican ideals. The expeditionary force arrived in Newport on July 11, 1780, and spent the next year there. Fersen as a fluent English speaker and excellent horseman was often used as a messenger between Rochambeau and Washington. His most important ride was to Newport in August 1781 to order Admiral Barras to join de Grasse's fleet at the mouth of the Chesapeake to interdict British resupply of Cornwallis's army. He was present at Yorktown. He was appointed *colonel-en-second* in the Deux-Ponts infantry regiment while still in America. He took part in the joint French-Spanish expedition to Venezuela to dislodge the British and then returned to Brest in June 1783.[2]

Fersen was rewarded with the Merite Militaire, the Protestant version of the Cross of Saint Louis and allowed to purchase the Royal-Suedois regiment for 100,000 livres from the Sparre brothers. The regiment provided an annual

_____

[2]Bod., 195.

income of 12,000 livres. Fersen was also appointed Captain-Lieutenant in one of the four Swedish lifeguard companies.

During the Revolution, he remained close to the French royal family and organized the abortive flight to Varennes which led to the abolition of the monarchy and France becoming a republic. Fersen returned to Sweden where he resumed his position in the Lifeguards. He served as the Swedish commissioner to the Congress of Rastatt and became Chancellor of Upsala University. He was appointed Grand Marshall to the Court and played a leading role in the government and in the writing and implementation of the 1809 Constitution, which is largely in place today. He was massacred in June 1810 for having supposedly taken part in the poisoning of the Crown Prince. Ironically his death paved the way for the pro-French party to put forward Marshal Bernadotte as a strong man who would restore order as heir apparent.

Founding US Engineers: Duportail and Fleury

Silas Deane and Benjamin Franklin were tasked with recruiting experienced foreign officers and ensuring that the Continental Army was supplied with critical weapons, ammunitions, and funds. Louis XVI ordered four engineering officers to take a two-year leave of absence and make their way to the American colonies in the autumn of 1776. The group was led by Le Begue du Portail and consisted of La Radiere, Gouvion, and Laumoy.

Duportail was admitted to the Mezieres engineering school on January 1, 1762.[3] He followed the usual program (discussed above). Duportail finished his course at Mezieres in 1765 and then spent the next decade serving in provincial garrisons, rising to captain. He came to the notice of War Minister Saint-Germain after submitting a plan for the reorganization of the engineering arm. He was called to the ministry to draft a royal ordonnance covering the reforms in July 1776, and this was promulgated that December to the discontent of many of his fellow officers. At this time, Duportail had started discussions with Franklin on joining the Continental Army, and the King's approval was obtained early in 1777.

Duportail's arrival in the US was delayed by a lack of shipping and poor weather. The first group to arrive was

---

[3]Serge le Pottier, *Duportail ou le Genie de George Washington* (Paris, 2011).

led by an artilleryman, Tronson de Coudray, and consisted of twelve officers from all arms, including Pierrc l'Enfant, future architect of Washington, D.C., and Teissèdre de Fleury. Duportail was appointed colonel and head of the corps of engineers. In May 1779 he submitted a comprehensive set of recommendations establishing the Corps of Engineers. They were accepted by Congress and largely implemented. The Corps was dissolved after the War but re-instituted at the express demand of President Washington in 1794.

Duportail was captured at Charleston and held prisoner by the British until November 1780. He oversaw the siege at Yorktown and was complimented by his British foes for the thoroughness of his preparations, which made Cornwallis' surrender inevitable.[4]

On his return to France, Duportail transferred to the infantry and was promoted to brigadier. He attended the Prussian army maneuvers with Lafayette and Gouvion in September 1785.[5] In June 1787, he became deputy chief of the new army general staff, which was full of American

---

[4]Schachtman, 70–71, 84, 104–05, and 140.
[5]Schachtman, throughout.

veterans. In March 1788, he was promoted to *maréchal de camp* and was appointed in early 1790 as commander in Flanders.

In November 1790, Duportail was appointed War Minister, replacing la Tour du Pin. He headed an army of 140,000, many of whom were absent from their units. In his thirteen-month tenure, he ensured that reforms were made in everything from the artillery to pay to the civil rights of soldiers. He abolished the ownership of regiments by their colonels and numbered each regiment. In August 1792 Duportail was accused of treason. He did not appear in court but went into hiding, eventually making his way to Philadelphia. He died while sailing back to France in 1802.

Teissèdre de Fleury had been a volunteer in the French Army and recruited as an engineer by Deane at the same time as Duportail. He was appointed captain after his bravery at Piscaway in May 1777. He fought at Brandywine and Germantown and was named major in the Pulaski Legion. Following his conduct leading the defense of Fort Mercer, he was promoted to lieutenant colonel in November 1777. Fleury led the successful bayonet charge on Stony

Point in July 1779.[6] Congress recognized his valor by awarding him one of only fourteen Medals of Honor granted during the War of Independence. He was the only foreign recipient.

He returned to France, becoming colonel of the Saintonge regiment with whom he served in Rochambeau's expeditionary corps, including at Yorktown. He was commander in chief of the Bourbon and Maurice islands in the Indian Ocean. Returning to France in April 1790, he was promoted to maréchal de camp on the recommendation of his old chief, Duportail. He was active in the initial campaigns of the Revolution but resigned after having been wounded for the third time in 1792.[7] The highest award to an American Army engineering officer is still today the Fleury Medal.

Louis XVI: America's Best Friend

Louis XVI was in contemporary American political parlance a "loser." He lost his head and after the reigns of his two

---

[6]Schachtman, 56, 87, 91, 101–03.

[7]Six, vol. 1, 454.

younger brothers ended a Bourbon dynasty that had lasted for over three centuries since the ascent of Henry IV. His family were a collateral branch of the Capetian dynasty that had ruled France since 987. For all his failings, he was an absolute monarch reigning over the most populous and important country in what today would be described as Western Europe. He was the great-great grandson of the Sun King Louis XIV who had terrorized Europe and the grandson of Louis XV. His grandfather left him with a diminished realm that had declared bankruptcy in 1770.

Louis XVI came to the throne unexpectedly in 1774 at age twenty.[8] He had outlived two heirs: his father and oldest brother, and his predecessor had died unexpectedly. He was not well educated but was diligent, working eight hours a day. Despite the infighting at court for positions and pensions, Louis surrounded himself with several outstanding statesmen.[9] His own interest was in foreign affairs, and he was ably served in that department by the

---

[8]Etienne Taillemite, *Louis XVI ou le navigateur immobile* (Paris, 2002), 49. Hereafter cited as Taillemite 4.

[9]James Perkins, *France in the American Revolution* (New York, 1970), 45–46. As early as September 1775 Bonvouloir was sent as an unofficial emissary to sound out the Americans' plans.

Comte de Vergennes.[10] He shared with his ministers and subjects an abiding hate for *Perfide Albion*,[11] which resonates to this day in France, and wanted revenge for the humiliating defeat in the Seven Years' War.

He inherited Choiseul as minister of the navy but was later advised by Sartine and de Castries who implemented more reforms. Choiseul's aim was to have a navy that could rival the British: eighty ships of the line and forty-five frigates.[12] At that time France had forty-three serviceable ships of the line and twenty-three serviceable frigates.[13] Vergennes tried to improve the odds of success by reinforcing the Family Compact between France and Spain by uniting their land and naval forces against Great Britain.

Louis XVI approved a vast increase in the naval budget to meet his ministers' aspirations. It rose from 17.7

[10]Petitfils, 399–402.

[11]*Perfide Albion* is the French term for their untrustworthy neighbor across the Channel. Even today syphilis is described as the English disease.

[12]A ship of the line was defined as having anywhere from 64 to 110 guns and 3 gun decks, although the French later eliminated the 64s as not being powerful enough. Frigates performed reconnaissance and escort duties.

[13]Taillemite 4, 70.

million livres in 1774 to 74 million in 1778.[14] Intendants or financial controllers were installed in each port and reported directly to the naval minister.[15] The navy realized that it would need the support of corsairs or privateers in the time of war to disrupt enemy shipping. Changes were made to make privateering more attractive: Notably the king gave up his third share of their prize money.[16]

The king gave leave for two years to four engineering officers, including the rising star in the corps, newly promoted lieutenant colonel Duportail to join the Americans.[17] He allowed Baron de Kalb,[18] a seasoned senior officer, to join the Continental Army and others to volunteer but threatened Lafayette with the Bastille, as his in-laws thought it was a bad idea for the newly married eighteen-year-old to go to America. Lafayette sailed anyway.

---

[14]Taillemite 4, 75.
[15]Taillemite 4, 91.
[16]Taillemite 4, 144.
[17]Schachtman, 70–71. Duportail would become War Minister at the end of the Ancien Regime and laid the basis for the successful armies of the Revolution, Consulate, and Empire.
[18]Schachtman, 58–59.

The king approved the sending of surplus rifles and cannons to America, as well as significant outright cash grants and loans.[19] Wenger estimates that the monetary value of the French contribution during the war was the equivalent of $745 million in 2010 dollars using the real price comparison calculator.[20]

American privateers were given access to French ports and to that of their Caribbean possessions. This could not have been done without the support of the king and his willingness to provoke Great Britain to war.

He approved the deployment of increased naval assets to America. The d'Estaing fleet of twelve ships of the line was sent to the West Indies in part to support the American rebels arriving at the mouth of the Delaware on July 7, 1778. D'Estaing failed at Saratoga in 1779 but took or retook several islands in the Caribbean.

---

[19]Richard Ketchum, *Victory at Yorktown: The Campaign that Won the Revolution* (New York, 2004), 17. Hereafter cited as Ketchum. The king authorized the dispatch of one million livres worth of surplus military equipment on May 12, 1776, using Beaumarchais's trading company as a cut-out.

[20]Wenger, 138. Using Wenger's figures, I have prepared a chart (see Appendix 2) showing the contribution of the Dutch, French, and Spanish which exceeded $1.3 billion.

Louis XVI approved the royal council's recommendation in February 1780 to send the Expedition Particuliere, which was originally to consist of 8000 men, to fight in America and approved the nomination of the Comte de Rochambeau as its commander.[21] Rochambeau had demonstrated his bravery at Minden in 1759 and his tactical abilities in the army maneuvers of 1778–79, which were a mock invasion of England. The expedition arrived in Rhode Island in July 1780.

In March 1781 de Grasse's fleet of 22 ships of the line, 3 frigates and 120 transports carrying over 3000 troops sailed for the West Indies from Brest.[22] Many of these troops who were slated for the invasion of Jamaica would form part of Saint-Simon's corps at Yorktown.

On October 19, 1781, General Cornwallis surrendered at Yorktown to the combined Franco-American forces. Despite having over 30,000 troops still on American soil the British soon realized the game was up.

---

[21]Petitfils, 462. For comparison he stated that the Continental Army had 14,000 men at this time; see Petitfils, 466. Schachtman sets the figure at 6000 for the expeditionary force; see Schactman, 207.
[22]Petitfils, 469.

Without the king's active support, the French would not have engaged the British as forcefully in America and off the American coast as they did. He provided the tools for the colonists to win their independence.

Miranda: Hero or Fake?

Francisco Miranda was born in Caracas in 1756 to a family that had emigrated from the Canary Islands. While his father was a successful businessman, the family were never considered part of the Creole elite, and Francisco travelled to Spain to find fame and fortune. His father purchased a captain's commission for him in the Princess Regiment in early 1773.[23]

He was posted to bases in Andalusia and North Africa where he fought against the forces of the Sultan of Morocco and was at the siege of Melilla in late 1774. He transferred to the Aragon regiment in April 1780 to

---

[23]Jacques de Cazotte, *Miranda (1750–1816) Histoire d'un seducteur* (Paris, 2000) and Karen Racine, *Francisco Miranda: A Transatlantic Life in the Age of Revolution* (Scholarly Resources 2003)

participate in the upcoming campaign in America against the British and was assigned to Havana.

He was named aide-de-camp to the acting governor of Cuba, Senor de Cacigal. He participated in the siege of Pensacola in March 1781, where, as one of the few English speakers, he was active in the surrender negotiations. He was promoted to lieutenant colonel in August. He claimed that he was instrumental in raising the funds needed to pay the French and American forces marching toward Yorktown later that year. He was due to be arrested for sedition and for being a spy for Britain, so he fled Havana for Europe via the United States where he became friends with George Washington, Alexander Hamilton, and Benjamin Franklin, among others. He later claimed that he had been appointed a brigadier general in the Continental Army.

He travelled extensively in northern Europe and Russia, where Empress Catherine appointed him a count, provided him with a stipend, and gave him the protection of her embassies abroad. While he spent significant time in England and later settled and married there, he was attracted to the political turmoil occurring in France.

Through the sponsorship of the mayor of Paris, Jerome de Petion and then Minister of War, Joseph Servan, he was appointed *maréchal de camp* based on his previous military experience in August 1792. They saw him as the vessel to spread French revolutionary ideas in Latin America and considered having him lead an expedition to the Caribbean. He served under Dumouriez in the Armée du Nord and was promoted to lieutenant general. He was arrested for incompetence after the battle of Neerwinden and for conspiring in Dumouriez's desertion to the Austrians and held in prison. At his trial in May 1793, Thomas Paine appeared as a character witness. The jury returned a not guilty verdict, and he was released. A warrant, however, for his arrest was again issued on July 5, and he was jailed in the La Force prison, along with many leading Girondins. He was finally released in January 1795.

His best-known political act was in December 1797, when Latin American exiles in Paris drafted the Act of Paris calling on Great Britain to secure the independence of the region working with the United States with Miranda serving as overall military commander. This was the first effort at coordinating the various independence movements in the region.

He fled France in January 1798, as he was on a list to be deported to Devil's Island (French Guyana). He returned to London, where he settled and married.

He organized an expedition of 180 men on the Leander out of New York City in early 1806 for Haiti. On August 3, 1806, he landed at Lavela de Coro and planted the Colombian flag. The expedition was doomed as the Spaniards had advance warning of his arrival. When it failed, he returned to London. In December 1811, he finally arrived home in Caracas. He was received with suspicion of being pro-British and not in tune with local conditions. He played an important role in the First Venezuelan Republic which ended with the peace of Monteverde in August 1812. He expected to be allowed to go into exile, but the royalists turned him and his colleagues over to the Spanish. They were initially held locally, before being transferred to a prison in Cadiz where he died in December 1812.

In summary, he was a career military officer, lucky enough to rise to high rank but consistently unsuccessful in the field and easily antagonizing his superiors. He was a revolutionary who spent most of his time in European salons, being financially supported by admirers. That being said, he was active in the three revolutionary movements of his day, and the Spanish authorities tried hard to keep him on their side despite repeated seditious behavior!

Rochambeau père et fils: French Patriots

Born in 1725 into a family whose ancestor had been killed in the First Crusade, Jean-Baptiste-Donatien de Vimeur was destined for the church as the third son and was singled out during his studies as a prospective bishop. Fate intervened with the premature death of his older brothers, and he was enrolled in the Paris Military Academy—the precursor to today's St Cyr or French West Point in 1740. While not from a wealthy family, he was able to purchase the Marche regiment in 1747. He was wounded at the Battle of Laufeldt and given the honor of riding in the king's coach. He made a love marriage, which also brought him a dowry of 300,000 livres in December 1749.

In 1759 he was made colonel of the Auvergne Regiment, one of the most prestigious infantry units in France. He was a hero at the Battle of Clostercamp, where he was wounded. He would face one of his adversaries in this battle at Yorktown: Cornwallis. He was promoted to *maréchal de camp* and named inspector general of the infantry. Eight years later he was awarded the Grand Cross of Saint Louis. He was promoted to lieutenant general and named head of the expeditionary force to support the American rebels in 1780.[24] For his success he was rewarded with the governorship of Picardie.

He was appointed by the king to command the Armée du Nord in 1792, the force defending France's vulnerable northern frontier. He resigned and was eventually imprisoned in the Conciergerie. He was released after Robespierre's fall.[25]

He was active in the Society of Cincinnatus and along with de Grasse recommended that some junior officers be given lifetime memberships in recognition of their contributions in America.

Rochambeau shared the distinction with Luckner of being the last two Maréchals de France appointed in the Ancien Regime in December 1791. He met Napoleon on several occasions. He pleaded the case of an émigré widow in an audience where Napoleon was surrounded by a few senior officers, including Maréchal Berthier. The emperor

---

[24]Bod., 420.
[25]Six, vol. 2, 378.

cried "General, these are your pupils." Rochambeau answered: "The pupils have far surpassed their master."[26]

His only son, Donatien Marie, served under him at Yorktown,[27] having risen quickly as a high noble and son of one of France's leading generals. He was a prisoner of the British for nearly nine years after surrendering in the West Indies in 1802, succeeding General Leclerc, Bonaparte's brother-in-law, as commander in chief of the army in Saint-Domingue, where it was putting down the slave rebellion. The British did not do him the courtesy of exchanging him early as his father had done for senior officers captured at Yorktown. After the debacle of the Russian campaign, Rochambeau fils was recalled as commander of the 19th Infantry Division at whose head he was mortally wounded at the Battle of Nations and died at Leipzig in 1813.[28]

His own son originally served in the navy in Saint-Domingue, transferring to the army in 1801. He was Murat's aide-de-camp at Friedland, where his bravery earned him the Legion of Honor. He also served in the Russian campaign.

---

[26] Arnold Whitridge, *Rochambeau* (New York, 1965).
[27] Bod., 419.
[28] Bod., vol. 2, 378–79.

Truguet: A Naval Survivor

Laurent François Truguet was born in 1752 to a brigadier or commodore in the navy in Toulon.[29] He joined the navy as a *garde de marine* in 1765 and was continuously on active service. By the American War of Independence he had risen to *lieutenant de vaisseau*. He saved the life of Admiral d'Estaing at the battle of Savannah despite being wounded. He was sent home to recover and then served on the *Languedoc* at the Battle of the Chesapeake and later aboard *Citoyen* at the Battle of the Saintes.[30]

He mapped out the Dardanelles as part of a hydrographic survey based in Constantinople from 1784 to 1786. He was promoted to *capitaine de vaisseau* in January 1792 and to *contre amiral* later that year. The following year he commanded a squadron against the Sardinian king, flying his flag on *Tonnant* and bombarded Nice and other cities. He failed to take Cagliari and was relieved and replaced by Trogoff.[31] In May 1793, he was discharged and imprisoned; he was released after the fall of Robespierre.

---

[29]Taillemitte, 514–15.
[30]La Jonquiere, 216.
[31]La Jonquiere, 216.

The Directory brought him back into service. He was promoted to vice admiral and Minister of the Navy (1795–97). He planned a two-pronged campaign to invade Ireland and recover parts of India that if successful would have stretched the resources of the Royal Navy. As a result of the failure of the Ireland expedition he was replaced as minister by Pleville Le Pelley and appointed ambassador to Madrid in October 1797.[32] Having taken his time returning to Paris from Madrid at the end of his appointment he was dismissed from the service and exiled to Holland. He was a keen advocate of the abolition of slavery and objected to Bonaparte's reestablishing the practice as First Consul.

Truguet returned to active duty as commander of the combined Franco-Spanish fleet at Cadiz in 1802. Two of the three of his squadron commanders had served in America: Bedout and Ganteaume. He returned to Paris after the Peace of Amiens. Truguet refused to sign a "spontaneous" petition from senior naval officers asking that Bonaparte take the imperial crown. He was punished by a loss of his awards. He was recalled in 1809 to command the Brest squadron, and the following year he headed the Dutch Navy which was

---

[32]La Jonquiere, 216.

under French command, defending Rotterdam in December 1813.

He served as commander of the Brest fleet under Louis XVIII. After the July Revolution he was named Amiral de France.[33] He died in 1839.

Unlucky admirals: Brueys d'Aigalliers & Villeneuve

François Paul, Comte de Brueys d'Aigalliers, was born in 1753. Like many aspiring officers, he joined as a volunteer in 1766 and participated in the Levant campaign. He served on several ships primarily in the Mediterranean from 1768 to 1776. In April 1777, he was promoted to *enseigne de vaisseau*. He served on *Le Zele* (1781–82), including at the Chesapeake and St. Christophe. After the war, he commanded several small ships. He was promoted to *capitaine de vaisseau* (January 1792). He was arrested, released, and resigned in 1793. He was reinstated in 1795 and made *chef de division* in charge of naval forces in the Adriatic. He was promoted to *contre amiral* (1706) and vice admiral (1798). He was named commander in chief of the Mediterranean fleet, flying his flag on *Orient*. The fleet was

---

[33]Six, vol. 2, 515.

tasked with ferrying and protecting Bonaparte's Egyptian army. Having taken Malta and then landed the army in Alexandria, he anchored in Aboukir Bay at Bonaparte's insistence, where he was attacked by Horatio Nelson on August 1. Brueys d'Aigalliers was nearly cut in half by a cannonball and died later that day.[34]

Pierre Charles de Villeneuve was born in late 1763 into a Provencal family whose ancestors had fought with Roland in the Pyrenees. He was the 91st member of his family who served as a knight of Malta.[35] He joined the navy as an aspirant *garde de marine* in 1778 and served successively on *Flore, Montreal,* and *Hardi.* Having been promoted to *enseigne de vaisseau,* he transferred to *Marseillais* and fought aboard it in five engagements including the Chesapeake and Saintes. He was promoted to *lieutenant de vaisseau* in 1786 and served extensively at sea. He was promoted to *capitaine de vaisseau* in early 1793 but was forced out of the navy as a noble later that year. He was brought back in May 1795 to serve as chief of staff of the

---

[34]Taillemite, 77.
[35]Adam Nicolson, *Seize the Fire: Heroism, Duty and the Battle of Trafalgar* (New York, 2005), 28–29. Hereafter cited as Nicolson.

Brest fleet. Promoted to *contre amiral*, his division was to have participated in the first Ireland expedition, In April 1798 he commanded *Guillaume-Tell* in Bonaparte's expedition to Egypt. At the battle of Aboukir he showed inertia and failed to assist admiral Brueys. He did escape with four ships to Malta after the battle, but he was taken prisoner when the island surrendered in September 1800. His behavior did little to harm his career: He went on to lead the West Indies squadron and then was made a vice admiral. He was named commander of the Toulon fleet, flying his flag on *Bucentaure*. He was to command the combined Franco-Spanish forces that were to sweep the British from the Channel, thus facilitating an invasion of England. After trying to draw Nelson to the West Indies, he returned to fight the indecisive battle of Cape Finisterre (July 1805). On October 21, he fought the battle of Trafalgar and lost 17 ships and 4000 killed.[36] He was forced to surrender. He was not up to the task of commanding a combined fleet and was let down by his senior commanders and the weak and ill-led Spanish fleet. After his release by the British, he returned to

---

[36]Taillemite, 532–33.

France and stabbed himself to death in a hotel room at Rennes in April 1806.

Unsung Heroes: Galvez, Gardoqui and Saavreda

Spain had similar motivations for helping the American colonists in their rebellion as France: revenge for defeat in the Seven Years' War and restricting British expansion overseas. The Spanish government reformed its army and navy in the 1760s and 1770s while appointing talented men to key government positions over aristocrats.

Bernardo Galvez[37] was born in July 1746 into a middle-class family in Andalucia.[38] His uncle Jose, however, had moved to Madrid and established himself as a lawyer and later entered the bureaucracy to become Minister for the Indies (1776–87). He was appointed lieutenant in the Royal Cantabre, a regiment raised under French officers. He volunteered for service in New Spain and served as a volunteer in a campaign in the American southwest against

---

[37]Paul A. Gilje, *Encyclopedia of Revolutionary America*, vol. 1 (New York, 2010), 337–38. Hereafter city as ERA.
[38]Gonzalo Quinto Sarava, *Bernardo de Galvez: Spanish Hero of the American Revolution* (Chapel Hill, 2018), 1–7. Hereafter cited as Quinto.

the Apaches in March 1769. In October 1772, he was promoted to captain of the 11th Infantry based in Seville. He soon became a student at the Avila Military Academy, which provided midcareer officers with training like the US Army's Command & General Staff College does today. At Avila he met Francisco de Saavreda, and they were part of a group of hardworking and scientifically inclined officers.[39]

In January 1777, he was promoted to lieutenant colonel and that fall was named governor of Louisiana and colonel of the Louisiana regiment. Louisiana's elite was mostly French creole, and he successfully got them onside. He was tasked with consolidating Spanish power in the region and making life difficult for the British in West Florida. He succeeded in taking Mobile. He led the combined Franco-Spanish assault at Pensacola,[40] which surrendered in May 1781. For this action he was promoted

---

[39]Quinto, 5.
[40]Desmarais, 210–14; Nathaniel Philbrick, *In the Hurricane's Eye The Genius of George Washington and the Victory at Yorktown* (New York, 2019), 133–34. Cited hereafter as Philbrick; Larrie D. Ferreiro, *Brothers at Arms American Independence and the Men of France and Spain who saved it* (New York, 2016), 248–54. Hereafter cited as Ferreiro; Schachtman 247–49.

to lieutenant general and later made a count. In February 1785 he was made governor of Cuba and then named Viceroy of New Spain (which included what is now the southwestern US, Central America, and Mexico) based in Mexico City where he died the following year.[41] Galvez is only the eighth foreign recipient of honorary US citizenship (2014), who include the Marquis de Lafayette, Winston Churchill, and General Pulaski.[42]

Don Diego de Gardoqui[43] was born in 1735 in Bilbao and was a merchant based there.[44] As he was fluent in English, he established trading relationships with North America in 1765. As a business associate of Eldridge Gerry, he was able to funnel supplies to the rebels in Massachusetts. He aided the Continental Navy and privateers in Bilbao and acted as a buyer and seller of prize goods. The Spanish court did not want to deal directly with Arthur Lee, whom Congress had sent as its emissary, so it charged Gardoqui

---

[41]Philbrick, 269; Quinto, 281.
[42]Quinto, 2.
[43]ERA, vol. 1, 339; Ferreiro, 39–61, 67–68, 309–10, and 334–35.
[44]Mark M. Boatner III, *Encyclopedia of the American Revolution* (Chapel Hill, 1976), 339. Hereafter cited as EAR.

with the negotiations. He also negotiated fruitlessly with John Jay regarding a potential cash grant of £100,000. He was later Spanish ambassador to the US. He died in Madrid in 1798.[45]

Francisco de Saavreda was born in October 1746 in Seville into a prominent noble family. He studied theology and obtained a doctorate at the University of Granada. He switched careers and joined the King's Regiment as a cadet. He later attended the Avila staff college with Galvez. They both served in the unsuccessful siege of Algiers in 1775. Jose de Galvez appointed him to a senior post in the Indies Ministry where he was responsible for trade relations with Spain's American colonies. In 1780 he was sent to Havana to straighten out the administration of Cuba and to work with Galvez on retaking West Florida from the British.[46] On his way to his new post, he was captured by the British and kept prisoner in Jamaica until January 1781, when he went to Havana. He was at the siege of Pensacola. He later met

---

[45]Ferreiro, 39–44, 67–68, 309–10, and 334–35.
[46]Ferreiro, 248–53, 257–62, and 277–79.

Admiral de Grasse and agreed on joint Franco-Spanish action in the Caribbean.[47]

As de Grasse was preparing to sail to meet the Franco-American forces in Virginia, he received word that the troops there had not been paid and that they needed supplies. Saavreda raised 500,000 pesos as a loan from Havana's merchants against the surety of the next bullion shipment in a day. After de Grasse's defeat at the battle of the Saintes in April 1782, joint operations against Jamaica were abandoned and Saavreda was appointed to Caracas as Intendant. He returned to Spain in 1788, serving first on the Supreme council and then as Finance Minister in 1797. He was made Chief Minister in 1798 and resigned due to ill health the following year. He was brought back as Chief Minister in 1810 after the French invasion of Spain. He died in 1819.

The Wild Geese: The Dillon Clan

Several Irish regiments served the French king, their officers and men having originally fled from their homeland during

---

[47] Philbrick, 277; Schachtman, 247–49.

the Jacobite Rebellion. They were known as the Wild Geese. The one of interest for this book is the Dillon Regiment, which was owned by the family whose name it carried. The Dillons were considered high nobility in France and were given the *honneurs de la cour* seven times.[48]

Five Dillons served as officers in America. Comte Arthur Dillon joined the regiment in 1765 and became its colonel in 1772. He commanded his regiment at Savannah and Yorktown.[49] He was promoted to *maréchal de camp* in 1783. He represented Martinique in the Estates General in Paris in 1789. He was named lieutenant general in January 1792 and commanded the left wing of the Armée du Nord under Lafayette. Dillon commanded a division under Dumouriez having been briefly suspended. Recalled to Paris, he was imprisoned and guillotined.[50] His daughter Fanny married General Bertrand, who followed Napoleon to Saint Helena.

Arthur's brother Theobald also served in the Dillon regiment and was at Savannah.[51] He was promoted to

---

48Bod., 147.
49Bod., 147–48.
50Six, vol. 1, 358–59.
51Bod., 149–50.

colonel commanding the family regiment in 1788 and *maréchal de camp* in 1791. He served in l'Armée du Nord and was killed by his soldiers at Lille in April 1792.[52]

Comte François Theobald Dillon was from a junior branch of the clan, as was Robert Guillaume. He did not start his career in the family regiment but served in what became the Lauzun Legion as a junior officer. He was an aide-de-camp to Chastellux at Yorktown.[53] He transferred to the family regiment as *major en second*. He commanded the family regiment, which was recreated in the Émigré Army and was promoted to *maréchal de camp* and later honorary lieutenant general for his services to the monarchy.

François' brother Robert Guillaume was a page to King Louis XVI. He also joined what became the Lauzun Legion and took part in the conquest of Senegal. He was promoted to *colonel-en-second* of the legion and served at Gloucester north of Yorktown.[54] He commanded the Lauzun Legion on its return to France in 1783. He resigned in 1787 after losing the use of his left arm in a hunting accident. He rejoined the army as colonel in command of the 3rd Infantry

---

[52]Six, vol. 1, 359.
[53]Bod., 148–49.
[54]Bod., 149.

regiment and then was advanced to *maréchal de camp* for retirement in March 1791. After the Restoration, he was appointed commander of the royal palace of Saint Germain and made an honorary lieutenant general (February 1816).

Guillaume Dillon, the brother both of François and Robert, was present at Gloucester north of Yorktown and died aboard the frigate *Neree* in 1788. Barthelemy Dillon served in the family regiment at Savannah and St Kitts, but his exact link to either branch of the family is unclear.[55]

Officers who served in America from either Irish-born or from Irish families established in France—were Conway, Humphrey, Jennings de Kilmaine,[56] Lynch, Macmahon, O'Keefe, O'Neill, and Stack de Croto. Lynch served in both the Dillon and Walsh regiments, while Humphrey, Mullens, O'Neill, and Stack de Croto served in the Walsh regiment, and Conway in the Clare regiment. Sheldon, while English-born, served in the Dillon regiment.[57]

---

[55]Bod., 148.
[56]Six, vol. 2, 6–7.
[57]Bod., *passim*.

Chapter 3: Sources and Methodology

The French contribution to the American War of Independence has been widely studied in France and much has been published in French. The objective here is to bring the higher-ranking army and naval officers who served ashore or at sea during the War within one work and to track their careers post-1783.

Sources

For the French army and volunteers, Lt. Colonel Gilbert Bodinier, a French army historian, prepared their biographies in the early 1980s.[1] He based his work on service records in the army archives and the work done previously by others, such as Balch, Cotenson, Lasseray, and Dawson. He later wrote a book analyzing the background and careers of officers serving in the American War of Independence and looked at their careers up to the start of the French Revolution.[2] He then wrote a multi-

---

[1]Bod.
[2]Bod. 2.

volume dictionary of the generals of the Ancien Regime,[3] and he finished his career by writing about the characteristics of officers under the Consulate and Empire.[4]

George Six was the authority on flag and general officers serving during the Republic and then under the Empire. His 1934 seminal work is still the standard,[5] and he later wrote a book on the general officers of the Revolution and Empire (1947).[6] I have supplemented his work with those of M and Mme Quintin, who focused on the colonels and *capitaines de vaisseau* under the Consulate and colonels under the Empire.[7]

Christian de La Jonquiere,[8] whose ancestor had served as a naval officer during the War of Independence, took the research done by Cotenson in the archives of the Society of Cincinnati and the biographical work done by Etienne Taillemite on naval officers and produced a list of

---

[3]Gilbert Bodinier, *Dictionnaire des Officiers Generaux de l'Armée Royale 1688–1772*, 4 vols. (Paris, 2013–2023) Hereafter cited as Bod. 4.

[4]Bod. 3.

[5]Six.

[6]Georges Six, *Les Generaux de la Revolution et l'Empire* (Paris, 1947). Hereafter cited as Six, 2.

[7]Quintin.

[8]La Jonquiere.

the original French naval members of the Society of Cincinnati and their careers (1988). The French Society of Cincinnati was very generous in awarding membership to officers who had neither risen to *capitaine de vaisseau* nor served in America. Unfortunately, La Jonquiere is vague on where an officer served and frequently lists the ships an officer served aboard but not always giving the dates. He also provides no information on service after the war except for promotions. I therefore supplemented La Jonquieres's work with Etienne Taillemite's work, where relevant. Taillemite was probably the best and most prolific French naval historian of his time.[9]

Some of the army related sources, such as Six and Bodinier, can be vague and refer only to "service in America." I ignored these entries unless they were confirmed by another reliable source. For this reason I omitted the glamourous Vicomte de Beauharnais, first husband of Empress Josephine and father to Prince Eugene.

---

[9]Etienne Taillemite, Etienne *Bougainville* (Paris, 2011). Hereafter cited as Taillemite 2. Taillemitte; Etienne Taillemite, *l'Histoire Ignoree de la Marine Française* (Paris, 1988). Hereafter cited as Taillemite 3. Taillemite 4.

Methodology

The initial challenge was to determine which officers had risen to the equivalent of colonel and *capitaine de vaisseau* or higher before, during, or after the American War of Independence and who had served in America or off the American coast. This effort generated over 400 candidates.

As this work is intended to be both a biographical dictionary and a series of essays, I decided to reduce the biographical component to those officers who eventually rose to general (175) or flag rank (93). This includes twenty-four volunteers and soldiers who achieved the rank of general. I also added biographies on notable figures who did not meet the rank criteria, such as l'Enfant who was an early volunteer engineering officer and designed the layout for Washington, D.C.

I supplemented the French research with the works done by Feirrero, Desmarais, and Schachtman over the past decade to bring the vast contribution of our allies in the war to the attention of the American reader.[10]

---

[10]Ferreiro; Desmarais; and Schacthman.

As part of the research, I developed a database with over 2500 entries covering the individuals in this book and the events in their lives ranging from the battle of Rocroix (1747) to Waterloo (1815).

The biographical entries are split into three sections: background, including membership in the high nobility represented by the *honneurs de la cour*; service in America; and post-war career. The major sources are given at the bottom of each entry. I listed the naval officers first in alphabetical order and then the army officers.

Chapter 4: Naval Biographies

Ache de Serquigny, Robert Vicomte d'

Background: Born in 1758, he was a garde de marine (1770). He served aboard *Dauphin-royal* at Ouessant.

American Service: He served on *Zodiaque* in the West Indies. He was aboard *Ville-de-Paris* (1781–82) participating in the actions at Fort-Royal, the Chesapeake, and St Kitts.

Post-American Career: He commanded *Clairvoyant* at Saintes. He was promoted to *capitaine de vaisseau* in 1784. He emigrated to Latin America but returned to France and was involved in the Cadoudal conspiracy. He tried to promote an uprising in Normandy and was reputedly killed by the police in 1809.

Notable fact: His uncle, Anne-Antoine, rose to vice admiral.

Sources: La Jonquiere, 19; Taillemite, 8.

Albert de Rions, François Hector Comte de

Background: He was born in 1728 to a noble Provençal family. He was a *cadet de marine* (1743), rising to *capitaine* *de vaisseau* (1772). He served in battle during the Seven Years' War including at the siege of Cartagena.

American Service: He commanded *Sagittaire* off Rhode Island (1778). He participated in the battles of St. Lucia and Grenada. He distinguished himself at Savannah. He returned to Toulon. In January 1781 he received command of *Pluton* in Grasse's squadron and participated in the Battle of the Chesapeake, where he captured HMS *Experiment*.

Post-American Career: He was in Vaudreuil's squadron at Saintes, where he fought off four British ships to try and protect the flagship *Ville de Paris*. He was port captain and commander of the vessels at Toulon and promoted to *chef d'escadre* (1784). He was sent by Louis XVI with a large squadron to Brest to assist the Spanish against the British. In 1792 he was promoted to contre amiral but resigned shortly thereafter. He joined the émigré navy where he was second in command to Comte Hector. He returned to France and retired in 1802, dying the same year.

Sources: La Jonquiere, 20; Taillemite, 8–9.

Albert de Saint-Hippolyte, François Auguste Chevalier d'

Background: He was a *garde de marine* (1741), rising to *capitaine de vaisseau* in 1771. He was director of the port of

Toulon (1777). He commanded *Victoire* in the battle against Rodney under Guichen.

American Service: He commanded *Victoire* at the Chesapeake and took part in the capture of HMS *Montreal*.

Post-American Career: He was promoted *chef d'escadre* in 1782 on retirement.

Source: La Jonquiere, 21.

Amblimont, Renard de Fuschamberg, Claude Marguerite Comte d'

Background: Born in 1736, he was *garde de marine* (1751), he served on the *Duc de Bourgogne* at Louisburg (1757). He successively commanded *Sardoine*, *Etourdie*, *Heroine,* and *Diligente* between 1762 and 1764. Afer promotion to *capitaine de vaissseau* (1772), he commanded *Diligente* and then *Vengeur* at Ouessant and took the corsair *St Peters* with the aid of *Belle Poule*.

American Service: He commanded *Hercule* under Guichen and then *Brave* under de Grasse.

Post-American Career: He was promoted to *contre amiral* (1792). He joined the Spanish navy and led a division at the Battle of Cape Saint Vincent off the Portuguese coast (1797) where he was killed by a cannonball.

Notable Facts: His father and grandfather were naval officers, with the latter serving as governor of the West Indies.

Sources: La Jonquiere, 22; Taillemitte, 11.

Saint-Germain, Etienne Joseph Chevalier d'Apchon

Background: Born in 1724, he was a *garde de marine* (1740), rising to *capitaine de vaisseau* (1770).

American Service: He commanded *Protecteur* in d'Estaing's squadron and later in Cordova's fleet at Cadiz. He was promoted to *chef d'escadre* (1781).

Post-American Career: Unknown.

Source: La Jonquiere, 23.

Arros d', Jean François Baron d'Argelos

Background: Born in 1726, he was a *garde de marine* (1744) and rose to *capitaine de vaisseau* (1772). He served on *Magnifique* at Ouessant.

American Service: He commanded *Palmier* at the Battle of the Chesapeake.

Post-American Career: He commanded *Languedoc* in de Grasse's squadron that was at Saintes. He distinguished himself at the battle of St. Kitts (1782). He was promoted to *chef d'escadre* (1784).

Source: La Jonquiere, 25.

Audibert de Ramatuelle, Joseph Jacques

Background: Born in 1759, he joined the navy as a *garde de marine* (1776) and was promoted to *enseigne de vaisseau* (1778).

American Service: He was aboard *Marseillais* and then *Cesar* in d'Estaing's squadron and participated at Grenada and Savannah.

Post-American Career: He was assigned to the Cadiz squadron (1781–82), serving on *Majestueux* and the *Robuste*. He was promoted to *capitaine de vaisseau* (1793) but was forced out as a noble. He emigrated and wrote a book on naval tactics dedicated to Bonaparte.

He served in the Neapolitan navy, rising to squadron leader and director of its naval academy. He returned to France and was kept on active service without a specific role. He was promoted to honorary *contre amiral* in 1824. He died in 1840.

Sources: La Jonquiere, 188; Taillemite, 19–20.

Bacqua, Luc Augustin

Background: Born in 1757, he studied surgery in Nantes and Paris and then joined the navy as a surgeon in 1779.

American Service: In March 1781, he transferred to *Scipion* where he was in action in the West indies, the Chesapeake and Saintes. At the battle of October 17, 1782, *Scipion* beat two British ships.

Post-American Career: He was promoted through to chirugien first class. He was arrested but released on the insistence of his colleagues. He died in 1814.

Notable Fact: He performed the first known Cesarian operation in which the patient survived in April 1797. Three years later he performed the same operation on the same patient successfully.

Source: Taillemitte, 23.

Barney, Joshua

Background: Born in Baltimore in 1758, he joined the Continental Navy in October 1775 as a 2nd lieutenant.

American Service: He commanded *Cincinnatus,* which took the American envoy to France, and then *Citoyen* on the return voyage, which brought Genet the French envoy to

America. He participated in seventeen engagements and was awarded a gold purse by Congress for capturing a larger frigate (April 1782). He was eventually promoted to captain in the US Navy.

Post-American Career: He was offered the command of one of the six new frigates built for the US Navy, but he did not take up the command due to issues of seniority.

He transferred to the French navy and was promoted to *capitaine de vaisseau* (1796) and to *chef de division* later that year. He commanded Meduse and a division of three ships under Admiral van Stabel in the West Indies. He resigned in 1801 and went to Pittsburgh. He ran unsuccessfully for Congress in Baltimore. He commanded the naval component at the battle of Bladensburg, the biggest defeat suffered by American forces during the War of 1812. He died in 1818.

Sources: Quintin, 339; ERA, vol. 1, 47–48; Ian Toll, *Six Frigates: The Epic History of the Founding of the US Navy* (New York, 2008), 433–34.

Barras de Saint-Laurent, Jacques Comte de

Background: Born in 1719 to a noble Provençal family, he was a *garde de marine*. He fought aboard *Boree* at the battle of Cap Scie (1744) and was employed in several convoys. On *Atalante*, he captured several prizes (1747). He fought in Canada, Minorca, and Gibraltar. He advanced to *capitaine de vaisseau* (1762) and commanded *Fier*, *Mignone*, *Provence*, and finally *Cesar* in the evolution squadron (1777). He was promoted to *chef d'escadre* (1778).

American Service: He commanded *Zele* and then *Tonnant* (1778–80) under d'Estaing in the battles of Grenada and St. Lucia and later at Savannah. He returned to France but was appointed to replace Ternay, who had died, as commander of the Newport squadron. He brought the artillery and supplies to the troops besieging Yorktown.

Post-American Career: He captured *Montserat* and *Nevis* from the British and was promoted to lieutenant general des Armées navales (1782). He refused the grade of vice admiral (1792), dying soon after.

Notable Facts: Admiral Barras was saved from the guillotine through the intervention of Paul Barras, his nephew, who served in India in the army as a *cadet gentilhomme*. He was involved in the taking of the Bastille. He was elected to the Legislative Assembly and then the Convention. He was a member of the commission of general safety and elected president of the Convention. He was one of the five members of the Directory. He resigned after Bonaparte's coup d'état.

Sources: La Jonquiere, 29; Taillemitte, 28–29; Norman Desmarais, trans., *The Road to Yorktown by L-F du Pont d'Aubevoye, comte de Lauberdiere* (El Dorado Hills, CA, 2021), 77, hereafter cited as Lauberdiere; ERA, vol. 1, 68; Schachtman, 305.

Barre dit de Saint-Leu, Jean Baptiste

Background: He was born in 1763 and entered the navy in 1783.

American Service: He served on American ships *Raleigh* and *Confederacy*. He was made a chevalier of Cincinnatus for having destroyed *Mediateur* (1784).

Post-American Career: He served in the Navy as a *sous-lieutenant de vaisseau* (1787) and then *capitaine de vaisseau* (1798). During the Revolution he was named governor of Saint Pierre et Miquelon but could not take up the post. He took refuge in the US under Washington's protection despite the request of French ambassador Genet to deliver him up to the French authorities. He was made an honorary rear admiral (1814).

Source: La Jonquiere, 30.

Bedout, Jacques

Background: Born in Quebec in 1751, he served in the merchant marine (1763-1777).

American Service: He was named *lieutenant de frégate* (1777) and given command of the privateer *Defense* armed in Boston and flying the Stars and Stripes. He then commanded *Congress* under the American flag and was captured. He escaped from New York and was appointed auxiliary officer in Orvilliers' squadron and on the *Railleuse*, taking part in the sieges of Tobago and Yorktown.

Post-American Career: He rose from *sous-lieutenant de vaisseau* (May 1786) to *capitaine de vaisseau* (August 1794). He commanded *Le Terrible* under Villaret-Joyeuse and then *Le Tigre,* in which he fought at Belle-Isle (June 1795).

He commanded *l'Indomptable* and a division of the fleet in the failed expedition to Ireland (December 1796). Promoted to *contre amiral* (April 1798), he led the Brest division which was sent to reinforce the Saint-Domingue expedition in May 1802, returning to France for health reasons (1803). He retired in January 1816 and died in 1818.

Sources: La Jonquiere, 34; Taillemitte, 39; Bod., 46–47; Six, vol. 1, 72–73; Quintin, 319.

Borda, Jean Charles Chevalier de

Background: He was born in 1733. He was a *lieutenant de port* and *garde de marine*. As a result of his mathematical ability, he was assigned to the Mezieres engineering school. He was promoted to engineer (1761), rising to *lieutenant de vaisseau* (1767). He was made a member of the *academie de marine* and took part in several scientific expeditions.

American Service: He was chief of staff to d'Estaing in the operations off of Rhode Island and took part in the siege of Savannah. He was promoted to *capitaine de vaisseau* (1780). He served as first officer on *Guerrier* (1781). He commanded the *Solitaire,* which escorted a convoy to Martinique. He fought against HMS *Ruby* and was taken prisoner in 1782.

Post-American Career: He was promoted *chef de division* (1784) and inspector of naval ship building. He was a key player in the naval reforms implemented in 1786–87. He died in 1799.

Notable facts: He was a well-known scientist and helped develop the methodology for measuring longitude and the meter. He has a crater on the moon named after him, as well as an asteroid.

Sources: La Jonquiere, 42; Taillemitte, 58–59.

Bougainville, Louis Antoine Comte de

Background: Born in 1729, he entered the Black Musketeers (1754). He was a lawyer and junior diplomat in London. As a cavalry captain, he served as Montcalm's aide-de-camp in Quebec (July 1756). He returned to France to obtain reinforcements but to no avail. Promoted to colonel (1759), he was blamed for his inaction on the Plain of Abraham.

He entered the navy as a *capitaine de vaisseau* (1763). He made his first exploration trip to Montevideo and the Falklands (1763-64) and is best known for his round the world trip of exploration in 1767–69. In 1778 he led a delegation to encourage the Iroquois to revolt against the British: His nephew was a member of the Iroquois delegation.

American Service: He commanded *le Guerrier* and *Languedoc* off Rhode Island. He was d'Estaing flag captain at Savannah. He was promoted *chef d'escadre* (1779) and led the attack at the Chesapeake on *l'Auguste*.

Post-American Career: He forced the capitulation of *Montserrat* (January 1782) and was at the Battle of Saintes. He was court martialed for that action and, while absolved, he was exiled from court. At the Revolution he was named commandant of Brest, which he refused. He then refused the post of Minister of the Navy and promotion to vice admiral (August 1792). He was arrested but released after the fall of Robespierre.

Notable Facts: He was a member of the Institut de France, where he was asked to preside over the scientific preparations for the Egypt expedition and the Royal Society (London). He was a grand officer of the legion d'honneur and comte d'empire. His heart is in the Pantheon. He has given his name to a Pacific Island, which he discovered and to a flowering shrub.

Sources: La Jonquiere, 44; Taillemite, 63; Lauberdiere; 152; Etienne Taillemite, *Bougainville* (Paris, 2011); Schachtman, 260.

Boulainvilliers de Croy, Henry-Louis Marquis de

Background: Born in 1735, he was a a *garde de marine* (1735), rising to *capitaine de vaisseau* (1757).

American Service: He was flag captain commanding *Languedoc* (1778-79) under d'Estaing in the Rhode Island campaign and at the siege of Savannah.

Post-American Career. He was promoted *chef d'escadre* in 1780 and immediately retired.

Sources: La Jonquiere, 44; Lauberdiere; 199.

Brach, Jean Louis Chevalier de

Background: Born in 1740, he was a *garde de marine* in 1757. He commanded *l'Eveille* at Ouessant.

American Service: He served aboard *Lion* (1779) and *Ville de Paris* (1780–82), the latter at the Chesapeake and Saintes, where he was taken prisoner.

Post-American Career: He was promoted to *capitaine de vaisseau* in 1786. He was later apparently named *chef d'escadre*. He was guillotined in 1794.

Source: La Jonquiere, 48.

Breugnon, Pierre Claude Hardenau Comte de

Background: Born in 1717 in Brest, he was a *garde de marine* (1733). He fought in Louisiana. He commanded *Sirene* (1756). He rose to *capitaine de vaisseau* (1757). He led a force against the Moroccan pirates and was named *chef d'escadre* (1767) and lieutenant general des Armées navales (1779).

American Service: As a division leader, he was aboard *Tonnant* and was involved in the battle of Saint Lucia and the actions off Newport. He commanded *Royal Louis* (1780).

Post-American Career: He was president of the court martial reviewing the loss at Saintes and was promoted vice admiral (1792) and massacred the same year in Paris.

Sources: La Jonquiere, 48; Taillemite, 72–73.

Briqueville, Bonchretien Marquis de

Background: Born in 1725, he was a *garde de marine* (1743) and advanced to *capitaine de vaisseau* (1772). He commanded *le Solitaire* at Ouessant.

American Service: He commanded *Northumberland* at the Chesapeake.

Post-American Career: He was named brigadier des Armées navales in 1782. He commanded *l'Aigrett*e and then *le Solitaire*. He was named *chef d'escadre* in 1784. He died in 1804.

Source: La Jonquiere, 49.

Bruix, Eustache

Background: Born in 1759 in Saint-Domingue where his father was serving in the army, he joined the navy as a *garde de marine* in 1778. He served on several ships. In March 1781 he was transferred to *Auguste*.

American Service: During the war, he served on the *Auguste* and was present at the Chesapeake. He was promoted *enseigne de vaisseau* in November 1781. He took part in the capture of St. Christopher.

Post-American Career: He was at Saintes, but his ship escaped. He remained at sea until October 1793 when he was relieved. His first command was the corvette *Pivert*, which took the oceanographer de Pusegur on a four-year mapping trip of Saint-Domingue and its environs. He commanded the frigate *Semillante* and was promoted to *capitaine de vaisseau* 2nd class in January 1793.

In October 1793 he lost his rank and was retired. Reintegrated, he was promoted to *capitaine de vaisseau* 1st class in January 1794 and was named major general/chief of staff of Villaret-Joyeuse's squadron at Brest.

He served in a similar position in the abortive Ireland expedition under Morard in November 1796. He was promoted to *contre amiral* (May 1797). In 1798 he commanded the Brest squadron which successfully resupplied Genoa.

He replaced Pleville Le Pelley as Minister of the Navy and Colonies from April 1798 to July 1799, during which time he was promoted vice admiral and took command of the Brest fleet whose mission was to relieve Malta and Egypt. Sailing to Toulon, he linked up with the Spanish fleet. When the relief of Egypt was aborted, he returned to Brest.

While Bruix was on way back he was replaced as Navy Minister and was assigned to build up the fleet based at Rochefort (March 1801). He left active service due to tuberculosis. He was appointed councilor of state but died in 1805 aged 46.

Sources: La Jonquiere, 50; Six, vol. 1, 164–65; Richard Humble, *Napoleon's Admirals* (Phialdelphia, 2019), 49–54; Taillemite, 77–78.

Brueys d'Aigalliers, François Paul Comte de

Background: Born in 1753 in Uzes into a minor noble family, he volunteered for naval service and participated in the Levant campaign (1766) and became a *garde de marine*

(1768). He served on several ships (1768–76), including in a campaign against the Barbary pirates. Serving in Saint-Domingue, he was gravely ill and sent home in 1773. He returned to the Levant aboard *Flore* and was later transferred to Provence, during which time he was promoted to *enseigne de vaisseau* (April 1777).

American Service: He served aboard *Le Zele* (1781–82) under de Grasse and participated in several battles, including the Chesapeake and St. Kitts. *Zele* was absent at Saintes due to a collision which required repairs prior to the battle.

Post-American Career: After the war, he received the order of Saint Louis and commanded several small ships. He was placed on half pay in June 1788 after having served in Martinique. He was recalled due to the mass emigration of officers and promoted to *capitaine de vaisseau* (January 1792), he commanded *Le Tricolore* in the Cagliari and Naples expeditions under Truguet. With the failure at Cagliari, he was arrested and stripped of his rank in May 1793. He was reinstated (June 1794) and promoted to commodore. He commanded the naval forces in the Adriatic and was promoted to *contre amiral* (September 1796). In July 1797 he led the successful taking of Corfu.

Promoted to vice admiral (April 1798), he was named commander of Toulon and concurrently of the Mediterranean fleet, flying his flag on *l'Orient*. His fleet of thirteen ships of the line, seven frigates and three hundred transports took Napoleon's expeditionary corps to Egypt. Brueys first took part in the siege of Malta on his way to Egypt. Having landed the army, he sought a safe anchorage at Aboukir Bay where he was attacked by Nelson on August 1, 1798. He was nearly cut in half by a cannonball and died. Luc Casabianca, Brueys' flag captain, and his ten-year-old son were killed when the *Orient* blew up.

Sources: La Jonquiere, 50; Taillemite, 77; Six, vol. 1, 163–64; Humble, *Napoleon's Admirals*, 65–70; Albert Soboul, *Dictionairre Historique de la Revolution Francaise*, vol. 2, 157. Hereafter cited as Soboul.

Bruyeres, Paul-Jacques Comte de Bruyeres-Calabre

Background: Born in 1734, he was a *garde de marine* in 1751, rising to *capitaine de vaisseau* (1777).

American Service: He commanded *Tonnant* in d'Estaing's squadron and reached Newport. He returned to the West Indies. He commanded *Zele* at Savannah.

Post-American Career: He returned to France. After being sanctioned for disobeying orders, he was given command of *l'Illustte*, which was ordered to join Suffren's squadron in the Indian Ocean. He was wounded in the battle of Trincomalee, and his ship returned to Brest to be decommissioned due to its poor state.

He was named *chef de division* in 1786, and he joined the Ocean fleet under Albert de Rions. With the Revolution, there was unrest in the fleet, and he resigned in 1792. He was arrested and released but did not emigrate. He was made a *contre amiral* in 1814 upon retirement.
Source: La Jonquiere, 50.

Caffarelli, Joseph Louis Marie Comte de

Background: He was born in 1760 into a noble Italian family that had moved to the Languedoc. He joined the Bretagne regiment as a cadet but soon switched to the navy.
American Service: He served aboard *Marseillais* in d'Estaing's squadron, including at the Chesapeake.
Post-American Career: He was at the Saintes. He left the navy for health reasons. In 1793 he joined the army as an engineer and fought in Spain at the battles of Roses and Figueres. He was made *prefet maritime* de Brest serving for

nine years and then was appointed to the navy council. He was a councilor of state. In January 1814 he was sent to organize the resistance to Wellington based in Toulouse. He died in 1845.

Notable Facts: His brother Maximilien was a general during the Egyptian expedition and died at the siege of Acre. Bonaparte's regard for him resulted in patronage for Joseph.

Sources: La Jonquiere, 53; Taillemite, 82–83; Six, vol. 1, 178.

Cambis, Joseph Vicomte de

Background: Born in 1748, he entered the military academy in 1755 but then joined the navy. He was a *garde de marine* (1764) and served on several ships. He was promoted to *enseigne de vaisseau* (October 1773) and then brigadier (November 1776).

American Service: He served on *Hector* (1778-80) under d'Estaing and distinguished himself at Savannah, where he was taken prisoner.

Post-American Career: He commanded *l'Aigrette* (1781–83), capturing *le Tarleton* (1782). He then commanded *La Galathee* (1791–92). He was promoted to *capitaine de vaisseau* (January 1792) and *contre amiral* (January 1793).

Serving in Saint-Domingue, he was relieved and returned to France for trial for having incited the sailors against the commissaires de la Republique. Imprisoned (November 1793), he was reinstated in September 1795. He was inactive and retired in March 1801 and died in 1825.

Sources: La Jonquiere, 54; Taillemite, 84; Six, vol. 1, 181–82.

Capellis, Hypolite Marquis de Fort

Background: Born in 1744, he joined the navy as a *garde de marine* (1758) and commanded *l'Epervier* in the Senegal expedition (January 1779). He was made a chevalier de Saint-Louis for his conduct.

American Service: He served as aide major to Ternay and the Destouches at Newport. He commanded *Ariele* at the battle of Cape Henry and was recommended for immediate promotion by Admiral Barras. He was in command of *Ariel* at Chesapeake. In command of *Danae*, he brought the Lauzun Legion back to France in 1783.

Post-American Career: He was promoted to *capitaine de vaisseau* (1786). He emigrated to Germany and then Russia, where he served in the Black Sea Fleet and as naval commander of Kronstadt and then St. Petersburg. He was promoted to *contre amiral* in the Russian Navy in 1799 and returned to France in 1801. He was briefly mayor of Avignon and died in 1813.

Source: La Jonquiere, 55.

Casabianca, Luc Julien

Background: Born in 1762 in Corsica, he went to the military academy in 1775. He became a *garde de marine* in 1778.

American Service: He served aboard *Terrible* and then *Zele* and took part in the battles of Fort-Royal, the Chesapeake, and St. Kitts.

Post-American Career: He was promoted to *lieutenant de vaisseau* in 1786. He was elected deputy to the Convention from Corsica in 1792 and was named *capitaine de vaisseau* in 1793. After serving on the Conseil de Cinq-Cents he rejoined the navy as a chef de division/commodore. He was Brueys's flag captain at Aboukir and was killed in the fighting, along with his ten-year-old son when the *Orient* blew up.

Notable Fact: Several French naval vessels have been named after Casabianca, including a nuclear attack submarine still in service.

Sources: La Jonquiere, 57; Taillemite, 86; Six, vol. 1, 196–97; Taillemite. 56.

La Croix, Anne Jean de Vicomte de Castries

Background: Born in 1756, he became a *garde de marine* in 1777.

American Service: He served aboard *Languedoc* (1778–79) under d'Estaing and was wounded at Grenada. He also served aboard *Neptune* and *Duc de Bourgogne*. He commanded *Ariel* (1782).

Post-American Career: He was promoted to *capitaine de vaisseau* in 1814 and to honorary *contre amiral* in 1825. He died in 1829.

Source: La Jonquiere, 58.

Castellane Majastres, Henri Cesar Marquis

Background: Born in 1733, he was a *garde de marine* (1749), rising to *capitaine de vaisseau* (1777).

American Service: Commanding *le Sagittaire* and then *le Marseillais* under de Grasse, he participated in all Grasse's engagements and was complimented for his sangfroid at the Chesapeake.

Post-American Career: He served at Saintes and returned to Brest with Vaudreuil's squadron. He was promoted to *chef d'escadre* and made a member of the *conseil de guerre* (1784). He died in 1789.

Source: La Jonquiere, 57.

Chabert Cogolin, Joseph Bernard Marquis de

Background: Born in 1724, he was a *garde de marine* (1741). He was aboard *Diamant* at the battle of Cap Scue (1744) and served on *Trident* and then *Esperance* in Martinique (1745). He was aboard *la Gloire* in the fighting against *Anson* and taken prisoner (1747). He was promoted *enseign de vaisseau* (1748) and sent on a scientific mission which earned him membership in the *academie de marine.* He commanded *Hirondelle* and then *Gracieuse* (1764–66) aboard which he made several research trips across the Mediterranean. He was advanced to *capitaine de vaisseau* (1771). He then commanded *Mignonne* and *Atalante.*

American Service: He commanded *Le Vaillant* (1778–79) at Rhode Island, St Lucia, Grenada, and at Savannah under d'Estaing. He commanded *Saint-Esprit* (1781–82) in the battle of the Chesapeake, where he was wounded under de Grasse.

Post-American Career: He was promoted *chef d'escadre* (1782) and then vice admiral (1792). He emigrated but returned to France in 1802 where he died in 1805.

Notable Facts: He published a memoir on a trip to America (1750–51) made on the orders of the king, as well as a treatise on marine clocks.

Sources: La Jonquiere, 59; Taillemite, 92–93.

Champagny, Jean Baptiste

Background: Born in 1756, he was a *garde de marine* (1771). He took part in the capture of Grenada on *Fier* (1779).

American Service: He served on *Emeraude* and then *la Couronne,* in which he participated in the Saintes where he was badly wounded.

Post-American Career: He commanded *Pandour* (1785). He was elected to the Estates General and then served on the maritime committee of the Constituent Assembly. He was imprisoned. He was recalled by Bonaparte, serving as a state councilor. He served as ambassador to Vienna and later as foreign minister. He was minister of state (1811). He died in 1834.

Sources: La Jonquiere, 61; Taillemite, 94–95.

Champion de Cice, Louis Toussaint Comte de Cice

Background: He was a *garde de marine* (1746), rising to *capitaine de vaisseau* (1772). He was first officer aboard *Zodiaque* at Ouessant.

American Service: He commanded *Solitaire* (1781–82) under Guichen and Grasse.

Post-American Career: He commanded *Zodiaque* at the siege of Gibraltar (1782) and was promoted *chef d'escadre* in 1784. He died in 1793.

Source: La Jonquiere, 61.

Charité, Charles Comte de

Background: Born in 1733, he was *garde de marine* (1749) and *capitaine de vaisseau* (1777).

American Service: He was flag captain to Rouchouart on *Duc de Bourgogne* in Orvilliers' squadron. He commanded *Bourgogne* under de Grasse and then *Northumberland*. He was at Yorktown providing Rochambeau with the pay for his troops.

Post-American Career: He was promoted to *chef d'escadre* (1784) and *contre amiral* (1792). He was made honorary vice admiral in 1814 and died in 1815.

Source: La Jonquiere, 62.

Chastenet de Puysegur, Antoine Hyacinthe Comte de Chastenet

Background: Born in 1752, he was a *garde de marine* in 1767. He took part in scientific expeditions, including in command of *l'Espiegle* in Borda's expedition off the African coast in 1776.

American Service: He served aboard *Languedoc* (1778–79). He commanded *la Bricole* at Savannah and was later taken prisoner at Charleston. He was promoted to *lieutenant de vaisseau* in 1780. He later commanded *Active* (1782), *Concorde*, and *Richmond* (1783).

Post-American Career: He was promoted to *capitaine de vaisseau* (1792), emigrated, and originally served with the army. He later transferred to the Portuguese Navy ,where he was appointed *contre amiral*. He died in 1806.

Source: La Jonquiere, 186.

Chaussegros, Martin Benoit

Background: Born in 1737, he was a *lieutenant garde cote* (1748) and *capitaine de vaisseau* (1780).

American Service: He served on *Vaillant* (1778–79) and then *Hector* (1780). He was flag captain under Chabert on the *Saint*-Esprit at the Chesapeake and in the same role on *Majestueux*.

Post-American Career: He commanded *Destin* (1783). He was promoted to *contre amiral* (1793).

Source: La Jonquiere, 64.

Chayla, Armand Simon Chevalier de Blanquet

Background: Born in 1759, he was an *aspirant de marine* (June 1775). As a *garde de marine*, he escorted the Comte de Provence during his visit to the Toulon naval base (June 1777). He served aboard *Hector*, *Zele,* and *Hector* again. He was promoted to *enseigne de vaisseau* (April 1778).

American Service: He served in the West Indies and America in d'Estaing's fleet and took part in the siege of Newport (August 1778). He was taken prisoner (November 1778), returning to France on exchange. He took part in the Battle of the Chesapeake aboard *Le Palmier*.

Post-American Career: He was wounded at Saintes, served continuously in the West Indies, North Sea, and the Levant, and was promoted to *lieutenant de vaisseau* (May 1786). He then served in the Mediterranean, including a battle with Albanian pirates (December 1788). At the siege of Gibraltar he commanded *La Fleche*.

He was promoted to *capitaine de vaisseau* (February 1793). He served as assistant to Navy Minister (May 1795–April 1797). He was promoted to *chef de division* and then *contre amiral* (September 1796). He commanded the 2nd squadron on *Le Franklin* in Brueys's fleet.

He took part in the siege of Malta and had his nose shot off at the Battle of Aboukir. He was taken prisoner by the British. He then retired in October 1803. He was made an honorary vice admiral (May 1816) and died in 1826.

Sources: La Jonquiere, 65; Taillemite, 149; Six, vol. 1, 107–08.

Cherisey, Charles Paul Comte de Nouroy

Background: Born in 1725, he was a *garde de marine* in 1742, advancing to *capitaine de vaisseau* in 1771.

American Service: He commanded *Scipion* (1779) and then *Invisible* (1781).

Post-American Career: He was promoted to *chef d'escadre* in 1782 and died in 1799.

Source: La Jonquiere, 66.

Cillart, Armand François Comte de Suville

Background: Born in 1730, he was a *garde de marine* (1746), rising to *capitaine de vaisseau* (1776). He took part in Ternay's expedition to Newfoundland. He commanded *Reflechi* at Ouessant. He then saved *Aurore* and a convoy going to Martinique in command of *l'Indien* (1779). He took part in the battles of Grenada and Martinique.

American Service: He took part in the battle of the Chesapeake.

Post-American Career: He commanded *Actif* in de Cordova's squadron (1782) at the battle of Cape Spartele. He was promoted to *chef d'escadre* (1786) and *contre amiral* (1792). He died in 1801.

Notable facts: His two brothers were naval officers, including Cillart de Villeneuve, who served in America and brought back the Duc de Lauzun to France with the news of the victory at Yorktown.

Source: La Jonquiere, 68.

Coetnempren, Guy Pierre Comte de Kersaint

Background: Born in 1742, he was a *garde de marine* (1755). Promoted to *enseigne de vaisseau*, he served on

Intrepide, which was commanded by his father in the Angolan and West Indies campaign (1757). He commanded *Lunette* in the Moroccan campaign (1767). He was promoted to *lieutenant de vaisseau* and to command of *Rossignol* (1771). He then commanded *Favorite* (1776–77) and *Iphigenie* (1778), aboard which he captured HMS *Lively* and HMS *Ceres.*

American Service: He commanded the frigate *Iphigenie* at Savannah and at the attack on Charleston.

Post-American Career: He led a successful campaign aboard with his squadron in the West Indies. He was involved in several technical issues relating to the navy including the coppering of vessels, a practice introduced by the British.

He was president of the Paris electors (1789). Promoted to *contre amiral* (1792), he was the administrator of the Seine department and a member of the Jacobin club. He was Paris's representative in the Legislative Assembly and then deputy to the Convention. He was promoted to vice admiral in 1793 and voted for the abolition of the monarchy. He briefly served as Navy Minister and was arrested and guillotined (1793).

Notable Facts: His father commanded *Thesee* at the battle of Quiberon Bay (1759). In trying to rescue his chief, his ship sank drowning the entire crew. His brother rose to *capitaine de vaisseau* and was *prefet maritime* of Antwerp. He was promoted to *contre amiral* and *prefet* on the Restoration.

Sources: La Jonquiere, 70; Six, vol. 2, 5–6.

Colbert, Edouard Charles Comte de Maleuvrier

Background: Born in 1758, he was a *garde de marine* (1775).

American Service: He commanded *la Guepe* (1780) off the coast of Rhode Island and at Cape Henry. *La Guepe* foundered without the loss of life. He then commanded *Ariel* (1781). He was aboard *Conquerant* at the Chesapeake and at Saintes.

Post-American Career: He commanded *Serpent* (1781–83), was promoted to *capitaine de vaisseau* (1792) and *contre amiral* in 1816. He died in 1820.

Notable Fact: He served as a deputy from Eure and Loire.

Sources: La Jonquiere, 72; Lauberdiere; 67.

Coriolis d'Espinousse, Jean Louis Marquis

Background: Born in 1726, he was a *garde de marine* (1741), rising to *capitaine de vaisseau* (1771). He commanded *Caton* (1778–79) and then *Destin* in Orvilliers's squadron.

American Service: He commanded *Cesar* at Chesapeake.

Post-American Career: He was named *chef d'escadre* (1782) and commanded *Bourgogne* (1781–82) at the Saintes and died in 1793.

Source: La Jonquiere, 73.

Coueret de Secqueville, Augustin Charles

Background: Born in 1749, he was a pilot on *La Folle* during its cruise to the Windward Islands (1763–65). He became a *garde de marine* (January 1766) and served on several ships in Europe and North America. He was promoted to *enseigne de vaisseau* (October 1773). He served at the battle of Ouessant under d'Orvilliers and was promoted to *lieutenant de vaisseau* (March 1779).

American Service: Under Guichen, he served on *l'Engageante* on its mission to Boston (1781).

Post-American Career: He served in the Windward Islands. Promoted to *major de vaisseau* (May 1786), he then commanded *la Railleuse*. He was acting commandant of Brest. He was promoted to *capitaine de vaisseau* (January 1792) and *contre amiral* (January 1793), and he was later Commander of *l'Orient*. He was suspended in January 1794 and then arrested and imprisoned in La Force. He was reinstated but without an assignment. He died in 1816.

Source: Six, vol. 1, 249.

Couturier, Joseph Comte de Fournoue

Background: Born in 1740, he was a *garde de marine* (1758). He was aboard *Vengeur* at Ouessant. He was first officer on *Vengeur* (1778) in d'Estaing's squadron.

American Service: He took part in the battle of Grenada and siege of Savannah. He took over command from de Retz and was involved in the battle for Martinique. He was promoted to *capitaine de vaisseau* (1780).

Post-American Career: He joined d'Estaing's squadron at Cadiz. He commanded *Lion* and then *Zodiaque*. He was promoted to *chef de division* in 1788 and sent with his division to support Tipo Sahib against the English. He was promoted to *chef d'escadre* and remained in the Indian Ocean. He retired in 1791 and died in 1801.

Source: La Jonquiere, 95.

Croizet, Jean Chevalier de Retz

Background: Born in 1725, he was a *garde de marine* in 1741, advancing to *capitaine de vaisseau* in 1772.

American Service: He commanded *Vengeur* (1779) under d'Estaing, *La Motte Picquet,* and then *Zodiaque* (1781) and *Robuste* (1782). He was wounded at the taking of Grenada.

Post-American Career: He was promoted to *chef d'escadre* in 1786 and died in 1789.

Source: La Jonquiere, 190.

Dampierre, Charles Picot Commandeur de

Background: Born in 1727, he was a *garde de marine* (1743) advancing to *capitaine de vaisseau* (1772). He commanded *Diademe* in La Motte Picquet's squadron, which saw off the British naval force in February 1780 and was at the battle of Grenada.

American Service: Still commanding *Diademe*, he was at the siege of Savannah. He later commanded *Bretagne* (1782).

Post-American Career: He was promoted to *chef d'escadre* (1784) and *contre amiral* (1792).

Source: La Jonquiere, 78.

Decres, Denis Duc

Background: He was born in 1761. He was a an aspirant *garde de marine* (1779).

American Service: He served aboard *Richmond* under de Grasse at the Chesapeake and at St. Kitts.

Post-American Career: He distinguished himself at the Saintes in towing *Glorieux* to safety. He was appointed *enseigne de vaisseau* as a result. He is promoted lieutenant (1786) and then *capitaine de vaisseau* (1793). He served in the Indian Ocean commanding *Cybele* which served as the flagship at *l'ile de Franc.* and was commander of the. Returning to France in command of *Atalante* to plead for more reinforcements, he was arrested and stripped of his rank (1794), but he was later released. He did not serve again until 1795 when he was assigned to Toulon under Martin and given command of *Formidable*.

He commanded *Formidable*, which served as Villeneuve's flagship which was to join the aborted Ireland expedition. Promoted to *contre amiral*, he commanded the frigates flying his flag in the frigate *Diane* in Brueys' squadron in the Egypt expedition. He escaped with four frigates from Aboukir and returned to Malta. He was ordered to sail to France in command of *Guillaume-Tel* to obtain reinforcements. He was attacked by four British ships and surrendered after a valiant fight which earned him the admiration of his British foes.

After being freed, he was given a sword of honor by Bonaparte and named maritime *prefet* at Lorient (1800). He briefly commanded the *Rochefort*, before being named Minister of the Navy—a position in which he served for fourteen years with absences for health issues. He was promoted to vice admiral (1804) and created Duc (1813). He retired in 1814 and then served during the Hundred Days as Navy Minister. He died in 1820 because of an assassination attempt by his valet, who placed a bomb under his bed.

Sources: La Jonquiere, 79; Taillemite, 129; Six, vol. 1, 305–06; Humble, 87–92.

Delmotte, Jean Louis

Background: Born in 1752, he joined the navy as a *mousse* (June 1761) aboard *Defenseur* serving in the West Indies, rising to *2eme pilote* (1776). He served on *Saint-Esprit* under Orvilliers (1779-80).

American Service: He transferred to the navy as an auxiliary officer on *Duc de Bourgogne,* which was part of Ternay's fleet bringing Rochambeau's corps to Newport (1780). He served at the battle near Bermuda and then in both actions at the Chesapeake.

Post-American Career: He served at the Battles of St. Kitts and Saintes. He later returned to North American waters and the US on *Le Courier* (1784–86). He was named a *sous-lieutenant de vaisseau* (May 1786). He commanded *La Loire*, *L'Espiegle,* and *Le Superbe* in the Mediterranean. He was promoted to *capitaine de vaisseau* (January 1793) and served as major general at Brest and then under Villaret Joyeuse aboard the flagship *Montagne*.

He was promoted to *contre amiral* (November 1793). He commanded the 2nd squadron aboard *Tonnant* under Martin in the Mediterranean (1794). He also served as commander of Brest (1796), chief of staff, and then interim commander of l'Armée de l'Ocean (1798–99).

He commanded the 2nd squadron under de Bruix (1799), serving as well as major general aboard *Alliance, Ocean,* and *Terrible.* He was briefly commander of the fleet aboard *Republicain* (1801) and then led the Lorient division aboard *Scipion* and three frigates in the Saint-Domingue expedition (November 1801–May 1802). He retired in September 1793 and died in 1816.

Sources: La Jonquiere, 79; Taillemite, 132; Six, vol. 1, 320–21; Quintin, 318.

Destouches, Charles Rene Sochet dit Chevalier Destouches

Background: Born in 1727, he entered the navy in 1743. He served in escorts to convoys to and from the Caribbean. He fought in Canada and Louisiana during the Seven Years War. He was a *lieutenant de vaisseau* commanding *Corisande* (1765) and promoted to *capitaine de vaisseau* (1772). He commanded *l'Artesien* at Ouessant.

American Service: He commanded *Neptune* under Ternay at Rhode Island (February 1780). He was acting squadron commander after Ternay's death until the arrival of Barras.

He commanded a ten-vessel force which tried to interdict Cornwallis in Virginia. He was defeated at Cape Henry.

His squadron sank ten British ships at the Chesapeake and captured *Romulus* which he brought to Newport. He played a key role in the landing of 3000 reinforcement for the Yorktown campaign. He took part in the successful siege of New York.

Post-American Career: He took part in the battle of Saintes and was taken prisoner along with de Grasse by Admiral Rodney. On his return to France, he was awarded the *grand croix de Saint Louis* and named *chef d'escadre*. Upon being promoted to *contre amiral* in January 1792, he immediately retired.

He was arrested as his son was serving in the Royalist army. Rescued, he served on the war council of the Vendean army. After the disaster at Savenay, he and his two nieces hid with a farmer. He died in 1793.

Sources: La Jonquiere, 213; Taillemite, 136; Philbrick, 61–68.

Dorre, Yves François

Background: Born in 1750, he joined the merchant marine as a sailor in 1765. In 1775 he was recruited to the navy as a chief petty officer.

American Service: He was lead helmsman on the *Languedoc* (1778–79) and was involved in all the actions including Rhode Island, St. Lucia, Grenada, and Savannah, where he boarded a British cutter. He was badly wounded in a storm when the ship lost its mast. The *Languedoc* sailed back to France in November 1779. He returned to the West Indies and took part in the actions in Martinique, Saint-Domingue, and S.t Kitts. He oversaw the destruction of British commercial establishments during the Hudson Bay expedition aboard *Astree* (1783).

Post-American Career: He advanced to *capitaine de vaisseau* (1794) and successively commanded *Temeraire*, *l'Auguste*, *Suffren*, *Tigre,* and *Eole* (1793–95). He was made *chef de division* in 1796 and then commanded several ships. He was put on the inactive list in 1801 and retired in 1803. He died in 1809.

Source: Quintin, 358–59.

Emeriau de Beauverger, Maurice Julien Comte de

Background: Born in 1762, he volunteered for the navy in 1776. He was aboard *Intrepide* at Ouessant under Orvilliers.

American Service: He served under d'Estaing and de Grasse aboard *Diademe* and took part in the capture of Grenada. He was wounded at Savannah. He was promoted to *lieutenant de fregate* (1781). He was wounded in the Battle of Martinique (March 1780).

Post-American Career: He was twice wounded at the battle of Saintes but escaped capture. He then returned to the merchant navy in which he served until 1786. He served on various ships in the West Indies until 1791 and was promoted to *lieutenant de vaisseau.* In 1793, he received his first command of *le Cerf.* He commanded *Embuscade* which was part of Vanstabel's squadron escorting 400 ships which brought grain back to France avoiding widespread famine (1793). He was promoted to *capitaine de vaisseau* (1794) and commanded *Jemappes* in the Ireland expedition.

He commanded a division aboard *Spartiate* at Aboukir, where he was wounded and taken prisoner. Promoted *contre amiral* (1802), he commanded a small squadron aboard *Duquesne* with *Indomitable* and *Mont-*

Blanc bringing reinforcements to the Saint-Domingue expedition in January 1803. He was instructed to replace Latouche-Treville if he was ready to return to France. He was *prefet maritime* of Toulon (1803–11) and was promoted *vice amiral* (1811) in charge of the Toulon fleet replacing Allemand. He retired in 1815 and died in 1845.

Notable Facts: He served in twelve engagements or sieges. He was made a *grand cordon* of the *legion d'honneur* and peer de France on the Restoration.

Sources: La Jonquiere, 86; Taillemite, 170; Six, 423–24; Quintin, 320; Humble, 101–05.

Estaing, Charles Henry Comte de

Background: Born in 1729 to a Rouergue noble family (1192), which received two *honneurs de la cour*. He was a musketeer (May 1738) and then appointed lieutenant in the Rouergue regiment (January 1748). He was wounded at the siege of Maastricht in command of his regiment. He fought in India and was taken prisoner at Madras. He was promoted to *maréchal de camp* (February 1761) and lieutenant general (July 1762). He was governor of Saint-Domingue and transferred to the navy as Lieutenant General des Armées navales (December 1763). The navy added a third position of vice admiral in 1777 so he could fill it.

American Service: He commanded the fleet sent from Toulon to America (April 1778) and failed to mount a joint operation with American forces in Rhode Island, partially due to a storm. In October 1779 he failed in the combined attack on Savannah. He was considered at fault for not being aggressive enough.

Post-American Career: He returned to France in late 1779 and commanded a joint French-Spanish fleet at Cadiz. He was a member of the *Assemblée des Notables* and commanded the National Guard of Versailles. He served as a simple soldier in Paris and was named admiral of France (January 1792) but refused and was renominated the following year but was not employed. He was arrested for owning medallions of the royal family. He was imprisoned and guillotined in 1794.

Notable Facts: Former French president Giscard d'Estaing claimed to be a lineal descendant and was a Son of the American Revolution. D'Estaing had never fought in a naval battle prior to the American War of Independence and was bitterly resented for his lack of experience in the navy.

Sources: La Jonquiere, 88; Taillemite, 172–73; Ketchum, 296; Six, vol. 1, 430; ERA, vol. 1, 275; Schachtman, 133, 152–56, 159–62, 308; Petitfils, 454–55.

Fleuriot de Langle, Paul Vicomte de

Background: Born in 1744, he became a *garde de marine* in 1758. He was chief of staff to the Duc de Chartres aboard *Saint-Esprit* at Ouessant.

American Service: He commanded successively *Hussard* (1779), *Aigrette*, *Resolue* (1781), *Experiment* (1782), and *Astree* (1782), which participated in the Hudson Bay expedition.

Post-American Career: He was promoted to *capitaine de vaisseau* in 1782. He commanded *l'Astrolabe* in La Perouse's round the globe expedition and was killed in Samoa in 1787.

Notable Facts: He was secretary and then director of the marine academy and contributed to several important scientific discoveries. He brought funds to the American rebels in 1781.

Sources: La Jonquiere, 93; Taillemite; 187.

Galaup, Jean François Comte de Laperouse

Background: Born in 1741 to a noble family (1558), he was a *garde de marine* (1756). He joined *Celebre* and took part in the resupply expedition to Louisburg. He was wounded at the Battle of Quiberon Bay (1759) while serving on the *Formidable* and was taken prisoner. He served on *Robuste* on the attack against the fisheries of Newfoundland (1762). He commanded *Seine* (1775) in the Indian Ocean.

American Service: He was appointed as captain of the *Amazone* (1778) and captured HMS *Ariel*. He fought under d'Estaing at Savannah, returning to France with Vicomte Rochambeau who was sent to obtain increased monetary and other support. He was part of Ternay's fleet convoying Rochambeau's corps to America. He commanded a frigate division aboard *Astree* under Latouche-Treville.

Post-American Career: He took part in the attack on St. Kitts (February 1782) and fought at the Battle of Saintes. He captured two forts in Hudson Bay. In 1785 he was appointed to lead a scientific expedition circumventing the globe. The objective was to complete the discoveries of Captain Cook. The Royal Society provided the expedition with the instruments used by Cook. He set off in August 1785,

rounded the Horn and made stops in Chile, Easter Island.
and was the first European to land on Maui. He went on to
Alaska and the US West Coast, where he learned that he had
been promoted to *chef d'escadre.*

He then crossed the Pacific and arrived at Macao. He
later sailed to the Philippines and Korea. He eventually
reached Australia in January 1788. He and his ships
disappeared on the trip back to France.

Notable Facts: Louis XVI is rumored to have asked "Any
news of Laperouse?" on the morning of his execution. The
fate of Laperouse is discussed in Jules Verne's *Twenty
Thousand Leagues under the Sea.*

Sources: La Jonquiere, 132; Taillemite, 303–04;
Lauberdiere, 44.

Glandevez de Castellet, Jean Baptiste Commandeur de

Background: Born in 1728 into a noble Provencal family,
he was a *garde de marine* (1741) serving with Suffren. He
served on board *Solide* at the Battle of Cap Scie (1744). He
served on *Ocean* at the Battle of Lagos off the Portuguese
coast, where he was wounded and taken prisoner in 1759.
He commanded *Souverain* under Guichen against Admiral

Rodney off Martinique in April and May 1780. He then returned to France.

American Service: Still commanding *Souverain*, he was in Grasse's squadron sailing back to the West Indies in March 1781. He was at Battle of the Chesapeake.

Post-American Career: He was at the Saintes and promoted to *chef d'escadre* (1784). He died in 1803.

Notable Facts: Both of his uncles were admirals.

Sources: La Jonquiere, 101; Taillemite, 215.

Granchain de Semervile, Guillaume Jacques

Background: Born in 1744, he joined the navy in 1757 as a *garde de marine* and embarked immediately on *Emeraude,* on which he was captured. He served on *Sphinx* and then *Normande*. He was promoted to *enseigne de vaisseau* (1765). He served on *Aigrette* in the Mediterranean (1775). He was promoted to *lieutenant de vaisseau* (1777) and was aboard *Actif* at Ouessant under Orvilliers.

American Service: He served on the *Duc de Bourgogne* in Ternay's squadron, escorting the convoy bringing Rochambeau's army to America. He was onboard *Duc de Bourgogne* at Cape Henry. At Yorktown he served as

Rochambeau's liaison officer with Washington. He helped draft the surrender documents.

Post-American Career: He was promoted to *capitaine de vaisseau* (1782) and served as a senior staff officer in the combined fleet at Cadiz under d'Estaing. He commanded *Nymphe* and then was major of the *escadre d'evolution* (1788). He was director of ports and arsenals in the navy ministry (1790). He resigned in 1791 and died in 1805.

Notable Facts: He was known for his scientific abilities and took part in several expeditions including with Borda, testing astronomical and hydrological instruments (1776).

Sources: La Jonquiere, 104; Taillemite, 221–22.

Gras, Charles Rene Chevalier de Preville

Background: Born in 1732, he was a *garde de marine* (1746), rising to *capitaine de vaisseau* in 1777.

American Service: He commanded *Engageante* in d'Estaing's squadron, captured HMS *Rose,* and took part in the operations at Newport. He was flag captain to Guichen aboard *Triomphant*. He returned to France. He commanded *Zele* in Grasse's squadron and took part in the taking of Tobago and Chesapeake.

Post-American Career: He served at the Saintes. He retired in 1786 and was executed in 1793 in Lyon.

Notable Facts: He wrote several works on astronomy and hydrology.

Source: La Jonquiere, 105.

Grasse du Bar, François Paul Marquis de Grasse-Tilly

Background: Born in 1722 to an ancient Provençal family, he was a *garde de marine* (1734) in the fleet of the Order of Malta until 1737. He was taken prisoner at the battle of Cape Ortegal (1747). He commanded *Zephye* (1757) and several other ships. He advanced to *capitaine de vaisseau* (1762) and *chef d'escadre* (1778). He commanded *Robuste* at Ouessant. He left Brest with a squadron of four ships of the line and several frigates to join d'Estaing in Martinique and participated at the battle of Grenada.

American Service: He was at Savannah and then returned to France. He commanded the squadron protecting the convoy bringing Rochambeau's corps to America. In August 1781, Grasse convoyed the troops of Saint-Simon to the Chesapeake to rendezvous with Rochambeau. On September 5 he engaged Admiral Graves at the mouth of the Chesapeake, which prevented the British from resupplying

Cornwallis's forces. Graves and his squadron returned to New York, leaving the French in control. He was promoted to *lieutenant general des forces navales*.

Post-American Career: He was defeated by Rodney at Saintes and taken prisoner. He was exonerated at the court martial reviewing the conduct of officers at the battle but was exiled from court. He died in 1788.

Notable Fact: His family owned the principality of Antibes in the Middle Ages. His son and four daughters were granted asylum in the United States, as well as citizenship and stipends. The US Navy commissioned a destroyer named for him which left service in 1998.

Sources: La Jonquiere, 105; Taillemite, 222–23; Lauberdiere, 77; Ketchum, 297; ERA, vol. 1, 354–55; Philbrick, Chapter 8 and at 270; Schachtman, 257–61, 309–10; Petitfils, 457–58, 473–74, 476–83.

Grasse-Limermont, Etienne Marc Antoine Comte de

Background: Born in 1757, he was a *garde de marine* (1771), advancing to *capitaine de vaisseau* (1771). He served on Toulouse at the battle of Toulon (1744). He took part in the siege of Minorca (1756).

American Service: He served on *Aimable* at the battle of Rhode Island (1778) and commanded *Pandour* at the battle of Fort Royal (1781) and took part in the invasion of Tobago.

Post-American Career: He commanded Pandour at the Saintes. He was promoted to *capitaine de vaisseau* (1792). He was commander of *Toulon* (1793) and surrendered it to the British. He was promoted to *contre amiral* (1816). He died in 1838.

Notable Fact: His father Etienne, who rose to *chef d'escadre,* also served in America.

Source: La Jonquiere, 106.

Grimouart, Nicolas Henry Comte de

Background: Born in 1743, he was a *garde de marine* in 1758. He served on several ships including under La Touche Treville and took part in the taking of *Larache,* which harbored Barbary pirates.

American Service: He served aboard *Charmante* (1778) and commanded *Minerve* (1778–79) under d'Estaing. He was first officer on *Actif* and *Magnifique* under de Grasse, including at Saintes. He was taken prisoner and released going on to command *Scipion*. He was considered one of the most successful captains during the war.

Post-American Career: He was acting commander of the third squadron at Brest (1787) and then commanded *le Brave* and *Felicité*. He was sent to Saint-Domingue in command of *La Borée* (1790–92). He was promoted *contre amiral* in 1792 and commander of naval forces in Saint-Domingue. He was released as a noble on his return to France and later promoted to vice admiral in January 1793 and named commander of the forces at Brest. He did not take up the appointment and resigned. He was arrested, tried, and guillotined on February 7, 1794.

Sources: La Jonquiere, 107; Six, vol. 2, 529; Taillemite, 224–25.

Huon de Kermadec, Jean Michel

Background: Born in 1744, he joined the navy in 1766 as a *garde de marine*, rising to *lieutenant de vaisseau* (1779). He was aboard *Sensible* at Ouessant (1778).

American Service: He served aboard *Diademe* at Grenada and at Savannah. He then served under Lamotte-Picquet.

Post-American Career: He was promoted to *major de vaisseau* (1786). He commanded *Esperance* and was charged with finding traces of La Perouse's expedition. He died in New Caledonia in 1793, unaware that he had been relieved of command as a noble.

Notable Facts: He gave his name to several islands in the Pacific. His father, Francis, was flag captain to Duchaffault aboard *La Couronne* at Ouessant. His brother Jean Marie also served in the navy in America and distinguished himself at the taking of Dominica in 1778.

Sources: La Jonquiere, 111; Taillemite, 249.

Infernet, Louis Antoine

Background: Born in 1756, he joined the merchant navy and had been on four voyages to the Levant (1770–75). He was a petty officer on the frigate *Atalante* (1776).

American Service: He served as co-pilot on *Vaillant* in d'Estaing's squadron and participated in the Saint Lucia and Grenada actions, as well as the siege of Savannah. He served as first pilot on *Cesar* at the Chesapeake and then at Saintes, where he was wounded when *Cesar* blew up.

Post-American Career: He served in the navy until 1785 when he joined the merchant fleet. He rejoined the navy in 1792 and was promoted to *enseigne de vaisseau* (1793). He served aboard *Minerva* and then commanded *Vestale*. He was promoted to *capitaine de vaisseau* (1798).

He commanded *Rhin* in Villeneuve's squadron and distinguished himself at Cape Ferrol. At Trafalgar, his ship was attacked by five British vessels, and he finally surrendered and was taken prisoner. He was presented to Napoleon by Decres, who made him a commander of the legion of honor. He commanded *Robuste* and then *Annibal,* which was in Ganteaume's squadron resupplying Corfu. He was appointed *contre amiral* for retirement in 1814 and died the following year.

Sources: La Jonquiere, 113; Taillemite, 252–53; Nicolson, 277–86.

Kergariou-Locmaria, Thibaut Rene

Background: Born in 1739, he was a *garde de marine* (1755). He was aboard *Orient* at the first battle of Quiberon Bay (1759). He commanded *Esturgeon* and other ships. He commanded *Danae* at Ouessant and then *Medee* in Guichen's squadron. He was promoted to *capitaine de vaisseau* in 1780.

American Service: He served on *l'Engageante* which brought the funds to pay for Barras's squadron and Rochambeau's corps to Boston in September 1781.

Post-American Career: He stayed in the navy and was promoted to *chef de division* (1786). He emigrated and took part in the failed Quiberon Bay landing.

Notable Facts: He and his older brother, Pierre were executed for their part in the Quiberon Bay fiasco in 1795. Pierre and their younger brother Raymond also fought as naval officers in America.

Sources: La Jonquiere, 117; Lauberdiere, 200; Taillemite, 273–74.

La Clocheterie, Jean Isaac

Background: Born in Quebec in 1741 into a naval family, he served as a *garde de marine* (1754). He was named *enseigne de vaisseau* (1757). He was aboard and taken prisoner aboard *Belliqueux* at the first battle of Ouessant (1758). In 1771 he commanded *Sylphide* which was the naval artillery school. He commanded *Belle Poule* in its combat against *Arethusa,* which created a fashion where women wore a miniature of the ship in their hair. He was promoted to *capitaine de vaisseau* for this action.

American Service: He commanded *Jason* in Ternay's squadron at Newport and commanded *le Jason* under Destouches at Cape Henry (March 1781).

Post-American Career: He commanded *Hercule* under de Grasse, fighting at Saint Christopher and Saintes, where he was killed.

Sources: La Jonquiere, 123; Taillemite, 286; Lauberdiere, 73; Desmarais, 139.

La Galissoniere, Athanase-Scipion Marquis de

Background: Born in 1739, he was a *garde de marine* (1755). He served on *Protee* and then onboard *Illustre,* where he was wounded at the battle of Pondichery (1759). He was serving aboard *la Blanche* when it fought off HMS *Jupiter* during a crossing from France to the West Indies.

American Service: He commanded *La Blanche* at Savannah and was later captured by admiral Rodney. He was promoted to *capitaine de vaisseau* (1780).

Post-American Career: He was promoted to *chef de division* (1786). He commanded *Leopard* in Saint-Domingue at the outbreak of the Revolution and was denied access to his ship. He emigrated but was later amnestied, returning to France where he died in 1805.

Sources: La Jonquiere, 125; Taillemite, 290–91.

La Laune de Saint Didier, François Xavier Ame de

Background: Born in 1746, he was a *garde de marine* in 1762.

American Service: He commanded *Serpent* (1778–81) and was wounded in combat in September 1780. He then commanded *Surveillante* (1782–84).

Post-American Career: He was promoted to *capitaine de vaisseau* in 1786 and to *contre amiral* in 1814.

Source: La Jonquiere, 127.

La Motte Picquet, Toussaint Guillaume Comte de

Background: Born in 1720, he was a *garde de marine* (1736). He served aboard *Mercure* (1744) and then *Renomme* (1746). He served in the West Indies and in the Louisburg campaign (1757). He was promoted to *capitaine de vaisseau* (1762). He commanded the frigate *Malicieuse* in 1763. In command of *Cerf-Volant*, he distinguished himself in the naval exercises under Admiral Orvilliers in 1772.

In December 1775 he was called to Paris to advise the navy minister Sartine on his proposed new regulations. He commanded *Solitaire* in 1776. He was advanced to *chef d'escadre* (1778). He commanded *Saint-Esprit* at Ouessant. He took thirteen prizes in the subsequent campaign.

American Service: He led a division at Savannah under d'Estaing and then returned to Martinique, where he defeated Admiral Parker's squadron. In 1781 he led a squadron which defeated the British, capturing twenty-six ships.

Post-American Career: In recognition of his victories, he was promoted to lieutenant general des Armées navales (1782). He died in 1791.

Notable Facts: In fifty-two years of naval service, he fought in thirty-four campaigns, fought in twelve actions, and suffered six wounds. As captain of *Robuste*, he recognized the US by firing a nine-gun salute in honor of John Paul Jones (December 1779).

Sources: La Jonquiere, 130; Taillemite, 296–97.

La Poype, Louis Armand Marquis de Vertrieux

Background: Born in 1754, he was a *garde de marine* (1738), rising to *capitaine de vaisseau* (1767). He commanded *Pleiade* in 1763 in a mission to attack Moroccan pirates based at Sale. He accidentally fired on an Algerian ship, creating a diplomatic incident which hampered his career.

American Service: He commanded *Marseillais* in d'Estaing's squadron, fought against HMS *Preston,* and was at the siege of Savannah. He was promoted to *chef d'escadre* (1781).

Post-American Career: He died in 1807.

Notable Facts: He was a deputy from the nobility to the Estates General. Suffren was his first officer on *Pleiade*.

Source: La Jonquiere, 132.

La Roche Kerandraon, François Yves

Background: Born in 1758, he was a *garde de marine* (1777).

Service in America: He volunteered for America and served in the Continental Army as a lieutenant colonel. He later rejoined the French Navy, serving under Orvilliers and de Grasse.

Post-American Career: He served on the *Temeraire* (1783). He was promoted to *lieutenant de vaisseau* (1786), advancing to *capitaine de vaisseau* (1814) and to *contre amiral* (1816). He died in 1822.

Source: La Jonquiere, 133.

Lavilleon de la Villevalio, Jean Baptiste Comte de

Background: He was born in 1740. He joined the navy and rose to *lieutenant de vaisseau* (1772). He was wounded at Ouessant.

American Service: He served on the *Neptune* in America (1778) and *Couronne* (1779–81) and was promoted to *capitaine de vaisseau* (1781).

Post-American Career: He was de Grasse's flag captain on *la Ville de Paris* (1781–82) at the Saintes. He was promoted to *contre amiral* (1792) and to honorary vice admiral on the Restoration. He died in 1820.

Notable Facts: His brother, Toussaint, commanded the Rohan regiment during the Quiberon expedition in 1795 and was captured and shot.

Sources: La Jonquiere, 137; Six, vol. 2, 77.

Lafargue, Armand

Background: He was born in Rochefort.

American Service: He commanded an American privateer in 1778 and had his arm shot off in action.

Post-American Career: He entered the French Navy in 1779 and served on *l'Argus* in the Indian Ocean campaign (1779–82). He commanded *la Bellone* (1792–94). He was promoted *capitaine de vaisseau* in 1795 and commanded *Dryade* and then *Patriote*, taking part in the Ireland and Bantry Bay expeditions. He was on medical leave, returning as port captain of Saint-Pierre in Martinique. He died there in 1803.

Source: Quintin, 381.

Landais, Pierre

Background: Born in 1734, he was a volunteer in the navy (1745) and *lieutenant de vaisseau* (1767) under Bougainville and was on the round the world cruise. He retired in 1777.

American Service: He joined the Continental Navy, commanding the 36-gun privateer *l'Alliance* in December 1777. He was with John Paul Jones when he fought off HMS *Serapis*. He was court martialed and dismissed from the Continental Navy.

Post-American Career: Promoted to *capitaine de vaisseau* (July 1792), he commanded *Le Patriote*. He was in command of the squadron bombarding Cagliari and made *contre amiral* (January 1793). His naval division mutinied so he returned to Brest. He was relieved of command in October 1798. He returned to the United States, dying there in 1802.

Sources: La Jonquiere, 130; Six, vol. 2, 51; Desmarais, 112; ERA, vol. 2, 466–67.

Latouche-Treville, Louis Rene Comte de

Background: Born in 1745, he was a *garde de marine* (1756). He served under his father at the battle of Quiberon Bay aboard Dragon. He became a musketeer and then a cavalry captain. Having resigned from the navy he returned as a blue officer in the rank of *capitaine de brulot*.

American Service: As captain of *Hermione*, he fought spectacular duels against British ships. Commanding *la Gloire* he delivered funds to the Americans in June 1782. He sank HMS *Hector* but was later taken prisoner at the entrance to the Chesapeake.

Post-American Career: He was director of the port of Rochefort and later assistant director of the port department at Versailles. He was elected to the Estates General and joined the Third Estate. He was made commander of *Languedoc* and a division of four ships. He was promoted to *contre amiral* in 1793. He was later arrested and then released. He successfully repulsed two attempts by Nelson to destroy the fleet which had gathered in Boulogne to support the invasion of England in August 1801.

He led the Rochefort-based division, consisting of ships of the line: *Aigle, Argonaute, Duguay-Trouin, Foudroyant, Heros,* and *Union,* along with four frigates on the Saint-Domingue expedition and took Port-au-Prince. He was naval commander in the West Indies until returning to France due to severe illness in July 1803. He was promoted vice admiral in 1804 and commander of the Mediterranean fleet which was to have led the decisive battle Napoleon sought with the British in preparation for an invasion of England in 1804–05. He died aboard his flagship in Toulon later that year.

Notable Facts: Historians speculate that if Latouche had been commander of the combined fleet at Trafalgar, which would have been the case due to his seniority and Napoleon's confidence in his abilities, he would have beaten Nelson as he had done in the past.

Sources: Taillemite, 310; Six, vol. 2, 66–68; Quintin, 318–21, 325; Six, vol. 1, 102.

Le Gardeur de Tilly, Armand

Background: Born in 1732, he was a *garde de marine* (May 1750), advancing to *enseigne de vaisseau* (October 1755). He captured HMS *Minerva* off Saint-Domingue in 1778. He commanded *La Concorde* and took HMS *Congress* (February 1779) but was wounded during the engagement.

American Service: He commanded *l'Eveille* off the American coast (March 1780–August 1782). He led a small squadron in February 1781, driving Benedict Arnold's naval support up the Elizabeth River and capturing HMS *Romulus*. He participated in the battle of Cape Henry in March 1781. While a stalemate, the British were able to provide Arnold with reinforcements and supplies. Le Gardeur came to the assistance of Ardent at Chesapeake. He was at Saintes.

Post-American Career: He was promoted to *chef de division* and then *contre amiral* (May 1791). His nomination to vice admiral was never ratified. On the inactive list, he retired in November 1796 and died in 1812.

Sources: La Jonquiere, 140; Taillemite, 321; Lauberdiere, 65; Six, vol. 2, 96; D, 137, 139–40; Philbrick, 45.

Le Saige, Jacques Chevalier de Villesbrunne

Background: Born in 1755, he was a *garde de marine*. He was aboard *Ville de Paris* (1779) in Orvilliers's squadron.

American Service: He commanded *Gentille* (1779–80) under first Guichen and then Ternay and was present at the capture of HMS *Romulus* at the entrance to Chesapeake in February 1781. He was promoted to *capitaine de vaisseau*. He took command of *Romulus* at Newport and participated in the battle of Cape Henry. He commanded the division that brought Viomenil's contingent from Annapolis to Williamsburg in September 1781. After Yorktown, he was left with a division to guard the Chesapeake.

Post-American Career: He was a *chef de division* in 1786.

Notable Facts: His brother, Servant Paul, served as a captain in the Agenais regiment at Pensacola and Yorktown and was killed at St. Kitts.

Source: La Jonquiere, 146.

Le Begue de Germiny, Jean Antoine Comte

Background: Born in 1727 to a noble family, he was a *garde de marine* (1748). Promoted to lieutenant (1761), he later advanced to *capitaine de vaisseau* (1776).

American Service: He was Ternay's flag captain aboard *Saint-Esprit* (1779) and then *Duc de Bourgogne*. He commanded *Neptune* (1781–82). He commanded *Magnanime* (1781–82) and participated in the battle of the Chesapeake.

Post-American Career: He was flag captain to Vaudreuil aboard *Northumberland* at Saintes and was twice wounded. He was cleared of dereliction of duty at the ensuing court martial. He died in 1808.

Source: La Jonquiere, 100.

L'Hermite, Jean Mathieu

Background: Born in 1766, he was a volunteer at age fourteen on *Pilote des Indes* which captured a British privateer in the Channel Islands (1780).

American Service: He joined the *Northumberland* under de Grasse before it set off for America and fought at the Chesapeake and St Kitts. He was transferred to *Medee* and therefore was not present at Saintes.

Post-American Career: As a reward for his service on *Medee* he was made an auxiliary on *l'Oiseau* (1783). With the reduction in force after the war, he spent three years as first officer on two merchantmen (1784–87). In early 1788 he returned to the navy as a *sous lieutenant de vaisseau* serving on *Achille* in American waters. He served briefly on several ships including as first lieutenant on a cruise to Saint-Domingue (1790–92).

He joined the Atlantic fleet moving between ships until he was assigned to *Resolue* in Allemand's frigate squadron (1793). *Resolue* made the first capture of a British warship when war resumed. *L'Hermitte* was put in command of that ship renamed *Thamise* and then promoted to *lieutenant de vaisseau* in early 1794. He had a small but significant role in the battle of the First of June.

He commanded *la Seine* off the Norwegian coast (1794–95), capturing or destroying several enemy ships. He took command of *Cocarde* but it became damaged, so he was transferred to *Vertu* and joined Sercey's squadron on its mission to the East Indies. He was promoted to *capitaine de vaisseau* (1796). He served in the Indian Ocean commanding *Preneuse* until ordered to return to France in June 1799. He fought in several engagements but was finally forced to surrender his ship off *l'ile de France* (1799). He returned to France in 1800.

On the resumption of war, he commanded *Brutus* (1801) and then served as flag captain to Truguet on

Alexandre at Brest. After *Ganteaume* replaced Truguet, he returned to *Lorient* and commanded *Republicain* and then *Regulus*.

Commanding a small squadron aboard *Regulus* (1805–06) he sailed in the southern Atlantic capturing fifty British ships, including the sloop *Favorite* valued at ten million livres d'or. While cruising in the West Indies his squadron was largely destroyed by a hurricane. He was promoted to *contre amiral* (1807) and made maritime *prefet* of Brest (1811–15). He flew his flag for the last time when he was tasked with bringing back the Duchess of Orleans from exile at Messina in June 1814. He was promoted vice admiral for retirement (1816) and died in 1826.

Sources: La Jonquiere, 149; Six, vol. 2, 120; Humble, 197–202; Taillemite, 337.

Lowenhorn, Poul de

Background: Born in 1751, he entered the Danish naval academy and was a junior lieutenant (1770). He sailed in the Mediterranean. He and nine other Danish naval officers volunteered to serve in the French navy on the outbreak of the American War of Independence.

American Service: He served under Verdun de Crene in d'Estaing's squadron and was promoted to *lieutenant de vaisseau*. He was shipwrecked and returned to Denmark.

Post-American Career: He retired to Denmark and commanded *Provence* (1782–83) in a year-long scientific expedition. He was made first director of the Naval Hydrographic and Oceanographic Service copied from the French *depot des cartes de marine* in 1784. He held several ship commands (1786–92), having been promoted to captain in 1789.

He served in several senior administrative roles in the Danish Navy and was promoted to flag rank in 1812. He died in 1826.

Notable Fact: He was a member of the Institut de France.

Source: La Jonquiere, 153.

Lucas, Jean Jacques

Background: Born in 1764, he joined the navy as an *officier auxillaire* (1779).

American Service: He served on *Hermione* (1779–82). He participated in five battles including the Chesapeake, in which he was wounded. He was in Laperouse's squadron in the Hudson Bay expedition.

Post-American Career: He was promoted to *lieutenant de vaisseau* (1794). He was at the battle of Algeciras and took command of HMS *Hannibal* which had been captured from the British. He was promoted to *capitaine de vaisseau* (1803).

He distinguished himself at Trafalgar where commanding *Redoutable* he came to the aid of his flagship *Bucentaure* by engaging HMS *Victory*. One of his marines mortally wounded Admiral Nelson. His ship was destroyed (522 of his 643-man crew were killed or out of action), and he was taken prisoner. He was presented to Napoleon and promoted to commander of the Legion of Honor. He commanded *Nestor* (1811–14). His honesty meant that he was never promoted to flag rank by either the Emperor or Louis XVIII.

Sources: La Jonquiere, 153; Taillemite, 340–41; Nicolson, 258–60.

MacCarthy de Marteigue

Background: He became a *garde de marine* in 1758.

American Service: He served on *Fendant* (1778–79) as a lieutenant. He was promoted to *capitaine de vaisseau* in 1780. He commanded *Actif* (1781–82) and *Magnifique*, which fought at Saintes and later foundered off the American coast. He was given command of the USS *America* as a gift of Congress to France (1783).

Post-American Career: He was promoted to *chef de division* in 1786.

Source: La Jonquiere, 155.

Medine, Magon de Charles Rene

Background: Born in 1763 to a Breton noble family, he joined the navy at age fourteen and was a *garde de marine* (1778). He served on *Bretagne* at the Battle of Ouessant and then in the English Channel on *Saint Esprit*. Promoted to *enseigne de vaisseau* (1780), he served on *le Solitaire* in the West Indies under Guichen.

American Service: He served aboard *Caton* in de Grasse's squadron fighting at the Chesapeake.

Post-American Career: He was taken prisoner on *Caton* at Saintes. He was posted to *Semillante* which served in the Indian Ocean (1783–98), commanding successively in *Amphitrite*, *Minerve*, and *Prudente*. On *Amphrite* he captured Diego Garcia for France (1786). He was promoted to *capitaine de vaisseau* (1794). He was acting commander of the naval forces in the Indian Ocean. In January 1798, he escorted two Spanish ships back to Europe in command of *Vertu*. He was dismissed from the service but reinstated by Brui and later named *chef de division*.

After a tour of duty in the Navy Ministry on the recommendation of Bruix, he commanded a squadron from Brest which landed Rochambeau's 2500 men at Saint Dauphin during the Saint-Domingue expedition. For his part in taking the fort there, he was promoted to *contre amiral*.

In 1803, he was ordered to Boulogne where he was to command one of the wings in the invasion of England. In March 1805 he commanded a division flying his flag on *Algeciras* at Rochefort under Villeneuve and commanded the rear guard at the Battle of Cape Finisterre. He was aboard Algeciras leading his squadron at Trafalgar where he was killed after five hours of fighting against HMS *Tonnant*.

Sources: La Jonquiere, 155; Taillemite, 345–46; Lauberdiere, 72; Six, vol. 2, 140; Quintin, 319; Humble, 107–14; Nicolson, 257–58.

Maistral, Esprit-Tranquille

Background: Born in 1763 to a Breton noble family, he was an ordinary seaman (1775), serving on *l'Oiseau* in the West

Indies. He was a volunteer on *Vengeur* at Ouessant and then in the West Indies under Guichen.

American Service: He served on *Scipion* in de Grasse's squadron fighting at Fort Royal, the Chesapeake, and St. Christopher.

Post-American Career: He served at sea continuously in the West Indies and American coast. He was promoted to lieutenant (1792) and the *capitaine de vaisseau* (1793). He commanded *Normande* and was sent to escort a convoy from the West Indies. He was arrested, released, and placed on inactive service. He was recalled to commanded *Terrible* and *Fougueux*, in which he took part in the Ireland expedition.

He commanded *Mont Blanc* and was briefly flag captain to Latouche-Treville. He commanded *Neptune* under Villeneuve and fought at both Cap Ferrol and Trafalgar. He was major general at Brest and promoted to *contre amiral* for retirement in 1814, dying the following year.

Notable Fact: His brother Desire rose to *capitaine de vaisseau* in 1800 and commanded the naval forces of the Kingdom of Italy until 1807.

Sources: La Jonquiere, 156; Taillemite, 348–49.

Maitz, François Louis du Comte de Goimpy

Background: Born in 1729, he was a *garde de marine* (1746), rising to *capitaine de vaisseau* (1772). He was taken prisoner aboard *Magnanime* (1748) at the first battle of Ouessant. In 1753 he was aboard *Comete* on a scientific trip to Portugal to observe a solar eclipse, having been named to the *Academie de Marine* the previous year. He served in the Canada campaign (1757). He commanded *Malicieuse* (1760) and took two British ships captive. He was aboard *Diademe* at the Battle of Martinique (1780) where he was wounded.

American Service: He commanded *Destin* (1780–83) at the Battle of the Chesapeake and at Saintes.

Post-American Career: He was promoted to *chef d'escadre* (1784) and retired shortly thereafter. He died in 1807.

Notable Fact: He wrote well received treatises on astronomy and naval construction.

Sources: La Jonquiere, 156; Taillemite, 154.

Marigny, Charles Vicomte de Bernard de Marigny

Background: Born in 1740, he was a *garde de marine* (1754). He commanded *Dorade* and then *Serin* on convoy protection.

American Service: He commanded the *Belle Poule,* which brough Silas Deane back to the colonies in January 1778. He commanded *Juno* which captured HMS *Ardent* in August 1779 and was in the squadron carrying Rochambeau's corps to Newport. He commanded *Ardent* at the battle of Cape Henry in March 1781 and was later part of Barras's squadron at Yorktown.

Post-American Career: He was promoted to *chef de division* and welcomed Louis XVI on his visit to Cherbourg. Major general at Brest, he was promoted to *contre amiral* (1791) and then resigned. He was arrested and freed after Thermidor. He was made a vice admiral (1814) and commanded the fleet at Brest. He died in 1816.

Notable Facts: He was a founding member of the Society of Cincinnati. His brother, Charles Louis, served as a *capitaine de vaisseau* in America and was killed commanding *Cesar* at the battle of the Saintes (1782). A cousin, Augustin, a former naval officer commanded the artillery in the Vendean army and was captured and shot in 1794.

Sources: La Jonquiere, 158; Taillemite, 355; Lauberdiere, 16; D, 139.

Martel, Leandre François

Background: Born in 1737, he entered the artillery (August 1754). He transferred to the navy as *garde de la marine* (February 1758). He served in the Levant and against the pirates of Sale (Morocco). Promoted to *enseigne de vaisseau* (August 1767) and then *lieutenant de vaisseau* (February 1778).

American Service: He served on *Flore* under d'Estaing (1778–79), on *Jason,* and *Pluton* under de Grasse. He was involved in three battles under Guichen (May 1779–October 1780). Returned to America aboard *Alceste* (1783).

Post-American Career: Promoted to *capitaine de vaisseau* (June 1792), he commanded *le Triomphant* based at Toulon. Advanced to *contre amiral* (January 1793). He was suspended and then reintegrated. He retired in September 1796 and died in 1817.

Sources: La Jonquiere, 160; Six, vol. 2, 159.

Martin, Pierre

Background: Born in 1752 in Louisburg (now Canada), his family relocated to France where he joined the merchant navy as a seaman. He advanced to 2nd pilot in 1774.

American Service: In March 1778 he was appointed pilot on *Magnifique* (1778–81) under d'Estaing, serving at Savannah. He transferred to *Ceres* and returned to France.

Post-American Career: He was appointed *officier bleu* and served as master pilot on the transport *Vigilante*. He served on *Desiree* and then *Rossignol* in the West Indies (1784–86). He commanded the corvette *Cousine* on the West African station (1786–91). He was promoted to *lieutenant de vaisseau* in 1792 and returned to Senegal in command of *Espoir*. He was made a chevalier of Saint Louis.

At the beginning of 1793 he led *l'Espoir* and two frigates patrolling the French coast capturing a ship off Jersey and was promoted to *capitaine de vaisseau* as a result. He commanded *America* and *Tortue* and was promoted to *contre amiral* ten months after becoming a captain. In February 1794, he was put in command of the Toulon fleet. He built up the fleet and restored the naval facilities following the insurrection and British occupation.

In February 1795 he sailed to Corsica with 3500 to reconquer the island for France. He failed to do so and fought an indecisive battle against a British squadron at Cape Noli. He was promoted to vice admiral (1796) handing over command of the Toulon fleet to Brueys. He returned to Rochefort as port commander and then *prefet maritime*. He died there in 1820.

Sources: Sixvol. 2, 160–61; Humble, 31–34.

Medine d'Isambert, Charles Comte de

Background: Born in 1736 to a noble family, he was a *garde de marine* (1754). He was promoted to *lieutenant de vaisseau* (1767), he advanced to *capitaine de vaisseau* (1779).

American Service: He was flag captain to Ternay in Saint Esprit (1779) and then on *Duc de Bourgogne* (1780). He captained *Neptune* at the Battle of Cape Henry and was wounded.

Post-American Career: He commanded *Experiment* at the Battle of Saint Kitts and *Reflechi* at Saintes. He was flag captain to Vaudreil on *Northumberland* (1783). He did not serve in the Revolution and was rewarded with promotion to flag rank, first as *contre amiral* and then as vice admiral on the *Restoration*. He died in 1819.

Sources: La Jonquiere, 165; Desmarais, 139.

Missiessy, Edouard Thomas

Background: He was born in 1756 into a naval family. Aged ten, he went to sea as a volunteer on *l'Altier* commanded by his father. Promoted to *garde de pavilion* or standard bearer while serving on *La Flore* in the Levant (1775–76). Promoted to *enseigne de vaisseau* in April 1777, he was involved in protecting shipping from the Barbary pirates serving aboard *La Sultane*.

American Service: He served aboard *le Vaillant* in d'Estaing's squadron and participated in the actions at Newport and Savannah. After returning to France, he shipped out on *Surveillante* and served in American waters. He was promoted to *lieutenant de vaisseau* (May 1781).

Post-American Career: He returned to France and then back to the West Indies in command of the cutter *Pygme* where he was taken prisoner by the British. He was first lieutenant on *le Reflechi* during the closing phases of the siege of Gibraltar. At sea in the Baltic commanding transport ships, he served in the Windward Islands and

Mediterranean, commanding frigates *La Belette* and *Modeste* (1783–92). As a *capitaine de vaisseau* (January 1792), he commanded *Le Centaure* under Admiral Truguet. He was made a *chevalier de Saint Louis*.

Promoted to *contre amiral* (January 1793), he flew his flag on *Centaure* under Truguet. He was arrested in May 1793 and then released. His hometown of Toulon revolted that August and was occupied by the British. As a result, he left the navy and went into exile in Italy.

After his return to France two years later he was the subject of a court of inquiry. He was acquitted. He served in staff jobs, including as director of naval construction in Paris until 1800. He acted as chief of staff to the combined Franco-Spanish fleet at Cadiz under Truguet's command (June 1801) and then was named *prefet maritime* of Cadiz. After a stint as maritime *prefet* at le Havre, he was a squadron commander under Truguet at Brest (1802–04).

He commanded the squadron at Rochefort and was sent to the West Indies to resupply the islands with troops prior to linking up with Villeneuve and Ganteaume (1805) in preparation for the decisive battle that was to precede the invasion of England. The invasion was cancelled. He was momentarily disgraced for not having captured Diamond

Head during the West Indies expedition and replaced by Allemand.

He was unemployed until 1808 when he was named commander of the Scheldt flotilla and was promoted to vice admiral in 1809. He successfully defended Antwerp against the allied forces. After the Restoration he was maritime prefect and commander of naval forces at Toulon. He served on the admiralty board before retiring. He was awarded the Grand Cross of the Legion of Honor and later made a chevalier of Saint-Esprit, the most prestigious royal order by the Bourbons. He finally retired in 1832 and died in 1837.

Sources: La Jonquiere166; Taillemite, 372–73; Six, vol. 2, 206–07; Humble, 15–18.

Montcabrier, Josep Saturnin Comte de Peytes de

Background: Born in 1741, he was a *garde de marine* in 1756.

American Service: He served on *Alcemene* in d'Estaing squadron and took part in the battle of Grenada. He transferred to *Triomphant* under Guichen. He was at St. Kitts and Saintes where he was wounded. He took command of *Triomphant* on the death of Captain du Pavillion. He was flag captain to Vaudreuil while he was in charge of protecting the New England coast. He was promoted to *capitaine de vaisseau* in 1782.

Post-American Career: He was promoted to honorary *contre amiral* in 1814 and died in 1818.

Source: La Jonquiere, 168.

Monier, Jean Baptiste Marquis de Castellet

Background: Born in 1732, he was a *garde de marine* (1748), rising to *capitaine de vaisseau* (1777).

American Service: He commanded *Cesar* off the Rhode Island coast. He was wounded at Grenada and took part in the siege of Savannah. He commanded *Sultane* (1780–81).

Post-American Career: He commanded *Suffisant* (1782–83) at Gibraltar. He was promoted to *chef d'escadre* (1786) and died in 1825.

Source: La Jonquiere, 57.

Montclair, Louis Augustin Comte de

Background: Born in 1727, he was a *garde de marine* (1743), rising to *capitaine de vaisseau* in 1772. He commanded *Solitaire* (1779).

American Service: He commanded *Hector* (1779) and then *Diademe* (1781) under de Grasse. Having been promoted to brigadier, he was wounded at the Chesapeake.

Post-American Career: He died in 1784.

Source: La Jonquiere, 169.

Monteil, François Aymar Baron de

Background: Born in 1725, he was a *garde de marine* (1741). He took part in the battle of Cape Scie (1746), for which he was promoted to ensign. He commanded *Anemone* (1755) and was promoted to lieutenant (1756). He took part in the battles of Cuddalore and Negapatam (1758) in Ache's squadron. He commanded *Sylphide* at the battle of Pondichery (1759). Promoted to *capitaine de vaisseau* (1762), he commanded several ships. He commanded *Conquerant* at Ouessant (July 1778). He was promoted *chef d'escadre* (1779).

American Service: In 1780 he was given command of the West Indies squadron. He led the French squadron of four ships of the line and two frigates at the Siege of Pensacola (May 1781). He commanded the *Languedoc* at the battle of the Chesapeake.

Post-American Career: He returned to Brest in 1782 and was promoted to lieutenant general des Armées navales (February 1783). He died in 1787.

Notable Facts: He was given a portrait of himself with a diamond frame by the King of Spain for his leadership at Pensacola.

Sources: La Jonquiere, 169; Lauberdiere, 49; Taillemite, 377.

Nauckhoff, Henrick Johann

Background: Born in 1744, he joined the Swedish Navy and volunteered to serve with the French Navy during the War of Independence.

American Service: He served aboard several ships with distinction under d'Estaing and de Grasse.

Post-American Career: He returned to Swedish service and participated in the battles of Hogland (1788) and Oland (1789) against the Russian Navy. He was later captured by the Russians. He was promoted colonel in 1793 and to rear admiral in 1797.

He commanded the Swedish squadron in the Finnish campaign in 1808. He was promoted to vice admiral in 1809, rising to admiral and head of the navy in 1817. He died in 1818.

Source: La Jonquiere, 173.

Parscau du Plessix, Louis Guillaume Seigneur de

Background: Born in 1725, he was a *garde de marine* (1744) and rose to *capitaine de vaisseau* (1772). He was flag captain to Orvilliers on the *Duc de Bretagne* and then commanded *Intrepide* under Guichen at the battle of Martinique.

American Service: He commanded *Intrepide* at the siege of Pensacola under Monteil. He commanded *Languedoc* at the Battle of the Chesapeake. He was sent to France to announce the victory at Yorktown with the Duc de Lauzun.

Post-American Career: He commanded *Guerrier* in the joint Franco Spanish fleet under Cordova (1782). He was made *chef d'escadre* in 1784 and died in 1786.

Notable Facts: He was considered one of the most able officers of his generation and his death was reported as a loss to the navy to Louis XVI.

Source: La Jonquiere, 178.

Pitray, Pierre Comte de Simard de

Background: Born in 1737, he joined the navy in 1756 as a *garde de marine*.

American Service: He served aboard *Neptune* and *Diademe* (1779–80) under La Motte Picquet and aboard *Brave* (1781–83) under de Grasse.

Post-American Career: He was promoted to *capitaine de vaisseau* in 1782 and to honorary *contre amiral* in 1814. He died in 1820.

Source: La Jonquiere,183.

Pleville Le Pelley, Georges Rene Comte de Pleville

Background: Born in 1726 to a bourgeois family which made its fortune in armaments. At twelve he ran away to sea from his boarding school, serving on a fishing vessel and then on a ship bound for America (1740). Appointed *garde de marine* (1743), he does not have the resources to take up the position.

In 1744 on the outbreak of war he joined a privateer, which lost a fight against a British ship during which engagement Pleville lost a leg. He was taken as a prisoner to Falmouth. In 1747, at the battle of Cape Finisterre, he lost his wooden leg! In May 1747 *L'Aimable Grelot* sails with Pleville and captured eight British ships. Pleville's share of the prize money was 2500 louis. He returned to the fishing trade for four years having failed to obtain a command.

He was at Marseille in 1757 and was given command of the privateer *Colibri*, owned by his new father-in-law. In 1758 *Colibri* was requisitioned into naval service. He then commanded *Hirondelle* (1758–62) as a *lieutenant de fregate*. He managed to capture three Indiamen but lost his second wooden leg doing so. He applied for shore duty for health reasons and was port commander at Marseille (1766–70).

As port captain of Marseille in 1770, he helped save the foundering HMS *Alarme,* whose captain was Jervis (future Earl of St. Vincent). The Lords of the Admiralty sent him a letter of thanks and a sterling silver soup bowl. He was belatedly promoted to *capitaine de port*.

American Service: In fitting out the fleet, d'Estaing requested that Pleville and his son serve on his flagship, the *Languedoc,* as it sailed to America. He served as d'Estaing's supply officer and was responsible for selling off prize ships. He was in Boston in 1778 purchasing supplies when a riot—

protesting at the inaction of d'Estaing—resulted in his being wounded and his deputy being killed. He was at Savannah.

Post-American Career: He was named *capitaine de vaisseau* in recognition of his service in America. He was one of the three members of the Maritime Commission looking into reforms of the navy. He was part of a peace delegation to end the war with Great Britain (April 1797) and appointed *contre amiral* (October 1797) and commanded the Adriatic fleet. He served briefly as Minister of the Navy (1797–98) being promoted to vice admiral. He resigned over the Egyptian expedition which he felt doomed to failure. Within six weeks he was appointed commander of the Adriatic coast. He was a senator. He died just before the battle of Trafalgar in 1805.

Notable Facts: His son was taken prisoner by the British and released without parole along with three other officers in recognition of his father's rescue of HMS *Alarme*. His nephew Pleville Dumanoir served in the Irish expedition under General Hoche (December 1796), was responsible for the transports in the Egyptian expedition, led at the first battle of Algeciras, and participated in the battle of Trafalgar, where his conduct was heavily criticized. His advancement was often ascribed to the achievements of his uncle.

Sources: La Jonquiere, 183; Taillemite, 425; Six, vol. 2, 319.

Ponteves-Gien, Henri Jean Baptiste Vicomte de

Background: Born in 1738, he was a *garde de marine* (1754) and was aboard *Fier* at the battle of Port Mahon (1756). He took part in many convoys in the Mediterranean during the Seven Years War. He commanded *Resolue* in 1778 and was promoted to *capitaine de vaisseau* (1779). He was part of the naval force under Vaudreil that attacked Senegal (1779).

American Service: As first officer on *Tonnant*, he participated in the campaigns off Rhode Island and at Savannah. He was flag captain on *Zele*.

Post-American Career: He commanded *Alcide* (1782-83) and was a major general at Brest. He was appointed *chef de division* in 1786. He commanded the Leeward Islands station (1788–90) and was acting governor of Martinique, dying aboard *Illustre* (1790).

Notable Facts: His brother, Jean Baptiste, and son, François, both served in the war. François rose to *contre amiral* in 1825.

Sources: La Jonquiere, 184; Taillemite, 428.

Quesne, Pierre Claude Marquis de Longbrun

Background: Born in 1751 in Martinique. He was a *garde de marine* (1766).

American Service: He served aboard *Rossignol* (1778) and was wounded in combat aboard *Hermione* (1779–82). He commanded *Guadeloupe* (1783).

Post-American Career: He was promoted to *capitaine de vaisseau* in 1792 and to honorary *contre amiral* in 1818. He died in 1834.

Notable Facts: His brother, Augustin, served as a naval volunteer in America.

Source: La Jonquiere, 187.

Racord, Pierre Paul

Background: Born in 1755, he worked as a carpenter at the Toulon naval base (1765–70). He joined the navy as a petty officer in December 1770 and served on several ships.

American Service: He was aboard *Vaillant* in d'Estaing's squadron and participated in the capture of St. Lucia and Grenada, as well as the siege of Savannah.

Post-American Service: He served as pilot on *l'éclair* and then *Hasard* which campaigned in the Levant. He was aboard *Centaure* in Truguet's squadron in the Sardinian campaign in early 1793. He was promoted to *capitaine de vaisseau* in 1796 and then commanded *Tonnant* and *Jean-Jacques Rousseau*. He commanded *Peuple Souverain* in the Egyptian expedition. He was badly wounded at Aboukir and taken prisoner. Upon being released, he returned to Toulon. He successfully escorted a convoy despite being attacked by the British. He retired in 1803.

Source: Quintin, 419.

Raimondis, Joseph Louis Chevalier de

Background: Born in 1723 to a noble family (1668), he was a *garde de marine* (1745) and promoted to *enseigne* (1747). He participated in the battle of Cape Finisterre and served in the West Indies (1751). He took part in the Minorca campaign and was promoted to *lieutenant de vaisseau* (1757). He sailed under his relative, comte de Broves. He commanded *La Gracieuse* (1775), having been promoted to *capitaine de vaisseau* (1772).

American Service: He commanded *Cesar* in d'Estaing's fleet to America. *Cesar* was separated from the fleet and fought HMS *Iris* during which Raimondis lost an arm to a cannonball (August 1778). He recuperated in Boston, where he received a sword of honor for his bravery.

Post-American Career: He and Lafayette then returned to France. He was promoted to *chef d'escadre* and made *commandeur* of *Saint Louis*. He died in 1801.

Notable Fact: He fought in twenty-five campaigns and seven battles and was wounded twice.

Source: La Jonquiere, 189.

Renaud d' Aleins, Laurent

Background: Born in 1734, he was a *garde de marine* in 1750, advancing to *capitaine de vaisseau* in 1777.

American Service: He commanded *Hector* at the Battle of the Chesapeake and Neptune at the Saintes. He later commanded *Hercule* under Vaudreuil.

Post-American Career: He was made a *chef de division* in 1786.

Source: La Jonquiere, 21.

Richery, Joseph de

Background: Born in 1757, he was a volunteer on *Sultane* (1766). He attended the naval academy at Le Havre (1774). He was made *garde de marine* (1777) and served on *Mignonne* and then *Fantasque*, the latter commanded by Suffren.

American Service: He was aboard *Hector* as an ensign under d'Estaing and distinguished himself at Newport.

Post-American Career: In 1781 he served aboard *Vengeur* in Suffren's squadron and fought at the battles of La Praya, Sadras, Negapatam, Provedien, Tricomale, and Gondelour. He commanded the *Maréchal de Castries* in the China Sea (1787) and encountered Laperouse at Macao on his round the world expedition. He was promoted to *capitaine de vaisseau* in January 1793 and given command of *Bretagne*. He was forced to resign as a noble.

Reinstated in 1795, he was named *chef de division*. In October he captured a convoy of thirty British ships which he forced into Cadiz. He was promoted to *contre amiral* (1796). In August of that year, he led a squadron which destroyed more than eighty ships off Newfoundland. He commanded *Pegase* and the light squadron in the Ireland expedition, which failed. He retired due to illness and died in 1798.

Sources: La Jonquiere, 191; Six, vol. 2, 369; Taillemite, 450.

Rigaud, Louis Comte de Vaudreuil

Background: Born in 1728, he was a *garde de marine* (1743) and advanced to *capitaine de vaisseau* (1772). He commanded *Magnanime* (1780).

American Service: He commanded *Sceptre* in Grasse's fleet and participated in the Battle of the Chesapeake. He later served under his eldest brother at the battle of Saintes.

Post-American Career: He was promoted to *chef d'escadre* in 1782 and then to lieutenant general des Armées navales (1791). He was named vice admiral in 1793. He died in 1803.

Source: La Jonquiere, 220.

Rossel, Elisabeth Paul Chevalier de

Background: Born in 1765, he was a *garde de marine* (1780).

American Service: He served on *Magnanime* under Grasse at the Chesapeake and later at St. Christopher and Saintes.

Post-American Career: He served in the Indian Ocean (1785–89) and was aboard *Resolution* when it made the first counter-monsoon trip between India and China. He was promoted to *lieutenant de vaisseau* (1787) and was aboard *Recherche,* which was sent to find the La Perouse expedition. He was promoted to *capitaine de vaisseau* in 1792 while commanding *Recherche* on a scientific mission searching for evidence of the Entrecsateaux expedition, which he found.

On returning to France, he was captured and held as a prisoner in the Shetlands until 1802. He was named an honorary *contre amiral* (1822) and was director of the *depots des cartes et plans* (1826). He died in 1829.

Sources: Taillemite, 465; La Jonquiere, 196.

Ruffo, Pierre Rene, Comte de Roux-Bonneval

Background: Born in 1741, he became a *garde de marine* in 1755.

American Service: He commanded *Alcmene* in d'Estaing's squadron and was at Newport and the capture of Dominica and St. Lucia, as well as the battle of Grenada. He was promoted to *capitaine de vaisseau* in March 1779. He was captured while escorting a convoy.

Post-American Career: In 1782 he commanded *Precieuse,* followed by *Minerve* and *Badine.* He was made *chef de division* in 1786 and was twice acting commander at Toulon. He died in 1814.

Source: La Jonquiere, 197.

Beaudot de Sainneville, Nicolas Chevalier de

Background: He was a *garde de marine* in 1755, advancing to *capitaine de vaisseau* in 1779.

American Service: Commanding *Nymphe* (1778–80), his was the first French war ship to visit Boston since the Seven Years' War in May 1778. He later commanded *Indien* (1781), *Puissant* (1782), and *le Robuste* (1783).

Post-American Career: He was made a *chef de division* in 1786.

Source: La Jonquiere, 19.

Sambucy de Luzenson, Pierre Louis, Chevalier de Sambucy

Background: Born in 1739, he was a *garde de marine* (1756).

American Service: He served aboard *Provence* at Rhode Island, Saint Lucia, Grenada, and Savannah. He was aboard *Caton* at the Chesapeake. He commanded *La Badine* (1781).

Post-American Career: He was promoted to *capitaine de vaisseau* (1782) and to honorary *contre amiral* (1816). He died in 1821.

Source: La Jonquiere, 203.

Saqui des Tourres, Henri Claude

Background: He was born in 1741 and joined the navy as a *garde de marine* (1756).

American Service: He served aboard *Languedoc* (1778–79) under d'Estaing. He commanded *Naiade* (1780–81) and was promoted to *capitaine de vaisseau* (1782).

Post-American Career: He was wounded at the siege of St. Lucia and commanded *Mignonne* (1782–83).

Source: La Jonquiere, 204.

Sercey, Pierre Cesar Marquis de

Background: He was born in 1753 near Autun. He was a volunteer at Brest at age twelve. He sailed in the West Indies and Indian waters was a *garde de marine* in 1769. He returned to the South Seas under Kerguelen. He was promoted to *lieutenant de vaisseau* for having sailed the damaged *Belle Poule* back to Brest in 1778.

American Service: He served on several ships in the West Indies during the War of Independence and commanded successively the cutters *Sans Pareil, Serpent,* and *Leverette.* While in command of *Sans Pareil* he was captured and later exchanged. He served under Monteil at Pensacola and was promoted to *lieutenant de vaisseau.* He was first officer and then commander of the frigate *Nymphe* which captured the British merchantman bring back the retiring governor of the West Indies.

Post-American Career: He commanded frigates and was promoted to *capitaine de vaisseau* (January 1792) and to *contre amiral* (February 1793). He was sent out from Brest that April with three ships of the line to escort a convoy gathering in the West Indies to return to France. When he reached Saint-Domingue, the rebellion had broken out and he gave what support he could to the colonists. He escorted the convoy back, making stops at Norfolk and New York. On his return to France he was arrested, imprisoned in the Luxemburg Palace, and stripped of his rank. He wasn't released and reinstated until early 1795.

He was appointed to lead a squadron of frigates and corvettes to disrupt British commerce in the South Seas in late 1795. He also carried 800 reinforcements and supplies for the Ile de France garrison. He sailed from Ile de France on July 14, 1796. He beat a more powerful British force off the Malacca Straight in early September. In January 1797 he failed to attack a large undefended British convoy in the Bali Strait. He was later taken prisoner and not released until the Peace of Amiens.

On his return to France, he was censored by Decres and decided to go to the Île de France (Mauritius), where he established himself as a planter. In 1810 he returned to France and remained on the inactive list. He was promoted to vice admiral on the Restoration and awarded a Grand Cross of both the Legion of Honor and Saint Louis. He retired in 1823 and died in Paris in 1836.

Sources: Six, vol. 2, 448–49; Humble, 39–45.

Paris, Claude Rene Comte de Soulange

Background: Born in 1732, he was a *garde de marine* (1751), advancing to *capitaine de vaissseau* (1777). He commanded *Sphinx* at Ouessant and took part in Vaudreuil's attack on Senegal (1779).

American Service: Still commanding *Sphinx*, he joined d'Estaing's squadron and participated in the siege of Savannah.

Post-American Career: He commanded *Protecteur* in the combined Franco-Spanish fleet (1782). He was promoted to *chef d'escadre* in 1785. He was arrested and executed in 1795.

Source: La Jonquiere, 207.

Suffren, Pierre Andre Bailli de Suffren

Background: He was born in 1729 in Provence. He was a knight of Malta and then a *garde de marine* (1743). He fought at Cap Scie aboard *Solide* (1744). He was taken prisoner aboard on *Monarque* (1747). He was in Malta (1749–51). In 1756 he fought at Port Mahon (1756). He was captured at the battle of Lagos. He was *capitaine de vaisseau* (1772) and commanded *Mignone* (1772–73).

American Service: He commanded *Le Fantasque* (1778–79) under d'Estaing, forcing the entrance to the bay of Narraganset during the siege of Newport in August 1778, and at the battle of Cape Henry in March 1781.

Post-American Career: He was captain of *Zele* (1780) when the combined fleet captured a large British convoy. He commanded *Heros* and a squadron of five ships in India (1781–84), beating the British at *la Praya* and ensuring that the British did not take the Cape Colony. In Indian waters, he won four victories: Sadras, Provedien, Negapatam, and Trincomalee. He was promoted to *chef d'escadre* in 1782 and then wintered off Java and captured HMS *Coventry* and fifty merchantmen.

He defeated a British squadron at Gondelour (June 1783). France created a fourth vice admiral berth for him, carrying the rank of *maréchal de France* in 1784. He returned to France and commanded the fleet at Brest in 1787 and died the following year.

Notable Fact: He was considered one of the three greatest sailors in the age of sail along with de Ruyter and Nelson.

Sources: La Jonquiere, 207; Taillemite, 491–92; Lauberdiere, 196; Harald Selesky, *Encyclopedia of the American Revolution*, 2 vols., vol. 2, 1122–23.

Tanouarn, Louis Marie Chevalier de

Background: Born in 1739, he was a *garde de marine* (1755). He served on *Neptune* and *Couronne* (1779) under Orvilliers. He commanded *Fine* (1780).

American Service: Commanding *Concorde* (1781–82) he brought the pay of Rochambeau's troops and Admiral Barras to Boston in May 1780. In June 1781, he was sent with the request for Grasse to provide naval support at Yorktown. He was promoted to *capitaine de vaisseau* (1781).

Post-American Career: He led a valiant fight against HMS *Valiant* and HMS *Courageous* (1781). He died in 1788 at sea commanding *Venus* in the Indian Ocean.

Sources: La Jonquiere, 209; Lauberdiere, 77.

Ternay, d'Arsac de Charles Louis Chevalier de

Background: Born into a noble family from Angers in 1723, he was a *garde de marine* (1723). He was aboard *Alcyon* at the battle of Cap Scie (1744). He participated in the battle of the Cardinals and distinguished himself by safely shepherding several ships back to Brest in view of the British fleet (1759). Promoted to *capitaine de vaisseau*, he commanded *Robuste* (January 1761), leading a division which ravaged Newfoundland and destroyed over five hundred ships. (1761). He captured St John's (May–June 1762), but he was forced to abandon the troops against superior British opposition. He was named commanding officer of the *Reunion* and *Ile de France* (1771). He was promoted *chef d'escadre* (1776).

American Service: He commanded *Saint Esprit* (1778–79) in Orvilliers's squadron and went to Boston. He returned to Brest. He commanded *Duc de Bourgogne* and the squadron carrying Rochambeau and his troops to Newport, arriving in July 1780. He died of disease and was buried at Newport in 1780.

Sources: La Jonquiere, 209; Taillemite, 498; Selesky, vol. 2, 1146.

Thierry de La Prevalaye, Marquis de

Background: Born in 1745, he was a *garde de marine* in 1762. He served aboard several ships under Orvilliers and then on *Ville de Paris* and *Saint-Esprit* (1780), *Bretagne* (1780–81), and several other ships.

American Service: He served on *Actif*, the first French ship to visit Boston since the Seven Years' War in 1778. He served under d'Estaing at Newport and fought at St. Lucia and Grenada. He commanded gun batteries at the siege of Savanah. As commander of *Poulette,* he brought the Treaty of Versailles to the US in 1783.

Post-American Career: He was promoted to *capitaine de vaisseau* in 1788 and then to *chef de division,* serving on the navy council. He was named *contre amiral* in 1814. He died in 1816.

Notable Facts: His father was the admiral commanding Brest, which prepared d'Estaing's squadron for America. His brother Charles led part of the Chouan army in the Vendee as a *maréchal de camp* and surrendered.

Source: La Jonquiere, 211.

Thomassin, Antoine Comte de Peynier

Background: Born in 1731, he was a *garde de marine* in 1744, serving in the Mediterranean. He commanded the frigate *Malicieuse* (1765) and rose to *capitaine de vaisseau* (1772). He was Guichen's flag captain aboard *Ville de Paris* at Ouessant.

American Service: He commanded *l'Artesien* at the siege of Savannah. He commanded *Fendant* which was sent to reinforce Suffren's squadron in India (1782). Suffren commended his conduct in combat.

Post-American Career He was promoted to *chef d'escadre* (1784) and replaced Suffren as squadron commander in the Indies until 1786. He was governor of Saint-Domingue (1789–90). He returned to France and advanced to *contre amiral* and then vice admiral (1792). He was appointed commander of the Brest fleet but refused the appointment. He was placed under house arrest. He died in 1809.

Source: La Jonquiere, 182.

Thy, Alexandre Chevalier de

Background: Born in 1732, he was a *garde de marine* (1751), rising to *capitaine de vaisseau* (1779).

American Service: He successively commanded *Aurore* (1778), *Lion* (1779), and *Sultane* (1779–80). He commanded *Citoyen* (1781–82) at the Chesapeake. He was promoted to *capitaine de vaisseau* in 1780.

Post-American Career: He fought on *Citoyen* at the Saintes where he was wounded and then under Vaudreuil. He was promoted to *chef de division* (1786). He died in 1804.

Source: La Jonquiere, 212.

Prevost de Sansac, Jean Baptiste Marquis de Traversay

Background: Born in 1754 in Martinique, he was a *garde de marine* (1766). He was aboard *Barbue* which foundered outside Penmarsh. He served aboard *Vengeur* at Ouessant. He was the first officer on *Iphigenie* and participated in the capture of HMS *Ceres* (1779), which he then commanded.

American Service: He served in Guichen and Grasse's squadrons and participated in the siege of Savannah and at the Chesapeake, where he played an essential role in scouting the British disposition and captured HMS *Richmond*. Commanding *Aigrette*, he successfully brought a million piastres to France from Havana. He took 222 prizes, including HMS *Richmond*.

Post-American Career: He was promoted to *capitaine de vaisseau* in 1786 and commanded *Active* in 1788. He served in Martinique and then returned to France. He took a leave of absence in Switzerland where he met his mentor, the Duc de Castries, who recommended him to Catherine the Great. He joined the Russian Navy and was given command of a squadron in the Baltic in 1791 and served successively as *contre amiral*, vice admiral, and Minister of the Navy.

Napoleon tried to get him to return to France after the treaty of Tilsit: Traversay refused and never saw his homeland again. He was appointed admiral and counselor of state and died in 1831.

Notable Facts: He sponsored the scientific expedition led by Bellingshausen (1819–20) in the Pacific, and he is credited for the good performance of the Russian Navy at Navarino (1827).

Sources: La Jonquiere, 213; Taillemite, 509–10.

Trogoff de Kerlessy, Jean Honore Comte de

Background: Born into a noble Breton family in 1751, he was a *garde de marine* (1767) and then *enseigne* (1773). He served under capitain Kerguelen during his second trip to Australia.

American Service: During the war he captured a British privateer and was promoted to *lieutenant de vaisseau* (1779). He was first officer on *Glorieux* and was at the Chesapeake.

Post-American Career: He took over as captain of *Glorieux* after Descars was killed at Saintes and fought off five British ships before striking his colors and being made prisoner. He was promoted to *capitaine de vaisseau* (1784).

He commanded *Le Duguay-Trouin* in Saint-Domingue and under Latouche Treville. He was wounded at the capture of Cagliari (January 1793). He was promoted to *contre amiral* (January 1793).

Named interim commander of the Mediterranean fleet at Toulon, he rearmed the fleet and ensured that convoys bringing wheat to France were safe. When Toulon declared for the Royalists, he refused to agree. He was, therefore, distrusted by both sides. He was declared an outlaw by the Convention (September 1793). He was able to arrange for the escape of several ships back to their home ports before leaving with the British fleet. He died in 1794. **Sources**: Taillemite, 512–13; La Jonquiere, 215; Six, vol. 2, 512–13; Six, vol. 1, 81.

Tromelin, Maurice Jean Chevalier de Launay

Background: Born in 1740, he was a *garde de marine* in 1756. He served aboard *Magnifique* (1778) and then *Protee* (1779) under d'Orvilliers.

American Service: He served on *Neptune* (1779–80) and *Ardent* (1780) under de Grasse. He was promoted to *capitaine de vaisseau* in 1781.

Post-American Career: He commanded *la Gentille* (1783). He was appointed honorary *contre amiral* in 1814.

Source: La Jonquiere, 216.

Truguet, Laurent François Comte de

Background: Born into a naval family in 1752, he was a *garde de marine* (1765). He sailed on several ships and was recognized for his navigational skills. He was made an *enseigne de vaisseau* (1773). He served aboard *l'Atalante* and *Hector* (1776–80). He took part in the battle of Saint Lucia. He was promoted to *lieutenant de vaisseau* (March 1779).

American Service: At Savannah he was badly wounded saving d'Estaing's life. He was named chevalier de Saint Louis for this act.

Post-American Career: He returned to France in March 1780. He served on various ships and commanded *le Tartelon* which took the new French ambassador to Constantinople, which allowed him to carry out hydrographic studies of the Dardanelles and Sea of Marmara. He was promoted to *capitaine de vaisseau* (January 1792) and *contre amiral* (July 1792), and he commanded the Toulon naval division flying his flag on

Tonnant, bombarded Nice but failed at Cagliari. Removed and arrested, he was released after the fall of Robespierre.

He was promoted to vice admiral (May 1795) and later Minister of the Navy and Colonies (November 1795– July 1797). He organized the failed expedition to Ireland. He was removed due to his perceived royalist ties and replaced by Pleville Le Pelley. He was ambassador to Madrid (1797– 98). He was temporarily promoted to admiral in 1802, but he resigned as he was against the establishment of the Empire and went into exile in Holland. He was recalled in 1809 and commanded the Toulon and Brest fleets despite his age and was taken prisoner at Rotterdam while serving as *prefet maritime* (end of 1813). He was confirmed as admiral and awarded a marshal's baton in 1832, dying in 1839.

Notable Facts: He was awarded the *Grand Cordon de la Legion d'Honneur* and *Grand Croix de Saint-Louis*. He received a marshal's baton from the king in October 1832 in recognition of his position as admiral.

Sources: La Jonquiere, 216; Six, vol. 2, 515; Humble, 3–6; Taillemite, 314–15.

Vallongue, Louis Marie Chevalier de

Background: Born in 1753, he was a *garde de marine* in 1770. He was promoted to lieutenant in 1781.

American Service: He served on several ships including on the *Royal Louis* (1781–82) in the combined Franco-Spanish fleet in Cadiz. He commanded *la Gloire,* which brought two million livres to pay Rochambeau's corps in May 1782.

Post-American Career: He was promoted to *capitaine de vaisseau* in 1783. He emigrated and returned in 1815, becoming mayor of Nimes and dying that same year.

Sources: La Jonquiere, 219; Lauberdiere, 234.

Rigaud, Louis Philippe Marquis de Vaudreuil

Background: Born in 1724, he joined the navy as a *garde de marine* (1740). He took part in the Battle of Toulon (1744) on *l'Heureux* which was captained by his father. Promoted to *capitaine de vaisseau* (1765), he commanded the squadron that took Senegal with the Duc de Lauzun's army detachment (January 1779). He commanded *le Fendant* at Ouessant.

American Service: He commanded a squadron as *chef d'escadre* sent to reinforce d'Estaing (1779). He commanded *Triomphant* and a division of Guichen's squadron. He served aboard *Spectre* at the Battle of the Chesapeake. He landed Lauzun's Legion and 800 of his own men at Gloucester.

Post-American Career: He saved the remnant of the French fleet at the battle of Saintes and took command after de Grasse's capture and sailed to Boston. He was preparing to attack Jamaica with John Paul Jones serving as a volunteer, but peace was signed. He was promoted to lieutenant general des Armées navales (1782). His squadron brought Rochambeau's corps back to France. He and several naval officers forced their way into Versailles to protect the king from the mob (October 5–6 ,1789). He emigrated to London, returning in 1801. He died in 1802.

Notable Facts: His uncle and grandfather were both governors of Canada and another uncle fought with Montcalm at the battle of Oswego. His father was an admiral, as was his brother, Louis, who also served under de Grasse commanding *Spectre* (1781–82).

Sources: La Jonquiere, 220; Taillemite, 523–24.

Vaugirard de Rosnay, Pierre Rene Comte de

Background: Born in 1741, he was a *garde de marine* (1755). He took part in the Battle of the Cardinals on *Orient* (1759). He was on *la Couronne* at Ouessant where he assisted his captain who was wounded. He was promoted to *capitaine de vaisseau* (1781).

American Service: He was chief of staff to de Grasse onboard *Ville de Paris* and took part in the battles of Fort-Royal, Tobago, the Chesapeake, and St. Kitts.

Post-American Career: He was taken prisoner at the Battle of Saintes. He was first officer on *Railleuse* (1785). He commanded *Gracieuse* and the Windward Islands station (1788). He emigrated and participated in the unsuccessful Quiberon expedition. He retired to England, only returning to France in 1814 where he was appointed vice admiral and governor of the Windward Islands. He was recalled in 1818 and died in 1819.

Sources: La Jonquiere, 220; Taillemite, 524.

Vence, Jean Gaspard

Background: He was born in 1747 in Marseille into a wealthy family of ship owners that owned plantations in Saint-Domingue, he served as a privateer with his brother in the West Indies and then served in the French navy. He returned to the West Indies in 1776.

American Service: Congress gave him a letter of marque so he could sail under the American flag. He took 211 ships in 40 combats. The British put a price of £2 million on his head as insurance premiums had risen by nearly a quarter! Once France entered the war, he was asked to scrap together a force to take Dominica, which he did in September 1778.

As a reward for taking Dominica, he was commissioned a *lieutenant de fregate,* joining d'Estaing's squadron. He served at the capture of St. Vincent and then led the assault on Hospital Bluff which led to the surrender of Georgetown in July 1779. He was port captain at Georgetown. He led a failed assault on Spring Hill at Savannah. He was named a *chevalier de Saint Louis* in recognition of his exploits (1780).

Post-American Career: He was forced to resign for irregularities at Georgetown. Returning to France to plead his case, his ship sank, losing him his immense fortune from his accumulated prize money.

Reintegrated into the navy as a *capitaine de vaisseau* (1792), he was given command of *l'Heureux* in Toulon. Sent to the Levant and Tunis to obtain wheat for a famished population, his squadron was bottled up. He eventually shepherded his eighty-ship convoy back to France and fought the British off Toulon. During his absence, his brother and nephew were guillotined as nobles. He was appointed *contre amiral* (1794). In March 1795 he was sent to Bordeaux to put together a supply convoy to sail for Brest. He was intercepted by a British squadron and forced to seek refuge at Lorient. He was named to command one of the squadrons in the Brest fleet poised for the invasion of Ireland under General Hoche, but he was relieved as he thought it would be unsuccessful, which was the case.

As commander of Toulon, he was responsible for outfitting de Brueys's fleet for the Egypt expedition. He was promoted to *maritime prefet* at Toulon by Bonaparte (1800). Consulted on the invasion of England, he was critical of the preparations and forced to retire in 1803, dying in 1808.

Sources: La Jonquiere, 221; Six, vol. 2, 538; Humble, 218–220; Selesky, vol. 2, 1193; Taillemite, 525.

Verdun de la Crenne, Jean Rene Marquis de

Background: Born in 1741, he was a *garde de marine* (1756) and advanced to *capitaine de vaisseau* (1779). He commanded *Flore* on a scientific expedition (1771–72) in the mid and north Atlantic. In 1776 he conducted another expedition in the Baltic Sea and met Catherine the Great, who invited him to return the following year to consult on the organization of the Russian Navy.

American Service: He commanded *Renommee* in 1778, when he rescued an American ship from a British warship. He served as d'Estaing chief of staff and commanded the *Royal Louis*.

Post–American Career: He was chief of staff to the combined fleet at Cadiz, commanding *Royal Louis*. He fought at Cape Spartel and was involved in the siege of Gibraltar before being promoted to *chef d'escadre* (1786). He emigrated and died after returning to France in 1805.

Notable Fact: He was a member of the Institut de France.

Sources: La Jonquiere, 222; Taillemite, 525–26.

Cillart de Villeneuve, Jean Marie Chevalier de

Background: Born in 1737, he was a *garde de marine* (1756). He was promoted to *capitaine de vaisseau* (1780). He commanded *Zephyr* at Ouessant.

American Service: He commanded *Surveillante* (1780-82) in Ternay's squadron. He served at Cape Henry. He defeated HMS *Ulysses*. He took part at the Chesapeake.

Post-American Career: He commanded *Sagittaire* (1782–83). He was killed in the abortive royalist landing at Quiberon in 1795 with his two nephews.

Notable facts: He brought back the Duc de Lauzun carrying news of the victory at Yorktown.

Source: La Jonquiere, 68.

Villeneuve, Silvestre de Pierre Charles

Background: He was born in 1763 into a minor noble family near Digne. He joined the navy as an aspirant *garde de marine* (1770). He served successively aboard *la Flore*, *le Montreal* (1779,) and *le Hardi* (1780).

American Service: Promoted to ensign, he transferred to *le Marseillais* aboard which he participated in the battles of Tobago, Martinique, and Chesapeake, as well as the Saintes where *le Marseillais* escaped so that its crew was not captured.

Post-American Career: He served on *Destin* and *la Blonde*. He was promoted to *lieutenant de vaisseau* and obtained the command of the *Badine* in February 1792. That August he transferred to *Tonnant*, the flagship of the Toulon fleet under Truguet. The fleet was tasked to attack the Sardinian cities on the coast and to capture Cagliari, which it failed to do. He was promoted to *capitaine de vaisseau* (1793) but did not receive a command. That November he was relieved as a noble.

He was reinstated in May 1795 and appointed to command *Peuple-Souverain* serving concurrently as port captain at Toulon. His success in the later position resulted in Admiral Martin's recommendation that he be promoted to commodore. He was promoted *contre amiral* in 1796. He was in charge of a division that was to join Morard in the abortive Ireland expedition by joining him at Brest. This failed and Villeneuve took his division in Lorient.

He flew his flag on *Guillaume-Tel* as a squadron commander in Brueys's fleet in the Egyptian expedition. He took part in the siege of Malta. He took little part in the Battle of Aboukir but managed to get four ships to safety in Malta. He was made prisoner when Malta surrendered to the British. He was promoted to vice admiral in 1804.

He replaced La Touche Treville as commander at Toulon on his death in 1804. Napoleon's strategy was to bring together most of the French and Spanish ships to fight a decisive sea battle which would open the way for the invasion of England. Most of the other French units missed the rendezvous, leaving Villeneuve to fight with a diminished Franco-Spanish fleet.

He fought an inconclusive action against the British at Cape Finisterre and then sought refuge at Cadiz. He was defeated at Trafalgar and taken prisoner. Franco-Spanish losses at the battle were ca. 14,000, including 7000 prisoners versus 1700 British ones, including Lord Nelson. Villeneuve was taken prisoner and stabbed himself to death on his return to France.

Sources: Taillemite, 532–33; La Jonquiere, 224; Six, vol. 2, 556–57; Humble, 55–64; John Terraine, *Trafalgar* (London, 1976), 162.

Chapter 5: Army Biographies

Aboville, François-Marie Comte d'

Background: He was born in January 1730 to a Norman noble family whose ancestor was killed at Poitiers in 1356. He joined the army in March 1744 as a supernumerary in artillery then aide-de-campto his relative, General Julien Aboville. He served in Flanders and at Fontenoy. He was at the siege of Munster. He steadily rose through the ranks, being promoted to colonel in April 1780. He was second in command of the artillery at Besancon.

American service: He was appointed commander of Rochambeau's artillery in America. He served at Yorktown and was promoted to brigadier of infantry in December 1781 in recognition of his service in America.

Post-American Career: On returning to France in 1783, he was appointed director of artillery at La Fere. He was promoted to *maréchal de camp* (September 1788). He was appointed inspector general of artillery (April 1791) and later served as head of artillery of l'Armée du Nord under Rochambeau (1792). Promoted to lieutenant general serving under Kellerman, he was present at Valmy. After serving as acting commanding general in l'Armée de la Moselle, he commanded a division. He was arrested in November 1793 as a noble. He was recalled by the Committee of Public Safety and appointed *commissaire du government* at Quesnoy. He was director of the Paris arsenal (July 1795) and concurrently served as president of the central artillery committee, a post last held by de Gribeauval. He fought for the introduction of interchangeable parts but was thwarted by Gassendi, who had been Napoleon's commanding officer. He was appointed to the Senate where he served as vice president and then retired. During the Empire he was recalled, heading various national guard units. He died in November 1817.

Notable Facts: He was the father of artillery generals Augustin-Gabriel and Augustin-Marie Aboville. He was a commander and later grand croix of Saint Louis and grand officier of the Legion of Honor. He was a count of the Empire and a peer of France under the Restoration. He accompanied Pius VII to France for the coronation of Napoleon. As a peer of France, he should have sat at Marshal Ney's trial before that chamber, but he abstained from participating due to age.

Sources: Bod. 13; Six, vol. 1, 2–3; Adler, 323–29.

Andigne, Louis Marie Comte d'

Background: Born in 1765, he started his career in the navy as a *garde de marine* (1779). He was present at Ouessant.

American Service: He served successively on *Amphitrite* (1779-81), *David,* and *Barboude* (81–85).

Post-American Career: He was promoted to *lieutenant de vaisseau* in 1786. During the Revolution he emigrated and later played an important role in the Vendean insurrection. He signed the peace with the French authorities in May 1796. When fighting resumed in 1799, he was second in command under Godet de Chatillon. He was arrested and escaped abroad.

On the Restoration he returned and was promoted to *maréchal de camp* and made a peer in 1814. He was made a lieutenant general in 1823. He refused to accept Louis Philippe as king and participated in a conspiracy to rebel against the new monarch. He was arrested.

Source: La Jonquiere, 23.

Andrault, Louis Alexandre Comte de Langeron

Background: He was born in January 1763 to lieutenant general Louis Theodore Andrault, who was from a noble family from Limousin known since 1336. His grandfather was also a lieutenant general.

He was named an ensign in the Gardes Françaises (August 1777). He was transferred as a second lieutenant to the Limousin regiment and subsequently served in that rank with the Condé and Bourbonnais regiments.

American service: He travelled to America on the *Aigle* as a replacement Bourbonnais officer in 1782.

Post-American Career: On his return to France, he was placed on half pay and eventually promoted to colonel in the Armagnac regiment (March 1788). After a duel killing the Bishop of Nevers, he passed into Russian service as a colonel, fighting the Swedes and Turks. He served briefly in the Austrian and Prussian armies.

Back in Russia, he was promoted to major general (June 1797) and lieutenant general (November 1798). He served under Kutuzov at Austerlitz as commander of the left wing. He was disgraced due to his conduct and joined the Moldavian army fighting the Turks (1806–11). He fought at the Berezina and Brest-Litovsk. He commanded a corps in the Prussian and French campaigns. He was named Governor General of New Russia (1822) and helped develop the city of Odessa. He served again against the Turks (1825–29).

Notable Facts: Among his many awards was the Order of Saint Andrew, the senior order in Russia. He wrote his memoirs.

Sources: Bod., 19–20; Mikaberidze, 218–20.

Anselme de la Gardette, Mathieu Joseph

Background: Born July 1748, he was named a lieutenant (August 1746) in what became the Soissonais regiment in which his brother and father were serving. He rose to captain (1769).

American Service: He served with his regiment in Rochambeau's corps.

Post-American Career: He was promoted to lieutenant colonel (July 1791) and resigned in 1792. He emigrated and served in Condé's army. He was promoted to *maréchal de camp* (1815) and died in 1820.

Notable Facts: His brother, Jacques, remained in France during the Revolution, rising to lieutenant general. He was suspended as a noble and retired.

Source: Bod., 22.

Anselme, Jacques Bernard

Background: Born July 1740 to a noble Florentine family that had settled in the Comtat Venaissin, he was named a lieutenant (September 1745) and then on half pay (1749). He served at Minorca (1756) and rose to captain in the Briqueville regiment (October 1760). He then served in several regiments in Germany and Corsica before being promoted lieutenant colonel in the Soissonnais regiment (July 1777).

American Service: He served with his regiment, including his brother, in Rochambeau's corps.

Post-American Career: He was promoted to *maréchal de camp* (March 1788). He served as principal aide-de-camp to Rochambeau (April 1792). He was promoted to lieutenant general in l'Armée du Midi (May 1792) and named its commander but never took up the post. He invaded Nice and was later suspended for plundering the city. He was put on half pay, eventually acting as inspector of the Armée du Midi before retiring in 1801. He died in 1821.

Sources: Bod., 22; Six, vol. 1, 16.

Angely, François Marie Baron d'

Background: He was born January 1735 into a family from Burgundy that had served in the army for eight generations. In 1751 he went to Germany and enlisted in the Anhalt regiment. He served as a captain in Prussia (1757–61) and then as major with the Danish Army (1761–69).

He was recruited into the Russian Army where he rose to colonel. He was commander of a fortress in which French officers fighting for the Poles were incarcerated. He was viewed as too lenient in their treatment and left Russia in 1774. He could not find a position in the French Army until named colonel of the Nassau volunteers in 1779.

American Service: He went to America as aide-de-camp to Baron de Viomenil. He led an attack on Fort Franklin on Long Island in July 1781.

Post-American Career: He did not serve on his return from America. He emigrated in 1791.

Sources: Bod., 20–21; Lauberdiere, 109.

Arlande de Salton, Louis François

Background: Born March 1753 in a family from the Haute Loire (recognized from 1327), he was a volunteer in the Bourbonnais regiment (May 1769). He was promoted to lieutenant (January 1777).

American Service: He served with Rochambeau in America and was promoted to captain (October 1781).

Post-American Career: He was decorated with the *croix de Saint-Louis*. He was promoted to lieutenant colonel and colonel in rapid succession (August 1792) of the 13th infantry (Bourbonnais). He served in the Spier expedition. He was named brigadier general in l'Armée Armée Armée du Rhin (July 1793). While commanding the camp at Nothweiler, he deserted to Prussia in August 1793 and was killed in battle a month later.

Notable facts: He had two brothers, one of whom served in America and the other made the first hot air balloon ascension in 1783. All three served in the Bourbonnais regiment.

Sources: Bod., 24–25; Six, vol. 1, 21.

Tuffin, Armand Charles Marquis de la Rouerie aka Armand

Background: Born in 1750 into a noble Breton family (1452), he was an ensign in the Gardes Françaises (October 1766), rising to 2nd lieutenant (April 1755). He was forced to emigrate after fighting a duel.

American Service: He travelled to American in April 1777 and was initially appointed as a lieutenant colonel in Pulaski's legion. He raised a legion of partisans as a colonel carrying his name. After Pulaski's death at Savannah, he took command of the legion which he renamed the Armand Legion. He was congratulated by Congress for his conduct at Camden. He returned to France on leave. He fought with Lafayette in Virginia and then at Yorktown. He was promoted to brigadier general (March 1783) and returned to France in 1784.

Post-American Career: He was treated shabbily on his return, although awarded the order of Saint-Louis. He was promoted to captain (June 1780). Finally named colonel, he refused the appointment.

Notable Facts: He was one of twelve Breton nobles who took their grievances to Versailles and were imprisoned in the Bastille (July 1788). He was involved in the revolt in the Vendee but died of illness in 1793, accelerated by the death of Louis XVI, before he could be arrested and tried for treason.

Sources: Bod., 455; Rufus Griswold, *Washington and the Generals of the American Revolution*, 2 vols. (Philadelphia, 1847) vol.1, 258–61, hereafter cited as WGAR; ERA, vol.

2, 792–93; Renee Critcher Lyons, *Foreign-Born American Patriots: Sixteen Volunteer Leaders in the Revolutionary War* (Jefferson, NC, 2014), 125–32; Schachtman, 314.

Attel de Luttange, Louis Alexandre

Background: Born in January 1745 into a Verdun family ennobled in 1541, he was a student at the Paris military academy and then an ensign in the Touraine regiment (March 1761). He was promoted to captain (April 1779).

American Service: He served at Yorktown and in the Caribbean.

Post-American Career: He was successively a major, lieutenant colonel, and colonel of the Auxerrois regiment (February 1792). He emigrated and served in the Bourbon and then Condé armies. He was promoted to *maréchal de camp* (February 1815). He died in 1819.

Source: Bod., 27–28.

Aubert du Bayet, Jean Baptiste

Background: He was born in April 1757 in Mobile (now Louisiana) to a nobleman serving as commanding officer there. He was appointed 2nd lieutenant in the Bourbonnais regiment and then lieutenant (February 1780).

American Service: He served in America.

Post-American Career: He was promoted to captain (June 1785), elected deputy to the Legislative Assembly (August 1791), and later promoted to lieutenant colonel (June 1792). He was president of the Legislative Assembly (July 1792). He served in the Rhine army and as commander of Worms. He was provisionally promoted to brigadier general (April 1793). He led the army of Mayence, which surrendered. He was released and forced to justify his conduct in front of the Convention. He was sent to fight in the Vendee.

Arrested after the defeats at Torfou and Pallet against the royalists, he was released and reintegrated into his rank. Retired, he was recalled by Kleber and promoted to *general de division* (February 1795).

He commanded the army based at Cherbourg (May to November 1795) when he was appointed Minister of War serving until February 1796. He was appointed ambassador to Constantinople, arriving in February 1797 and dying later that year.

Notable Facts: He was replaced by Carra Saint-Cyr in Constantinople who married his widow.

Sources: Bod., 29; Six, vol. 1, 25–26.

Barazer de Kermorvan, Gilles Jean

Background: Born into a noble family, he was a lieutenant in the Brie regiment (June 1758). Reformed, he served in the Turkish army (1772–75) under Pulaski and was made a colonel by the sultan.

American Service: Recruited by Barbeu-Dubourg, he volunteered for America where he was appointed lieutenant colonel and engineer in the Continental Army (April 1776). He returned to France in 1778.

Post-American Career: He was promoted to captain (June 1780) and named adjutant general in October 1792. He was appointed *maréchal de camp* in the Belgian Army (November 1792) and then in the French Army (March 1793). He was suspended (July 1793). He died in 1817.

Sources: Bod., 35; Six, vol. 2, 5; Six, vol. 1, 74.

Baville, Armand

Background: Born in 1757, he was a soldier in the Bourbonnais regiment (February 1776), rising to sergeant (October 1778).

American Service: He was with Rochambeau (1780–83) and served with his regiment at Yorktown.

Post-American Career: He rose to lieutenant in the Auxerrois regiment (April 1792) and was rapidly promoted through lieutenant colonel to brigadier general (June 1795). He was on half pay (January 1797). He later served in administrative capacities until he retired in May 1813. Recalled as the Allies pushed the Grande Armée back, he was mortally wounded at Lubnitz in 1813.

Notable Facts: He was governor of the Invalides (January 1796) and *Commandeur de la Legion d'Honneur*.

Source: Six, vol. 1, 63.

Beaumont d'Antichamp, Antoine Joseph Comte de

Background: He was born in December 1744 to a noble family from Dauphine (1250) which received the *honneurs de la cour* eleven times. He was a volunteer in the Roi-Cavalerie (1759). He rose to lieutenant colonel in the Aquitaine regiment (April 1776). He became colonel of the Agenais regiment (October 1779)

American Service: With Rochambeau commanding his regiment, he was promoted to brigadier for his conduct at

Yorktown. He then served in the Caribbean, including the Battle of Saint Christopher.

Post-American Career: He returned to Saint-Domingue. He was promoted to *maréchal de camp* (January 1784) and commander of an infantry brigade. He resigned (January 1790) and emigrated. He served in his brother's regiment as lieutenant colonel. He returned to France in 1802 and was made an honorary lieutenant general (August 1814). He served as governor of Chateau de Saint Germain.

Notable Facts: His three brothers were also in the army. One served at Yorktown and died of wounds sustained at the Battle of Saintes. The other two were generals in the Vendean emigré army.

Source: Bod., 43.

Belley, Jean Baptiste

Background: Born in 1747 at Gore in Senegal, he was deported to Saint-Domingue as a slave two years later. He bought his freedom at age seventeen.

American Service: He was a volunteer in and served at Savannah. He was given the family name of Mars in recognition of his bravery.

Post-American Career: He returned to Saint-Domingue and was part of the free Black population which actively supported the republican commissioners, Saintonax and Polverel, who were sent to take over the island. He fought as a captain against the white colonists in the actions of June 9–11, 1793, and was wounded. He was elected as one of the two Black representatives along with Joseph Boisson to the Convention: The island sent two representatives each from the white, Black, and mulatto communities. He travelled via the US to France, arriving in Lorient in January 1794. He was denounced along with a fellow deputy by colonists and briefly arrested. He was admitted to the Convention on February 3, and slavery was abolished the following day.

He was named *chef de battalion* in 1795 at the insistence of General Felix du Muy in May 1795. He was made a member of the *conseil de Cinq-Cents* in October 1795 and sat on that body until May 1797. In July 1797 he was promoted to *chef de brigade* and head of the Saint-Domingue gendarmerie. He went on a mission under General Hedouville to Saint-Domingue to persuade Toussaint l'Ouverture to bow to French control. This effort failed, and he returned to France. Toussaint later declared independence. Belley joined the expedition under General

Leclerc to retake Saint-Domingue. Leclerc had him arrested for sedition and forcibly returned to France in 1802. He is held under house arrest as were several other Black officers who were considered untrustworthy, and their pay was suspended. Belley died in August 1805 in a prison hospital.
Source: Quintin, 90–91; Desmarais, 201.

Berthier, Louis Alexandre Prince de Neuchatel and Wagram

Background: He was born in November 1753 in Versailles to a family ennobled in 1763. His father was a senior *ingenieur geographe,* so Berthier was appointed to that corps in January 1766. He obtained a commission as a lieutenant in the Flanders Legion (1770). He served in the cavalry as a captain and then obtained permission to transfer to the Soissonnais regiment which was earmarked to serve in America.

American Service: He served as a senior staff officer to Rochambeau for the entire campaign.

Post-American Career: On his return to France, he was part of the Custine mission to Prussia to study their tactics. He served on the newly created general staff, rising to lieutenant colonel (April 1791). He served as chief of staff to Besenval who commanded the troops in the Paris region,was appointed major general of the Versailles national guard (July 1789) and escorted the king's great-aunts to safety. He then transferred to the Paris national guard. He was promoted to colonel and tasked with training thirty new infantry battalions. He was appointed *maréchal de camp* in May 1792 and served as chief of staff under Rochambeau, Luckner, and Kellerman in l'Armée du Nord (May 1792). He was suspended in September 1792 but allowed to serve as a volunteer.

He was recalled to serve as chief of staff with the rank of brigadier general in l'Armée d'Italie in March 1795. He was promoted to *general de division* in 1795 and served as Bonaparte's chief of staff in l'Armée d'Italie. During this time, he developed the staff system which would be used throughout the Napoleonic era. He and Massena led 1000 volunteers across the bridge at Lodi (1796), which turned the battle in Bonaparte's favor and led a cavalry charge at Rivoli (1797). He commanded l'Armée d'Italie (December 1797) and took Rome.

He was elected to the *Conseil des Cinq-Cents* (April 1798). He served as Bonaparte's chief of staff in Egypt and was Minister of War (November 1799–April 1800). He formed the Armée de reserve based at Dijon to invade Italy and was nominally in command during the campaign, as Bonaparte was legally unable to do so as First Consul. He fought at Montebello and was wounded at Marengo. Sent as an ambassador to Madrid, he successfully negotiated the treaty of San Idelfonso. On his return he was reappointed Minister of War, a position he held until September 1807.

He was promoted to *Maréchal d'Empire* (May 1804) and was considered the most senior officer. He was Major General of the Grande Armée (August 1805-1814) and subsequently of other armies. He was sent as French ambassador to Vienna to negotiate Napoleon's marriage with Archduchess Marie Louise (1810). He served in the Russian campaign and was wounded at Brienne during the 1814 French campaign. He adhered to the Bourbons and was struck off the list of Napoleonic Marshals. He was appointed captain of the Royal Guards and died in 1815.

Notable Facts: He either had an accident or was murdered in Bamberg by falling from a window. He married the daughter of the Duke of Bavaria and served as Great Huntsman to Napoleon. His two brothers, Louis Cesar and Victor, were generals in Napoleon's armies.

Sources: Bod., 55–56; Ketchum, 294; Six, vol. 1, 87–88; Chandler, 42–56; Pattison, 1–22; Frederic Hulot, *Le Maréchel Jourdan* (Paris, 2010); Samuel F. Scott, *Dictionary of the French Revolution* (Westport, CT, 1985), vol. 1, 78–79.

Besse, Martial

Background: Born in 1759 in Saint-Domingue, he was a soldier in the Royal Auvergne regiment (1779–83).

American Service: He served at Savannah with the *chasseurs volontaires de Saint–Domingue.*

Post-American Career: Having returned to Saint-Domingue, he was placed on the inactive list in 1783. He was named district commander with the rank of lieutenant colonel by commissioner Santhonax (1793) and then held several other commands. In August 1794 he arrived in France.

A year later he was named *general de brigade.* He returned to Saint-Domingue but did not see much service. Having parlayed with the insurgents, he was considered unreliable and transferred back to France in 1802. He was held under house arrest but managed to escape. He eventually returned to Saint-Domingue in 1804.

Notable Facts: When visiting Charleston in an official capacity in 1797 he was required to post a bond as was required of all Black visitors. The French consul complained that Besse was a general in the French army and had served at Savannah. The requirement was waived.

Sources: Six, vol. 1, 93; Desmarais, 201, 205.

Bethisy, Jules Jacques Vicomte de

Background: He was born in 1748 to lieutenant general Eugene Marquis de Bethisty from a noble Artois family (1375) and received three *honneurs de la cour*. He was named a *garde de marine* (1756) and captain of dragoons (1768). He was attached to the Royal-Etranger regiment and promoted to *colonel-en-second* (February 1778).

American Service: He was wounded at Savannah as deputy commander of the Gatinais regiment.

Post-American Career: He refused the rank of *maréchal de camp* at the beginning of the Revolution. He emigrated and served as lieutenant colonel in his brother's regiment. For his services to the Bourbon cause, he was promoted to *maréchal de camp* and then lieutenant general (February 1815). He died in 1816.

Notable Facts: He returned to France in 1797 and was imprisoned in the Temple. Condemned to death, he was saved by his niece who had the case thrown out.

Source: Bod., 58–59.

Beville, Pierre François

Background: Born in 1721, he was a volunteer in the Nivernais regiment (1744–45). He was named a lieutenant in the Lowendal regiment (June 1746). He served as an aide-de-camp to Maréchal de Broglie (1757) and was then promoted to captain (August 1758). He held staff positions at various army headquarters. He was promoted to lieutenant colonel (April 1761) and brigadier (September 1778).

American Service: He was *maréchal general de logis* or chief staff officer in Rochambeau's corps. He was promoted to *maréchal de camp* (December 1781).

Post-American Career: He did not serve after America and retired in 1792.

Notable Facts: He served with his two sons, who were both staff officers at Yorktown.

Sources: Bod., 59–60; Lauberdiere, 17.

Beville de Pont, Charles

Background: Born in 1757, he was named a 2nd lieutenant in the Limousin regiment (April 1773) and then captain in the Noailles-Dragon (March 1779).

American Service: He served as an *aide maréchal de logis* in Rochambeau's corps under his father, Pierre François.

Post-American career: He joined the general staff on its creation (June 1783). He was promoted to major (May 1784) and lieutenant colonel (July 1788). He was appointed adjutant general colonel (April 1791) but resigned although he did not emigrate. He died in 1827.

Notable Facts: He served with his father and brother at Yorktown.

Source: Bod., 59.

Binet de Marcognet, Pierre Louis

Background: He was born November 1765 to a noble family settled in Aunis (1531), and he was a student at the Pontlevoy military academy (1777) and a cadet in the Bourbonnais regiment (March 1781).

American Service: He served with Rochambeau.

Post-American Career: He advanced to captain in March 1792, fought with distinction in numerous actions with l'armée du Rhin, and was wounded at Bodenthal, Fillingen, and Wissenbourg. He was suspended in December 1793 but reinstated in July 1795. He served in the Armée de l'Ouest and then du Rhin until 1801, having been wounded and captured at Hohenlinden (December 1800). He was promoted to brigadier general (August 1803). He commanded a brigade of the 3rd division in the grande Armée (1806-07) under Ney and was transferred with Ney's corps to Spain, where he distinguished himself at the battle of Oviedo (1808–11).

He was promoted to *general de division* (August 1811) and created a baron of the Empire. He commanded the 14th military division at Caen (1812). He commanded successively the 2nd division under Prince Eugene and the 4th division serving in Italy. Upon the Restoration he was put on the inactive list. He commanded the 3rd infantry division at Waterloo. He finally retired in 1832, dying in 1854.

Notable Facts: He served under every government from that of Louis XVI to the Second Republic.

Sources: Bod., 61; Six, vol. 2, 153.

Blanchard, Claude

Background: Born in 1742, his pre-American Service is unknown.

American Service: He served as principal *Commissaire de Guerre* in Rochambeau's corps and was promoted to major-general (November 1781).

Post-American Career: He was deputy from the Pas-de-Calais (1791-92). He served as chief military judge (October 1791) and deputy Minister of War. He served in the Sambre et Meuse and Interieur armies as *commissaire ordonnateur*. He held the same post at the Invalides where he died.

Sources: Bod., 63; Lauberdiere, 151.

Boyvin de la Martiniere, Guillaume baron de

Background: Born in 1745, he was a student at Bapaume artillery school (July 1766) and advanced to captain (June 1779) with the Auxonne regiment.

American Service: He served with his regiment under Rochambeau (1780–83).

Post-American Career: He served in the army of the Two Sicilies (1787–90) by order of Louis XVI, rising to colonel. He was promoted to lieutenant colonel in the La Fere regiment (August 1792). He served in the Armées du Centre and Nord (1792–93), including as second in command of the artillery in the expedition to Holland under Dumouriez. He was at the sieges of Breda and Gertruydenberg and commanded the arsenal at Douai.

In November 1802 he was made commander of the artillery and engineering school at Metz. He was promoted to brigadier general (February 1805) and served in Italy (1805–06). He commanded the reserve artillery of the grande armée and then the 10th corps artillery at Danzig. He later served in Germany and commanded at Wurzburg. He was created Baron of the Empire upon his retirement in August 1809. He died in 1820.

Sources: Bod., 76; Six, vol. 1, 155.

Brentano, Joseph Frederic Baron de

Background: Born February 1746 to François Xavier Minister of the Elector Palatine, he was named 2nd lieutenant in the Alsace regiment. He did not serve in his regiment but joined Viomenil in Poland, rising to captain (January 1774). He passed into Turkish service where he fought against the Russians.

American Service: He served as aide-de-camp to Viomenil in America.

Post-American Career: He served with the Turkish Army (1785–87) and advanced to colonel (November 1788). He resigned and went into Swedish service. He was Swedish ambassador to Constantinople. He died in 1798.

Source: Bod., 76–77.

Bressoles, Gilbert de

Background: Born in 1739, he was a lieutenant in the Touraine regiment (1757), rising to lieutenant colonel (1777).

American Service: He served in America with Rochambeau, including at Yorktown.

Post-American Career: He was promoted to *maréchal de camp* for retirement in 1791. He did not emigrate.

Source: Bod., 77.

Broglie, Charles Louis Prince de

Background: He was born in 1756 into a noble Piedmontese family (1360) that had received thireen *honneurs de la cour*. He was named a second lieutenant in the Limousin regiment (October 1771). He rose from captain to *colonel-en-second* in the Saintonge regiment (June 1779). He served as a senior staff officer in the Armée de Bretagne and then as *colonel-en-second* of the Aunis regiment (1779).

American Service: He arrived in America in September 1782 as a replacement officer until the war ended.

Post-American Career: He commanded the Bourbonnais regiment (July 1783) and was chief of staff of the Metz garrison. He was elected deputy to the Estates General from Colmar. He served as secretary to and later president of the Constituent Assembly.

He was promoted to *maréchal de ca*mp (November 1791) and then chief of staff of l'Armée Armée du Rhin but was sacked in August 1792, as he did not recognize the removal of the king. He was dismissed, arrested, and then guillotined in June 1794.

Notable Facts: His father the Duc de Broglie was a *maréchal de France* and minister of war. Three other relatives were marshals of France.

Sources: Bod., 78–79; Lauberdiere, 294; Six, vol. 1, 160; J. Balteau et al., *Dictionnarie Biographie Française*, 19 vols. (Paris, 1933–), vol. 7, 410, hereafter cited as DBF.

Buchold, Claude

Background: He was born in 1759 and joined as a soldier the Schomberg-dragons (1745). He exchanged into the Berkeley regiment as a sergeant in 1760.

American Service: He served in America with the Dillon regiment at Grenada, Savannah, and St. Kitts.

Post-American Career: He rose to lieutenant and then retired in 1786. He was elected lieutenant colonel of the 1st volunteer battalion du Nord (September 1791) and served as governor of Doullens. He was promoted to acting brigadier general (October 1793). He was arrested, tried, and guillotined in 1794.

Sources: Bod., 80–81; Six, vol. 1, 172.

Casteras de Seignan, Raphael

Background: Born in 1763, he was a musketeer in 1772. He was a cadet in the Bourbonnais regiment (1779), rising to 2nd lieutenant.

American Service: He served in America with Rochambeau.

Post-American Career: He was promoted to lieutenant. He resigned and joined the Spanish army and was promoted to

colonel in 1811, serving until 1822 and was made an honorary *maréchal de camp* the same year. He died in 1843.
Source: Bod., 92.

Chabannes, Jean Frederic Marquis de la Palice

Background: He was born August 1762 into a noble family from l'Angoumois (1395) which received five *honneurs de la cour*. He was a 2nd lieutenant in the Chartres-Dragon regiment (July 1777) and then a captain in the Royal-Pologne Cavalerie (June 1780).

American Service: He served as aide-de-camp to Baron de Viomenil (1782–83) in Rochambeau's corps.

Post-American Career: He was promoted to colonel (April 1788). He was elected to the Estates General from Moulins. After spending time in Naples and Smyrna, he returned to France before emigrating in 1792. He was aide-de-camp to Louis XVIII but then disgraced. He went into exile in London and died in 1836.

Notable Facts: He applied for promotion to lieutenant general on the basis of having helped Louis Philippe to the throne, but his request was refused! His two sons, Hughes and Alfred, rose to brigadier general.

Sources: Bod., 96–97; Lauberdiere, 249.

Chandeon de la Valette, Charles François Chevalier

Background: Born into a family ennobled for services to the crown in 1731, he was appointed lieutenant in the Bourbonnais regiment (October April 1746) and promoted to captain (September 1780). He was a major and then lieutenant colonel (February 1774) in the Saintonge regiment.

American Service: He served with his regiment in America as lieutenant colonel and was named brigadier (December 1781) for his bravery at Yorktown. He was left in command of the rearguard and siege artillery after the battle.

Post-American Career: He was promoted to *maréchal de camp* (March 1788). He remained in the army until the end of December 1791 when he retired.

Sources: Bod., 100; Lauberdiere, 121.

Chapuis de Tourville, Charles Bertin

Background: Born January 1740 into a noble family from the Vivarais, he was a volunteer in the Grenadiers de France (June 1755). He advanced to the rank of major in the Gatinais regiment (April 1776).

American Service: He served at Yorktown with his regiment.

Post-American Career: He was promoted to lieutenant colonel (April 1786). He remained in the army during the Revolution and was promoted to *general de division* (March 1793). Suspended as a noble, he was recalled at the insistence of General Jourdan and others. Suspended again, he retired. He died in 1809.

Notable Facts: A younger relative served in the Gatinais regiment at Savannah and in the émigré army.

Sources: Bod., 101; Six, vol. 2, 506; R.P. Dunn-Pattison, *Napoleon's Marshals* (1977), 251–58, hereafter cited as Pattison; Hulot, *Biography*.

Beauvoir de Chastellux, François Jean Chevalier then Marquis

Background: He was born May 1734 into a noble family from Burgundy (1339) which received *honneurs de la cour* four times. He advanced to the rank of colonel of the Marche regiment (March 1759) and then of the Guyenne regiment. Promoted to brigadier (January 1769), he later resigned.

American Service: He was *maréchal de camp* and deputy to Rochambeau (March 1780).

Post-American career: He held senior inspection posts and died in 1788.

Notable Facts: He was an *habitue* of Parisian literary salons and wrote a well-received memoir of his time in America: *Voyages en Amerique...*

Sources: Bod., 45; ERA, vol. 1, 133.

Chaussegros, François Comte de Lery

Background: Born in 1754 in Quebec, he was a student at the Mezieres engineering school in 1773, rising to aspirant in 1777.

American Service: He volunteered and was appointed a lieutenant of engineers in the Continental Army.

Post-American Career: He was in the West Indies until 1793. He was made a *chef de brigade* (December 1795) while serving in l'Armée de Sambre-et-Meuse. He was promoted to *general de brigade* in 1799 and assumed the position of inspector general of engineers the following year. He held senior engineering assignments in several theaters of operations.

He fought at Friedland. He was appointed chief engineer of l'Armée d'Espagne in 1808. He remained on active service until retiring in 1815. He died in 1824.

Notable Facts: His father-in-law was Marshal Kellermann.
Source: Six, vol. 2, 109–10.

Choin de Montchoisy, Antoine Louis

Background: Born into the high bourgeoisie of the Dauphine in 1747, he was an artillery student (1765), captain of colonial troops (1778), and major (1779). He joined what became Lauzun's Legion.

American Service: He served in America with Rochambeau.

Post-American Career: He was named colonel of the 98th infantry regiment (Decembre 1791) and then *maréchal de camp* (March 1793). Arrested, he was released after Thermidor and returned to the army. He was promoted to *general de division* (September 1795). He served under the Empire as commander of the Genoa military division (June 1805) and was made a baron of the Empire; he rallied to the Bourbons. He died in 1814.

Sources: Bod., 106–07; Six, vol. 2, 216–17.

Choisy, Claude Gabriel Marquis de

Background: He was born in January 1723 into a family of *noblesse de la robe* in Moulins. He joined as a soldier, serving in Flanders, and was wounded at Fontenoy and the siege of Brussels. He advanced to lieutenant colonel (1767). He served in Poland and captured Krakow, which he held for three months against the Russians. While in Poland he was promoted to brigadier (1772) and made a commander of the order of Saint Louis.

American Service: As a brigadier he commanded the troops at Gloucester that cut off Cornwallis's escape from Yorktown and was promoted to *maréchal de camp* for his conduct.

Post-American Career: He remained in the army during the Revolution, commanding troops in Alsace and Grenoble and went on to command l'Armée du Midi. Promoted to *general de division* (1791?) and awarded *Grand Croix de Saint Louis* (March 1792), he retired for health reasons. He may have died in 1799.

Notable Fact: He claimed to have participated in twenty-two campaigns as an infantryman holding a rifle, making him unique as an officer in Europe.

Sources: Bod., 107; Lauberdiere, 37; Six, vol. 1, 236–37; DBF, vol. 8, 1227–28; Schachtman, 268–69.

Clark, Georges Roger

Background: Born in Virginia in 1758, his pre-war activities are unknown.

American Service: He was commissioned as an officer in Virginia state forces (1776) and later appointed colonel of Illinois regiment and commander of troops west of the Allegheny mountains (1781). He was made a brigadier general (1782) and later major general in charge of the Mississippi independent legion. He took Colonel Hamilton prisoner.

Post-American Career: He was confirmed as brigadier general by the Directory (November 1796) and may have died in 1799.

Source: Six, vol. 1, 242.

Closen de Haydenbourg, Jean-Christophe Baron

Background: He was born in 1755 to a Bavarian noble family which received the *honneurs de la cour* in 1784. He was named a 2nd lieutenant (September 1769). He advanced through to captain (April 1780) in the Royal Deux-Ponts regiment.

American Service: He served as aide-de-camp to Rochambeau throughout the campaign and was at Yorktown. Due to his command of the English language, he often acted as a courier between Rochambeau and Washington.

Post-American Career: He was promoted to major in his regiment (April 1788). He again served asaide-de-camp to Rochambeau (April 1791). He was promoted to colonel (November 1791) and then *maréchal de camp* (July 1792). The Duc de Deux Ponts threatened to confiscate his estates if he continued to serve the French. He resigned. Under the Empire, he served as *sous-prefet* of Zimmern (1803). He died in 1830.

Notable Facts: He wrote his memoirs of his time in America, which were translated by Evelyn Acomb.

Sources: Bod., 109–10; Ketchum, 295; Six, vol. 1, 247; Evelyn Acomb, *The Revolutionary Journal of Baron Ludwig von Klosen* (Chapel Hill, 1958), *passim;* Philbrick, 268; Schachtman, 253.

Cocherel, Nicolas Marquis de

Background: He was born in 1741 in Saint-Domingue; he served in various militia units, rising to captain in the chasseurs volontaires de Saint-Domingue.

American Service: He served at Savannah with his unit.

Post-American Career: He returned to France in 1782. He represented Saint-Domingue in the Estates General and later in the National Assembly. Returning to Saint-Domingue, he raised and was colonel of a regiment of British chasseurs (1794). He returned to France in 1814 and was named *maréchal de camp* the following year.

Notable Fact: He was one of the richest men in Saint-Domingue with properties valued at 1.2 million livres.

Source: Bod., 110.

Coigny, François-Marie de Franquetot Duc de

Background: He was born in 1737 to Maréchal of France Coigny, who served at Minden.

Service in America: He served in America (1780–82) with Rochambeau.

Post-American Career: He was promoted to brigadier in September 1782 in recognition of his service in America.

His father and thus he resigned from their hereditary position of Premier Ecuyer du Roi because of the reform of court positions. He was made *maréchal de camp* in March 1788. He was promoted to lieutenant general at the First Restoration. He died in 1816.

Notable Fact: He is known for memoirs he did not write.

Source: DBF, vol. 9, 154.

Collot, Georges Henry

Background: Born in 1750, he was a volunteer in the Chamborant Hussards. He advanced to captain (February 1778).

American Service: Promoted to lieutenant colonel, he served as a senior staff officer to Rochambeau. He was captured by the British.

Post-American Career: He was promoted to colonel in the adjutant corps (April 1791) and then to *maréchal de camp* (December 1791). He was governor of Guadeloupe (May 1792–April 1794), which he surrendered to the British. He served in the War Ministry (October 1801). He died in 1805.

Sources: Bod., 111–12; Six, vol. 1, 254.

Conway de, Thomas

Background: Born in 1733 to a Welsh noble family that settled in Ireland (1602), he was a lieutenant in the Clare regiment (December 1767) and advanced through to colonel (1772).

American Service: He was authorized to join the Continental Army with his brother-in-law Langlois de Bouchet. He was named brigadier general (May 1777). He participated in the battles of Brandywine and Germantown. He was a leader in a cabal to replace Washington as commanding general with Horatio Gates. He resigned in April 1779.

Post-American Career: On his return to France, he was promoted to brigadier (March 1780) and named colonel of the Pondicherry (India) regiment. He was named *maréchal de camp* (January 1784) and served as governor of the French establishments in India and subsequently other territories. He resigned In July 1790. He later commanded the 6th regiment in the Irish Brigade in the British forces. He died in 1795.

Sources: Bod., 113–14; WGAR, vol. 2, 266–68; Schachtman, 307.

Cromot de Bourg, Marie François Baron de

Background: Born in 1756 to a family from Burgundy ennobled for military service (1765), he was a volunteer in the Rochefoucault-Dragons regiment (1768). He was promoted to lieutenant in the Monsieur-Dragons (March 1774) and commanded a company of that regiment.

American Service: He landed in Boston (July 1781) and served as aide-de-camp to Rochambeau.

Post-American Career: He was appointed to the general staff as a major (June 1783) and advanced to colonel (November 1788). He resigned and emigrated, serving as aide-de-camp to the Comte de Provence. He was made honorary *maréchal de camp* in 1815. He died in 1836.

Source: Bod., 121–22.

Crublier d'Opterre, Henry

Background: Born into an old bourgeois family in 1739, he was a 2nd lieutenant of artillery (1757). He transferred to the engineer corps and advanced to captain (November 1770). He was posted to Martinique (1768–75).

American Service: He served with Rochambeau in America and was at Yorktown.

Post-American Career: He took part in the sieges of Minorca and Gibraltar (1781–82). He was promoted to lieutenant colonel (December 1791). He was a deputy to the Legislative Assembly and elected as its secretary. He served in senior engineering roles, being promoted to *chef de brigade* and then brigadier general (April 1795). Retired in August 1795, he died in 1799.

Sources: Bod., 123–24; Six, vol. 1, 273–74.

Custine de Sarrebeck, Adam Philippe Comte de

Background: He was born in 1742 to a noble family (1423) which received *honneurs de la cour* six times. He was an infantry lieutenant (June 1747) and advanced through to brigadier (March 1781). Having observed the annual Prussian military maneuvers, he advocated a Prussian system for the French Army.

American Service: He served in America as colonel of the Saintonge regiment, commanding it at Yorktown.

Post-American Career: He was promoted to *maréchal de camp* (December 1781) and appointed governor of Toulon (April 1782). He attended the Prussian military maneuvers with Berthier on his staff. He represented the Metz nobility in the Estates General, sitting with the Third Estate.

Promoted to lieutenant general (September 1792), he commanded the Vosges army and captured Spier, Worms, Mainz, and Frankfurt. He held various army commands until relieved, tried, and guillotined in 1793.

Notable Fact: His aide-de-camp wrote his memoirs, which were published in 1831.

Sources: Bod., 124–25; Six, vol. 1, 277–78; Scott, *Dictionnary*, vol. 1, 281–82; Edouard Ebel, *Les Ministres de la Guerre, 1792–1870* (Rennes, 2018),124.

Dallemagne, Claude Baron

Background: He served as a soldier, rising to sergeant in Hainault regiment.

American Service: He served at the siege of Savannah and was wounded at Saint Lucia.

Post-American Career: Sergeant major in 1786, he took part in the repression of the Nancy mutiny in 1790. Made 2nd lieutenant in 1791, he advanced to captain, commanding the grenadiers at the siege of Toulon. He was promoted to brigadier general (December 1793).

He served in l'Armée d'Italie and played a crucial role in the battle of Lodi (May 1796) and led the 32nd demi brigade at the siege of Mantua for which he received a saber of honor. Promoted to *general de division* (August 1796), he held various division commands in Italy and Germany, taking Koblenz. He commanded the 25th military division and then the 1st division in the army of Holland.

He was created a baron d'empire. He was a deputy to the Corps Legislatif (March 1802), serving as its vice president and again in 1813, dying shortly thereafter.

Source: Six, vol. 1, 281–82.

Dalmas de Pracontal, Joseph François

Background: Born in 1749, he was an artillery aspirant at Grenoble, rising to lieutenant (1771).

American Service: He served in America with Rochambeau.

Post-American Career: He was promoted to captain in 1785. He took part in the defense of the Tuilleries and was kicked out of the army. He did not emigrate but was imprisoned for nine months. He was recalled to active service and commanded the Toulon artillery park as a colonel (1816) and was promoted to *maréchal de camp* (1822). He died in 1825.

Source: Bod., 126.

Damas d'Antigny, Charles-Cesar Comte de and the Duc

Background: He was born in 1758. He joined *l'infanterie du roi* in 1771, rising to the rank of captain in 1778.

American Service: He was aide-de-camp to Rochambeau.

Post-American Career: In 1788 he was promoted to colonel, commanding the Comte de Provence's dragoons. He escorted the king in his flight to Varennes and encouraged him to press on or give him the Dauphin to take to safety. The king refused and was captured and returned to Paris.

He was arrested and then released. He emigrated and served in the aborted expedition to l'Ile d'Yeu and was promoted to *maréchal de camp* (1795). At the Restoration he was promoted to lieutenant general and created Duc in 1827 by Charles X.

Notable Facts: He was a second cousin to Talleyrand. His younger brother Roger served against the Turks in the Austrian Army and then switched to the Russian one where he captured the Turkish admiral's flagship and offered the flag to Empress Catherine. He commanded the Legion Mirabeau in the emigré army. He served as lieutenant general in the army of Naples fighting against the French.

During the Restoration he was successively governor of Lorraine and Alsace.

Sources: Bod., 127; Lauberdiere, 32.

Dardenne, Charles Ambroise

Background: Born in 1756, he was a student at Mezieres engineering school (1778).

American Service: He was with Rochambeau in America, serving on the staff (February 1779–August 1782).

Post-American Career: He resigned on his return to France. He was appointed 2nd lieutenant in the Belgian Army, advancing to lieutenant colonel (January 1793). He was suspended, tried, and acquitted (March 1794). He then served as a volunteer in l'Armée du Nord. He was promoted to brigadier general and adjutant general (June 1795). He served in the Netherlands and later retired for health reasons.

Sources: Bod., 128; Six, vol. 1, 286–87.

Arrot, Rene Marie, Vicomte d'

Background: Born in 1754, he was a second lieutenant in the Legion of l'Ile de France (1767) and then a lieutenant in the Pondicherry regiment (1772), which he did not join. He was named a colonel in Saint-Domingue in 1774. He took part in the Senegal expedition and was then named colonel in the Lauzun Legion (1780).

American Service: He served with the Lauzun Legion under Rochambeau.

Post-American Career: He was appointed vice governor of Guyana. He was promoted to *maréchal de camp* (1790). He emigrated in 1792 and took several soldiers and officers from the Guadeloupe regiment with him. He returned to France in 1802 and died in 1821.

Source: Bod., 129.

Daurier, Charles Baron

Background: Born in 1761, he was a soldier in the Gatinais regiment (March 1777).

American Service: He served in America (1777–83), including at Yorktown. He was promoted to sergeant (February 1780).

Post-American Career: He advanced to provisional brigadier general (May 1794) having served in the revolutionary armies in the north. He served temporarily as division commander under the Empire. He was the military governor of Venice (October 1813), after which he retired

(January 1816). He was made a baron of the Empire (January 1812). He was appointed chevalier of Saint Louis and honorary lieutenant general on the Restoration.

Notable Fact: He committed suicide in Nancy.

Source: Six, vol. 1, 293.

Delmas, Jean Joseph

Background: Born in May 1768, he enlisted in the Touraine regiment at age eleven and rose to captain in the *chasseurs volontaires de Saint-Domingue* in March 1779.

American Service: He fought at Yorktown where he was badly wounded.

Post-American Career: Because of his political views, he was forced out of the army in 1788. He was elected commander as of the 1st Correze volunteer battalion and proved himself with l'Armée du Rhin. Promoted to general de brigade, he came under suspicion and was sent to Paris. He was released and sent to lead a division under Moreau. Wounded, he was sent home. He was transferred to l'Armée d'Italie and distinguished himself at Magnano. In 1801 he was given command of the troops stationed in Piedmont.

He was publicly against the Concordat and was sent into disgrace. He offered his services to Napoleon in 1813 and was mortally wounded fighting at Leipzig, as was Rochambeau *fils*.

Source: John R. Elting, *Swords around a Throne: Napoleon's Grande Armée* (New York, 1997), 160, hereafter cited as Elting 2.

Denis de la Ronde, Philippe Ambroise

Background: He was born in Quebec in 1752 to a family ennobled by Henri III. He was a cadet in the Quebec troops (May 1764). He transferred and advanced to lieutenant in the Guyana troops (November 1768).

American Service: He served in the siege of Savannah.

Post-American Career: He transferred to the Martinique regiment, where he was promoted to captain. He was made a brigadier general in September 1793 and promoted to *general de division* two weeks later. He was forced to resign in June 1795. He was involved in the 13th Vendemiaire. He retired February 1796 and died in 1813.

Sources: Bod., 135; Six, vol. 2, 62–63.

Desandrouins, Jean Nicolas

Background: Born in 1729 into a family ennobled in the eighteenth century, he was named lieutenant in the Beauce regiment (December 1746) and promoted to captain (February 1756). He served in Canada (1756–60). He was promoted to lieutenant colonel in 1774 and colonel (April 1779).

American Service: He served as Rochambeau's chief engineer but was absent at Yorktown due to illness. He was promoted to brigadier (December 1781).

Post-American Career: Promoted to *maréchal de camp* (March 1788), he retired in April 1791 and died the following year.

Sources: Bod., 136; Lauberdiere, 32.

Desbordes, Silvain François

Background: Born in 1747, he was an *ingenieur geographe* (February 1772), 2nd lieutenant, and then lieutenant in the *canoniers-bombardiers a la Martinique* (March 1777).

American Service: He served at the siege of Savannah.

Post-America Career: He advanced to colonel (January 1794) and was promoted to *maréchal de camp* on retirement

(December 1814). He was director of artillery at Mezieres on his death in August 1817.

Source: Bod., 137.

Des Hayes de La Radiere, Louis Guillaume

Background: Born in 1744, he was a student at Mezieres and was promoted to captain (1775).

American Service: He was one of four engineering officers sent by Louis XVI to America in 1776. He was named lieutenant colonel and later promoted to colonel in the Continental Army. He died in October 1779.

Post-American Career: Unknown.

Sources: Bod., 140–41.

Devrigny, Denis Felix

Background: Born in 1754, he was a dragoon and then standard bearer in the Lauzun Legion.

American Service: He served with the Lauzun Legion in America and was promoted to lieutenant (April 1782).

Post-American Career: He rose to brigadier general (June 1793), was suspended for being noble, and reinstated. He served in the Armée du Rhin and des Grisons. He captured the entrenchments at Zernetz (December 1800). He was transferred to the West Indies and died of yellow fever while serving in Martinique in 1811.

Source: Six, vol. 1, 354.

Dezoteux de Cormatin, Pierre Marie "Baron de"

Background: Born in 1751, he failed to enter the engineering academy twice but was named an officer despite not being noble thanks to the patronage of the Comte d'Estrees. He was a 2nd lieutenant in the Royal Navarre-cavalerie (1772), rising to captain (1779). He travelled extensively throughout Europe and became a talented linguist.

American Service: He served as aide-de-camp to Baron de Viomenil in America.

Post-American Career: As a major he was assigned to the new general staff in 1784. He held several staff positions including under Bouille during the Nancy insurrection. He was promoted to adjutant general lieutenant colonel in 1791. He was accused of facilitating the king's flight and decided to emigrate to England.

He landed in Brittany and became head of the Chouans after Puisaye (1794–95). He negotiated with Hoche but was considered unreliable so was arrested. He was condemned to deportation but spent seven years in jail before being freed in1802. He died in 1812.

Source: Bod., 146.

Digonet, Antoine

Background: He was born in 1763 and served as a soldier in the Ile de France regiment (August 1779).

American Service: He served with Rochambeau in America and was wounded at Yorktown.

Post-American Career: He advanced to lieutenant colonel in the Landes regiment (May 1793) and to brigadier general (April 1794). He served in the Vendee, defeating Charette near Saint-Fulgent, and later in l'Armée du Rhin and d'Italie, as well as commander of military districts in France. He briefly commanded a division in the attack on Venice (November 1805).

Source: Six, vol. 1, 358.

Dillon,Arthur Comte de

Background: He was born in 1750 to a noble Irish family (1343), and they received seven *honneurs de la cour*. He was appointed a cadet in the Dillon regiment (May 1765), rising to a colonel commanding that regiment in May 1772.

American Service: He served at the siege of Savannah and commanded the Dillon regiment at Yorktown.

Post-American Career: He was promoted to brigadier and then *maréchal de camp* (June 1783). He represented the nobility of Martinique at the Estates General (September 1789). He was named lieutenant general (January 1792) and commanded the left wing of l'Armée du Nord under Lafayette. He commanded a division under Dumouriez after a brief suspension. He was recalled to Paris, imprisoned in the Luxemburg palace, and guillotined.

Notable Facts: His daughter Fanny was the wife of General Bertrand, who followed Napoleon into exile at St Helena.

Sources: Bod., 147–48; Six, vol. 1, 358–59.

Dillon, François Theobald Comte de

Background: Born in 1764 to a noble Irish family (1343), which was a cadet branch to that of Arthur and Theobald. He was a 2nd lieutenant in the *volontaires etrangers de la marine* (January 1779), which became the Lauzun Legion.

American Service: He served at the Lauzun Legion in America and as aide-de-camp to Chastellux at Yorktown.

Post-American Career: He was advanced to *major-en-second* in his family's regiment (June 1789). Emigrating, he commanded his brother Edouard's regiment in the Armée des Princes. He was promoted to *maréchal de camp* (February 1815) and then to honorary lieutenant general (May 1825). He died in 1837.

Notable Facts: Both his brothers served in America. Guillaume Henry, known as Billy, was at Gloucester and died on board the frigate *la Neree* (1788). Guillaume is listed below.

Source: Bod., 148.

Dillon, Robert Guillaume

Background: He was born in 1754 into a noble Irish family (1343) ,which was a cadet branch to that of Arthur and Theobald. He was a page to Louis XV (1770). He was named 2nd lieutenant and then captain in the Lorraine regiment (June 1778). He transferred to the *volontaires etrangers de la marine* (1779). He took part in the conquest of Senegal. He was promoted to *colonel-en-second* in the Lauzun Legion (April 1780).

American Service: He served with Rochambeau in America and was wounded at Gloucester. He was at

Yorktown and took command of the legion on Lauzun's return to France.

Post-American Career: He resigned in October 1787 after a hunting accident cost him his left arm. He was promoted to colonel in the 3rd regiment and then to *maréchal de camp* (March 1791) upon retirement. He died in 1837.

Notable Facts: After the Restoration he was commander of the Palace of St. Germain and made honorary lieutenant general (February 1816).

Source: Bod., 149.

Dillon, Theobald Chevalier

Background: He was born in 1750 into a noble Irish family (1343) which received seven *honneurs de la cour*. He was appointed a cadet in the Dillon regiment (May 1762), rising to captain in the regiment commanded by his brother, Arthur (May 1772).

American Service: He served at the siege of Savannah and was later awarded the Order of Cincinnatus.

Post-American Career: He was advanced to colonel, commanding his family's regiment (March 1788). Promoted to *maréchal de camp* (August 1791). He served in l'Armée du Nord and was killed by his soldiers at Lille (April 1792).

Notable Facts: His heart was buried in the Pantheon, and his mistress was awarded a state pension in recognition of his services to the Revolution.

Sources: Bod., 149; Six, vol. 1, 359.

Houx de Viomenil, Antoine Charles Baron du

Background: He was born in 1728 into an ancient noble family whose antecedents are murky. They twice had *honneurs de la cour*. He was a lieutenant in the Limousin regiment where his father and later brother served (September 1741). He was advanced to captain (March 1747) and named colonel of the *volontaires du Dauphine* regiment (February 1759). He was promoted to brigadier (July 1762). He served in Corsica (1768–69) and Poland in 1771, where he fought in the siege of Krakow. He was promoted to *maréchal de camp* (January 1770).

American Service: He served as Rochambeau's 2nd in command in America and then commanded the expeditionary force on Rochambeau's return to France.

Post-American Career: He was promoted to lieutenant general (June 1783). He resigned at the beginning of the Revolution. He was badly wounded defending the Tuileries on August 10, 1792, and subsequently died of his injuries.

Notable Facts: He was awarded the *Grand Croix de Saint-Louis* (limited to eight holders). His brother, Comte Joseph, served in the émigré, Portuguese, and Russian armies and was made a *maréchal de France* in 1816. His son Charles also emigrated and served in the Portuguese Army as a colonel and was reintegrated into the French army. He returned to France and was arrested for his political views. He was promoted to *maréchal de camp* following the Restoration.

Sources: Bod., 162–63; Ketchum, 305.

Houx de Viomenil, Charles Gabriel du

Background: He was born in 1767 into an ancient noble family whose antecedents are murky. They twice had *honneurs de la cour*. He was named a 2nd lieutenant cavalry (September 1779).

American Service: He served as aide-de-camp to his father in America.

Post-American Career: He was promoted to captain (February 1786) and then put on half pay in spring 1792. He emigrated and was a *colonel a la suite* in Condé's army and aide-de-camp to his uncle. He was a colonel in Portuguese service (March 1802). His rank was confirmed by Napoleon, and he served in French army in Spain. After his return to France in 1811, he was arrested for his political views and imprisoned for nearly three years. On the return of the Bourbons, he was promoted to *maréchal de camp* and served in the army until November 1817. He died in 1831.

Source: Bod., 164–65.

Houx de Viomenil, Antoine Louis Chevalier du

Background: He was born in 1745 to a cadet branch of the ancient noble family de Viomenil. He was named a cavalry cornet (May 1760) and then 2nd lieutenant and captain in the Legion of Lorraine (July 1771). He served in Poland with his cousin and distinguished himself at Krakow. He was promoted to lieutenant colonel of cavalry (June 1779).

American Service: He served as aide-de-camp to his cousin, Baron de Viomenil, in America.

Post-American Career: He was promoted to lieutenant colonel in the Brie regiment and then promoted to *maréchal de camp* upon retirement in March 1791. He did not emigrate. He died in 1821.

Notable Fact: His son was killed in 1793 fighting in Condé's army.

Source: Bod., 163.

Houx de Viomenil, Joseph Hyacinthe Marquis du

Background: He was born in 1734 into an ancient noble family whose antecedents are murky. They twice had *honneurs de la cour*. He was named a lieutenant in the Limousin regiment where his father and later brother served (June 1747). He served in the Netherlands during the War of the Austrian Succession. He was advanced to captain (April 1759) and served in Germany (1756–63). He was colonel of the *volontaires du Dauphine* (July 1761). He led a 1500-advance guard in the Corsican operation (1769). He was promoted to brigadier (January 1770) and *maréchal de camp* (March 1780).

American Service: He served under Rochambeau in America, commanding the Bourbonnais brigade at Yorktown.

Post-American Career: He served as governor of Martinique, but his brutality led to his recall. He was named commander of Basse Alsace but did not take up the position due to significant opposition. He emigrated and served in Condé's army. He was named lieutenant general in Russian service and served in Portugal 1801–02. On his return to

France, he commanded several military divisions and was promoted to *maréchal de France* (July 1816).

Notable Facts: He was the highest ranking "American" officer outside of the two Napoleonic marshals, Rochambeau, and three admirals and received the *Grand Croix de Saint-Louis* (limited to eight holders).

Sources: Bod., 163–64; Ketchum, 305.

Du Lau d'Allemans, Pierre Marie Vicomte

Background: He was born in 1752 into a noble family (1372) which had received seven *honneurs de la cour*. He was a *garde du corps* in the Noailles company (1766), eventually rising to *colonel-en-second* in the Agenais regiment (1778). He embarked with his regiment for Saint-Domingue and assumed command when the colonel, Dupleix de Cadignan, died. He commanded a district of Saint-Domingue and returned to France.

American Service: He rejoined the Agenais regiment and served with it at Yorktown.

Post-American Career: He was promoted to colonel of the Saintonge regiment (1783) and then to *maréchal de camp* (1792). He emigrated and commanded the company of officers of his regiment in Condé's army. He went to Saint-

Domingue to look after his wife's financial interests and ended up serving with the British (1794–98). He returned to France and was named an honorary lieutenant general (1814). He died in 1816.

Source: Bod., 165.

Du Portail, Lebegue de Presle Louis

Background: Born in 1747 to a family ennobled in the seventeenth century, he was a student at Mezieres engineering school (January 1762). He was involved in a dispute at the school which resulted in him being cashiered and imprisoned for a year. He was re-instated as an engineer and then captain (August 1773). He was asked by War Minister Saint-Germain to develop an engineering manual. He was given leave for two years to look after his personal affairs.

American Service: The leave allowed him to travel to America with three other engineers to serve in the Continental Army. He arrived in late 1776 and was named a lieutenant colonel in the Continental Army, rising to brigadier general and chief engineer. He served at Brandywine, Germantown, Monmouth, and Charleston where he was taken prisoner. After being exchanged, he directed the siege operations at Yorktown. He was promoted to lieutenant colonel in the French Army (April 1780) and major general in the Continental Army (November 1781).

Post-American Career: He returned to France and was promoted to brigadier and appointed to the general staff as his fellow engineers were jealous and did not want him to hold an important position in their corps. He attended the Prussian military maneuvers with Lafayette in the summer of 1785. He was sent to Naples with other officers to train its army. He was named *maréchal de camp* (March 1788). He served as War Minister (November 1790–December 1791) on the recommendation of Lafayette.

He was named lieutenant general in January 1792 and appointed to command the 21st military division. He did not take up his post and went into hiding for two years. He fled to the United States and bought a farm at Valley Forge. He died sailing back to France in 1802.

Notable Facts: He was one of the five highest ranking Frenchmen in the Continental Army as a major general. He was responsible for implementing a series of reforms as War Minister which laid the groundwork for the army's later success.

Sources: Bod., 291; Lauberdiere, 129; ERA, vol. 1, 247; Serge le Pottier, *Duportail ou le Genie de George Washington* (Paris, 2011), *passim.*,; Schachtman, 307–08; Bod. 2, 183–88.

Du Buysson des Aix, Charles François Chevalier and then Vicomte

Background: Born in 1752, he was an aspirant in the artillery (August 1768). He served as 2nd lieutenant in the Noailles-Dragons (November 1772) and was placed on half pay in 1776 but then appointed captain in the colonial forces.

American Service: He travelled with Lafayette and Kalb to America and was confirmed as captain. He served as de Kalb's aide-de-camp and was appointed lieutenant colonel in the Continental Army. He was wounded at Camden trying to save Kalb's life and taken prisoner. He was promoted to brigadier general on his return and served with the North Carolina Militia.

Post-American Career: He was promoted to colonel on his return from America in late 1781. He was named vicomte and awarded the Croix de Saint-Louis.

Notable Facts: He is known for memoirs—which were ghost written and published in 1913 and was a founder of the French branch of the Society of Cincinnatus.

Sources: Bod., 157; Lauberdiere, 39.

Dumas, Mathieu Comte

Background: Born in 1753, he became an *aspirant de genie* (1768) and later lieutenant in the Medoc regiment. He served as aide-de-camp to the Marquis de Puysegur who was slated to command the army assigned to the invasion of England. He was advanced to captain (1780).

American Service: He embarked for America as aide-de-camp to Rochambeau.

Post-American Career: In 1784 he was sent to Amsterdam to defend Holland against the Prussians. He escorted Louis XVI and the royal family back from Varennes after their unsuccessful flight. He successively served Maréchal de Broglie and Lafayette as aide-de-camp. Promoted to *maréchal de camp* in 1791, he commanded the 3rd military division at Metz and ensured that any unrest among the troops was limited. He was elected to the Legislative Assembly and served as its president (1792). He fled to England as he was concerned for his safety. He later sat on the Conseil des Ancients but was proscribed as a noble and fled to Hamburg.

He returned in 1799 when Napoleon became First Consul and was tasked with organizing the reserve army, which distinguished itself in the conquest of Italy. He was promoted to *general de division* (1805). He served as war minister in Naples under King Joseph Bonaparte after serving bravely at Austerlitz. He fought in the 1806 Spanish campaign after Joseph Bonaparte had become king of Spain. He fought at Wagram, where he was deputy chief of staff under Berthier. He served as intendant of the Grande Armée (1812) and was severely ill during the Russian campaign. He was wounded and captured at Leipzig in 1813.

On the first Restoration he was tasked by Louis XVIII with reorganizing the army for a peacetime role. Napoleon recalled him to head the national guard. He was in disfavor but appointed to the council of state in 1818. He died in 1837.

Notable Facts: He had the idea for the Legion of Honor as a replacement for royal decorations. On the night of July 30, 1830, he was one of a delegation of twelve sent to tell Louis Philippe that he had been appointed lieutenant general of the realm. He also wrote nineteen volumes of the war (1798–

1807) but stopped due to poor eyesight. This did not prevent him from translating Napier's *Peninsula War* into French! His son finished and published his memoirs in 1839.

Sources: Bod., 166; Lauberdiere, 11, 186; K, 296; Six, vol. 1, 393–94; Soboul, vol. 2, 376–77; Ebel, 150, 181, 189, 253.

Durand, Jean Baptiste

Background: Born in 1753 to a noble family (1702), he was a student in the artillery school (July 1771) and promoted to lieutenant (November 1774).

American Service: He served at Yorktown.

Post-American Career: He was promoted to captain (January 1787). He emigrated and served as colonel of the Hollenlohe regiment. He was appointed *maréchal de camp* (August 1814) but relieved by Napoleon during the Hundred Days. Reinstated, he served until March 1819. He was named honorary lieutenant general (December 1824). He died in 1829.

Source: Bod., 176.

Duval, François Raymond

Background: Born in 1756, he served as an infantryman in the navy and was taken prisoner.

American Service: He was captain of the troops aboard the *Bonhomme Richard* commanded by John Paul Jones (1778). He was made prisoner, exchanged, and then served until 1783.

Post-American Career: He became a priest. He rejoined the army in October 1791, rising to brigadier general (July 1793) and later suspended for not implementing the scorched earth policy in the Vendee. He returned to active duty in August 1809, commanding various military posts, including Porte-Ferrajo on Elba where he received Napoleon as he entered exile. He retired in 1815.

Source: Six, vol. 1, 418.

Enfant L', Pierre Charles

Background: Born in 1754, he studied art at the Royal Academy where his father was a professor.

American Service: Recruited by Beaumarchais, he served as an engineer in the Continental Army. He was promoted to captain (April 1779). He served at Valley Forge, where he illustrated von Steuben's army manual. He was at the siege of Savannah and was captured at Charleston. He spent the rest of the war on Washington's staff and was promoted to major (May 1783).

Post-American Career: He set up a civil engineering firm in New York City, where he redesigned City Hall. He designed the medal of the Society of Cincinnati. He was appointed to design "Federal City," now Washington, D.C., by President Washington (1791). He was professor of engineering at West Point (1813–17). He died in poverty, living with a benefactor in 1825, never having been properly paid for the plans for Washington, D.C.

Notable Facts: He designed the insignia for the Order of the Cincinnati. In 1909, his body was exhumed to lie in state in the Capitol before being buried in Arlington National Cemetery.

Sources: ERA, vol. 2, 489; Schachtman, 57.

Oyre, François Ignace Comte Ervoil d'

Background: Born in 1739, he was an engineering student at Mezieres. He was named 2nd lieutenant (June 1756), rising to captain (1765).

American Service: He served in America under Rochambeau.

Post-American Career: He rose from major to *maréchal de camp* (1792). He was captured at the siege of Mainz in 1793. On his return to France, he retired. He died in 1799.

Notable Fact: He left a journal of his American service to the Society of Cincinnati.

Source: Bod., 184.

Esebeck, Louis Eberhard Baron d'

Background: Born in 1747 to a noble family from Zweibrucken (recognized 1276), he served as an ensign in the Fersen regiment (1747) and in Holland. He transferred as a captain to the Deux-Ponts regiment (March 1758), rising to lieutenant colonel (April 1778).

American Service: He served with his regiment under Rochambeau in America.

Post-American Career: He rose to *maréchal de camp* on retiring in March 1791. He emigrated and served in Bourbon army before becoming minister of the Duchy of Deux-Ponts (February 1795). He died in 1817.

Notable Facts: He was one of three brothers in the Deux-Ponts regiment, including Henry Louis who served with the regiment in America as a captain. He retired in 1784.

Source: Bod., 185–86.

Ethis de Corny, Dominique Louis

Background: Born in 1736 he was in the intendance department at Besancon (1766). He was appointed *commissaire de guerre* (April 1767) but did not exercise this function until 1772.

American Service: He accompanied Lafayette in March 1780 to prepare for the arrival and supply of Rochambeau's corps. Congress named him a lieutenant colonel (June 1780). He returned to France in March 1781.

Post-American Career: He served as *commissaire principal de guerre* for the Swiss Guards (August 1784). His position was eliminated, but he organized the Paris militia. He was delegated to obtain the arms from the Invalides and Bastille. He was not involved in the taking of the Bastille but recommended that the fortress be demolished.

Notable Fact: He was sent to London to retrieve a pamphlet attacking the Queen from the Comtesse de la Motte. He was a Freemason.

Source: Bod., 188–89.

Eustace, Jean-Skey

Background: He was born in New York in 1762.

American Service: He served as aide-de-camp to General Lee (1775) and as a 2nd lieutenant in the Continental Army and then major (November 1777). He was named colonel and chief of staff of Georgia state forces (August 1781).

Post-American Career: He was taken into French service as a colonel (April 1792) and appointed *maréchal de camp* (September 1792). He was arrested for insubordination but released.

Sources: Six, vol. 1, 432–33; Six, vol. 1, 67.

Felix d'Olliere, Jean Baptiste Comte de Saint-Mesme and then Muy

Background: Born in 1755 to a family ennobled in the sixteenth century, he was a 2nd lieutenant in the cavalry (July 1769) and then captain (May 1771), joining the Soissonnais regiment.

American Service: He served with Rochambeau's corps, including at Yorktown.

Post-American Career: He was named brigadier (January 1784), rising to *maréchal de camp* and then lieutenant general (February 1792). He was charged with organizing l'Armée du Midi and then commanded the troops facing the Lyon insurrection (1793). Suspended, he retired but later rejoined the army and served in Egypt under Bonaparte and held important posts under the Empire. He died in 1820.

Notable Fact: He voted for the death of Marshall Ney when the chamber of peers condemned Ney to death.

Sources: Bod., 193–94; Lauberdiere, 121; Six, vol. 2, 246–47.

Fersen, Hans Axel Count

Background: He was born in 1754 to a noble Swedish family from present-day Lithuania. He served in Swedish Army, attaining the rank of captain and then moved to Paris.

American Service: He served as aide-de-camp to Rochambeau throughout the campaign.

Post-American Career: He purchased the Royal-Suedois regiment in 1783, serving as its colonel. He returned to Sweden, serving against the Russians (1788). He was appointed major general in the Swedish Army (1792), rising to Grand Marshall in 1801. Accused of having poisoned the Swedish crown prince he was massacred while in prison on June 20, 1810.

Notable Facts: He organized the royal family's flight to Varennes and was arrested. He may have been Marie-Antoinette's lover. He was a Freemason.

Sources: Bod, 195; Lauberdiere, 29; Ketchum, 296.

Fleury Teissèdre de, François Louis

Background: Born in 1749, he was a volunteer in the Rouergue regiment (May 1768). He served in Corsica and was appointed captain-engineer (1776).

American Service: He joined in the American forces, rising to lieutenant colonel in the Continental Army (1779). He fought at Germantown and the siege of Fort Mifflin and led the assault at Stonypoint. Reintegrated into the French Army as a major in the Saintonge regiment (March 1780). He distinguished himself at Yorktown.

Post-American Career: He was made colonel of the Pondichery regiment (January 1784). He was promoted to *maréchal de camp* (June 1791) and served in l'Armée du Nord. Wounded at the retreat from Mons (April 1792), he retired shortly thereafter.

Notable Facts: He was one of only eight officers to receive a medal from Congress for his actions during the War of

Independence and the only non-American. The US Corps of Engineers' highest award is named after him.

Sources: Bod., 442; Lauberdiere, 131; Six, vol. 1, 454; Selesky, vol. 2, 1144–45.

Fontanges, François Vicomte de

Background: He was born in 1740 into a noble family (1433) from Auvergne, which twice received *honneurs de la cour*. He was a lieutenant in the Poitou regiment (January 1756) and then captain. He was wounded at Rossbach (1757) and appointed major in the Cap regiment (May 1775).

American Service: He served as d'Estaing's chief of staff at Savannah, where he was badly wounded.

Post-American Career: He was promoted to lieutenant colonel and then colonel in the Cap regiment (January 1784) and later to *maréchal de camp* (May 1780). He resigned in April 1790 and later fled to Hispaniola. He served as *maréchal de camp* in the Spanish army and was captured by the French (December 1808). He was promoted to lieutenant general (August 1814). He died in 1822.

Notable Fact: His wife, a relation of the Beauharnais family in Saint-Domingue, served as lady in waiting to Napoleon's mother (1809).

Source: Bod., 199–200.

Fontbonne, Alexandre Louis de

Background: Born into a noble family in 1750, he served as a 2nd lieutenant and then lieutenant in the Auvergne regiment (July1775). He advanced to captain in the Gatinais regiment (January 1780).

American Service: He took part in the siege of Savannah and was wounded at Yorktown.

Post-American Career: He rose from lieutenant colonel to *maréchal de camp* (March 1793). After being suspended, he returned to service as a *general de division* (June 1795) in l'Armée d'Italie. Forced into retirement, he was assassinated near Frejus in 1796.

Sources: Bod., 200; Six, vol. 1, 457.

Forbach des Deux-Ponts, Christian Comte and the Marquis
de

Background: Born in 1752, he was the oldest son of Christian IV, Duke des Deux-Ponts, and of a French actress. As a result of this marriage, he and his brother were excluded from succeeding to the dukedom. He rose from 2nd lieutenant to colonel (July 1772) in his family regiment of Deux-Ponts and took command in 1775.

American Service: He and his regiment were with Rochambeau throughout the campaign, and he commanded it at Yorktown.

Post-American Career: He was promoted to brigadier and then *maréchal de camp* (March 1788). He was removed as commander of the Deux-Ponts regiment and placed on half pay (March 1791). He served in the Bavarian army under the Duke of Brunswick, achieving the rank of lieutenant general. He died in 1817.

Source: Bod., 201–02.

Forbach des Deux-Ponts, Guillaume Philippe Vicomte and then Comte

Background: Born in 1754, he was the second son of Christian IV, Duke des Deux-Ponts and of a French actress. As a result of this marriage, he and his brother were excluded from succeeding to the dukedom. He rose from 2nd lieutenant to captain in the Schomberg-Dragon regiment (April 1772). He was appointed lieutenant colonel in his family regiment of Deux-Ponts in October 1777.

American Service: He and his regiment were with Rochambeau, and he commanded a combined unit of Gatinais and Deux-Ponts soldiers at Yorktown where he was wounded. He was sent back to France to announce the victory.

Post-American Career: He continued to serve in the Deux-Ponts regiment until resigning (June 1791). He served in the Bavarian Army, achieving the rank of lieutenant general. He died in 1807.

Notable Fact: He was a Freemason, as was his older brother. While waiting to sail with Rochambeau to America at Brest, he went AWOL to Nantes where he was wounded twice in a duel. Rochambeau confined him to quarters during the sea voyage.

Source: Bod., 202.

Gau de Voves, Joseph François

Background: Born in 1748 to a recently ennobled Alsatian family (1772), he was named *Commissaire des Guerres* (February 1777).

American Service: He served under Rochambeau as his *Commissaire de Guerre* responsible for the artillery.

Post-American Career: He served in the Ministry of War and head of central administration. He retired in 1792 and was arrested during the Terror. Reinstated, he assisted Aubry in reorganizing the army. He was a deputy to the *Conseil de Cinq-Cents*. He could not take his seat as the relative of an émigré until 1797. He was forced into hiding.

He served as Treasurer of the War Ministry under the Consulate. He served on the Conseil d'Etat under both Napoleon and the Restoration. He died in 1825.

Source: Bod., 211–12.

Gaultier de Kerveguen, Paul Louis

Background: Born in 1737, he was a naval engineering student (1755), rising to lieutenant geographer. He served in the Rio de Janeiro expedition in 1763 and was d'Estaing's aide-de-camp on Saint-Domingue (1764) and returned to France in 1767, where he was employed in the cartography section at Versailles. He was promoted to captain in the infantry (1769). He was re-employed in 1768 and later was assigned to the Auxerrois regiment.

American Service: He served as a senior staff officer to d'Estaing and took part in the capture of Grenada during which he was wounded, as well as in the battles of Saint Lucia and Savannah.

Post-American Career: He was promoted to lieutenant colonel (1780) and adjutant general colonel (1791). He was named *general de brigade* in 1793 but suspended as a noble. He was re-instated and served as chief of staff of l'Armée d'Italie, being made a temporary *general de division*. He was replaced by Berthier and commanded several Italian cities, including Florence. He was named *inspecteur en chef des revues* in 1800 and retired in 1807.

Sources: Bod., 213; Six, vol. 1, 487.

Gauthier de Murnan, Jean Bernard

Background: Born in 1748, he was an aspirant engineer (1769) in the Garde du Corps to the Comte d'Artois (November 1773). He passed into Russian service as captain of engineers but could not take the climate.

American Service: He went to America as a volunteer and was appointed a major of engineers in the Continental Army. He was in Sullivan's expedition against the Six Nations and participated at the Battle of Newton. He directed the American sappers and engineers at Yorktown and was promoted to lieutenant colonel (September 1783). He resigned from the Continental Army in February 1784.

Post-American Career: On returning to France, he was not initially employed but was later promoted to lieutenant colonel (April 1791) and colonel of 35th infantry regiment (August 1792). Promoted provisional brigadier general (April 1793), he was imprisoned and saved by the events of Thermidor. He died in 1797.

Sources: Bod., 213; Six, vol. 2, 244–45; Six, vol. 1, 74.

Gimat de Soubadere (Jean Joseph)

Background: Born in 1747 to a noble family (1536), he was an ensign, rising to lieutenant (June 1776) in the Viennois regiment.

American Service: He was allowed by the king to accept a commission as a major in the Continental Army (December 1776). He was aide-de-camp to Lafayette in America. He was named lieutenant colonel (1778) and commanded an American light infantry battalion in the assault on redoubt no. 9 of British lines at Yorktown, where he was wounded.

Post-American Career: He was promoted to captain and then major while in America. He was advanced to colonel of the Martinique regiment (August 1782) and governor of Saint Lucia (June 1789). Siding with the royalist party, he was replaced. Leading a 1100-émigré corps landed by the British in Martinique (June 1793), he was mortally wounded.

Sources: Bod., 218; Lauberdiere, 166–67.

Gontaut, Armand Louis Duc de Biron and then Lauzun

Background: He was born in 1747 into a high noble family which received *honneurs de la cour* twelve times. He entered the Gardes Françaises at age twelve. He rose to lieutenant and aide major (February 1766). A spendthrift and gambler, he lost most of his fortune. He rose to colonel (October 1767). He became the owner in 1778 of the *corps volontaires etrangers de marine*, later known as the Lauzun Legion. He led an expedition to Senegal and Gambia in 1779 capturing the fort of Cap Blanc.

American Service: He served in America at the head of the combined cavalry-infantry legion he had raised. He played an important role in the siege of Yorktown and at Gloucester, where he fought a cavalry duel with Tarleton. For his courage he was designated to bring the news of the victory to France along with Count Forbach.

Post-American Career: He was promoted to *maréchal de camp* (June1783). Elected to the Estates General from Quercy, he sided with the Duc d'Orleans against the king. His motivation may have been that he was denied command of the Gardes Françaises, which he felt was his right. He was chief of staff to Rochambeau in l'Armée du Nord and promoted to lieutenant general (January 1792). He commanded l' Armée du Rhin and beat the Piedmontese at Sospel. He tried repeatedly to resign. He was arrested and guillotined on December 31, 1793. His wife was guillotined six months later.

Notable Facts: As a young man he was a favorite of Madame de Pompadour. He died bravely, offering his executioner a glass of fine wine. His memoirs were published in 1822. His father and grandfather were both lieutenant generals. He was a Freemason.

Sources: Bod., 224–25; Ketchum, 300; Six, vol. 1, 104–05; DBF, vol. 6, 519–20; Philbrick, 273; Schachtman, 310–11.

Goullet de la Tour, Jean Pierre

Background: Born in 1730, he was an artillery student (1745), rising to lieutenant colonel in 1780.

American Service: He was the second in command of Rochambeau's artillery serving at Yorktown.

Post-American Career: He returned to France in 1782 and was named *colonel directeur d'artillerie* in 1782. He was promoted to *maréchal de camp* on retirement (1791). He died in 1809.

Source: Bod., 225–26.

Gouvion, Jean-Baptiste

Background: Born January 1747, he was an officer candidate at the Mezieres engineering school (1769–70) and was promoted to *ingenieur ordinaire* in January 1771.

American Service: He was sent by Louis XVI with other engineering officers to America in February 1777. He was named captain and later major and lieutenant colonel in the Continental Army. He served at Yorktown. At General Washington's insistence he was advanced to colonel and chief engineer in November 1781.

Post-American Career: He was promoted to lieutenant colonel in 1783 and awarded the order of Saint Louis in 1784. He was appointed major general in the Paris Garde Nationale under Lafayette in 1789. He was promoted to *maréchal de camp* in June 1791. He was elected deputy to the Legislative Assembly in September 1791 and served on its military commission.

He resigned after the flight to Varennes and the killing of his brother by the garrison at Toul. He rejoined to the Armée du Centre and was killed at Maubeuge leading the advanced guard in June 1792.

Notable Fact: As a peer of France, he voted for deportation during Marshal Ney's trial before that chamber.

Sources: Bod., 226–27; Lauberdiere, 260; DBF, vol. 16, 839; Six, vol. 1, 515.

Grenier de Cauville, Jacques François

Background: Born in 1752, he was a student at the military academy and then joined the Bearn regiment, rising to lieutenant in 1775. He transferred to the Agenais regiment in 1776.

American Service: He may have served with his regiment at Yorktown.

Post-American Career: He returned to France in 1782 and was named *colonel directeur d'artillerie* in 1782 and was promoted to *maréchal de camp* on retirement (1791). He died in 1809.

Source: Bod., 229–30.

Guerin de la Chaise, Jean Pierre

Background: Born in 1744 to a noble family from Perigord (1531), he was an ensign (April 1761) in the marine regiment, rising to captain (May 1778).

American Service: He commanded the Auxerrois detachment at Savannah and served in the West Indies.

Post-American Career: He was promoted to major in the Armagnac regiment, rising to colonel (February 1782). He emigrated and served in the army as a company commander. He was promoted to *maréchal de camp* (December 1798).

Notable Fact: He was the Venerable of the Freemason Lodge of the Armagnac regiment.

Source: Bod., 232.

Jennings de Kilmaine, Charles Edouard

Background: Born in 1751 to an Irish noble family, he joined the Austrian Army, rising to 2nd lieutenant and was a *gentilhomme* in the Royal-Dragon regiment (1774) and then adjutant in the *volontaires etrangers de la marine* (September 1778), which became the Lauzun Legion. He served with his unit in Senegal and then as 2nd Lieutenant in the Lauzun Legion (April 1780).

American Service: He served with Lauzun's Legion in America.

Post-American Career: He returned to France, serving in the Lauzun Hussards and rising to colonel (November 1792). He was promoted brigadier general and then *general* *de division* (May 1794). He was arrested and imprisoned for fifteen months. He later served in l'Armée d'Italie as head of the cavalry and then as acting commander in chief between Bonaparte and Berthier. He finally served as general in chief of l'Armée d'Angleterre. He died in December 1799.

Sources: Bod., 252; Six, vol. 2, 6–7; Jean Tulard, *Dictionnaire Napoleon* (Paris, 1989), vol. 2, 116.

Jourdan, Jean Baptiste Comte de

Background: Born in Limoges to a surgeon in 1762, he was an apprentice silk worker and then enlisted in the Auxerrois regiment (April 1778).

American Service: He served with his regiment at Savannah.

Post-American Career: He returned to France due to illness and was discharged from the army in July 1784, becoming a haberdasher in Limoges. He was elected captain in the Limoges national guard (July 1789) and soon after to lieutenant colonel in a 2nd Haute Vienne volunteer battalion, serving at Jemappes with distinction. He was promoted to brigadier general (May 1793) and then *general de division* (July 1793). He led his division at Hondschoote (September

1793), which was a tactical victory for the French and was wounded.

He was then named commanding general of l'Armée du Nord. He won the battle of Wattignies against Coburg and then relieved Maubeuge (October 1793). Relieved of duty in January 1794 and arraigned before the Committee of Public Safety, he barely escaped the guillotine. He returned to Limoges but was recalled that March. He led successful campaigns in what is now Belgium, including the successful siege of Charleroi, winning the battle of Fleurus (1794) and losing at Wurzburg, Germany. He resigned following this defeat and returned to Limoges.

Elected to the *Conseil des Cinq-Cents* in April 1797, he served as its president twice. During his term on the Cinq-Cents he drafted the first universal conscription law enacted in France: It bears his name and put the entire male adult population aged 20–25 in the service of the Republic and later the Empire.

He was named commander of the Armée Armée de Mayence in November 1798 and then of a combined army which was defeated at Stockach by Archduke Charles. Ill, he was relieved by Massena and reelected to his seat on the Cinq-Cents. He opposed the Brumaire coup due to his strong

Republican sympathies but was nevertheless appointed as Inspector General of the infantry (April 1799). After the string of defeats in Italy culminating in the loss at Novi, Jourdan and Bernadotte were involved in a Jacobin plot to overthrow the government, which came to nothing in the end.

He was named *maréchal d'Empire* (May 1804). He served in Naples as governor, advising King Joseph, and then as chief of staff in Spain. He was defeated by Wellesley at Talavera and recalled to France. He returned to Spain, serving as governor of Madrid and chief of staff of l'Armée du Centre (July 1811). He then was chief of staff of l'Armée d'Espagne and was beaten in July 1813 at Vitoria by Wellington.

He was recalled to France. After retiring, he pledged allegiance to the Bourbons and was named Governor of the Invalides in 1830. He died in 1833.

Notable Facts: He was appointed president of the court martial of Marshall Ney, but the court managed to recuse itself, forcing the trial to be moved to the chamber of peers, which condemned Ney to death. Jourdan received the Grand Eagle of the Legion of Honor.

Sources: Six, vol. 1, 608–09; David Chandler, *Napoleon's Marshals* (New York, 1987), 156–78; Frederic Hulot, *Le Maréchal* Jourdan (Paris, 2010*),* passim.; Scott, Dictionnairy, vol. 1, 83; Souboul, *Dictionnaire,* vol. 2, 601; Tulard, *Dictionnaire,* vol. 2, 90–9;1 Ebel, *passim.*

Kalb, Jean Baron de

Background: Born into a Franconian noble family in 1726, he was a lieutenant in the Fischer Chasseurs (September 1743). He transferred to the Lowendal regiment where he rose to lieutenant colonel (May 1761). He was sent by Choiseul to America to report on conditions there in 1768.

American Service: Recruited by Silas Deane with the tacit approval of Louis XVI, he travelled to America with Lafayette and was named major general in the Continental Army. He served under Gates in the Southern Department, taking part in the battles of Brandywine, Valley-Forge, and Monmouth. Promoted to brigadier general in the French army (March 1780), he was killed at the Battle of Camden in 1780.

Post-American Career: None.

Notable Facts: Two of his sons served in the French army, including one with the Deux-Ponts in America, and both emigrated. One, Frederick, returned to France and was guillotined in November 1793.

Sources: Bod., 257; Lauberdiere, 39; DBF, vol. 18, 1077; DAR, 741; WGAR, vol. 2, 269–71.

La Barre, Andre

Background: Born in 1749 at Fort Missouri in Louisiana, he was an aspirant and later lieutenant in the Condé Dragoons (December 1776).

American Service: He served with d'Estaing and was wounded at Savannah.

Post-American Career: He held various staff and line appointments, rising to lieutenant colonel in the 15th Dragoons (July 1791). He served in l'Armée d'Italie and was made brigadier general (August 1793). He served in the Siege of Toulon and died near Roses (Catalunya) leading a cavalry charge (June 1794).

Sources: Bod., 259–60; Six, vol. 2, 16–17.

La Croix, Armand Charles Comte de Charlus

Background: He was born in 1756 into noble family from the Languedoc (1487), which received six *honneurs de la* *cour*. He was named as an artillery second lieutenant (November 1769) so he could attend the courses at Mezieres. He then obtained a company and then served in the Schomberg-dragoons. He was named *mestre de camp en second* in the General-cavalerie. With the impending departure of the Rochambeau expedition, his father had him transferred to the Saintonge regiment (March 1780) as second in command.

American Service: He served with his regiment at Yorktown, where he was commended for his bravery and was presented to Washington. He returned to France after the battle.

Post-American Career: He was promoted to *maréchal de camp* (March 1788) and created a duc. He was elected to the Estates General and served with the right wing of the nobility known as the ultras. He fought a duel with Alexandre Lameth on the abolition of privileges. As a result, the family's Paris mansion was burned to the ground. He emigrated after the king's flight to Varennes. He raised a regiment bearing his name, which served under British command in Portugal (1797–1802). He was promoted to lieutenant general (August 1814). He supported the July

Monarchy and was involved in the return of Napoleon's ashes from Saint Helena. He died in 1842.

Notable Facts: He succeeded his father, who had served as a reforming Navy Minister (1780–87) following the Seven Years' War as Duc de Castries. His fellow tutee at the family's Paris townhouse was Jean-Nicolas Pache, who became mayor of Paris and War Minister during the Revolution. Lacroix He voted for Ney's death.

Lafitte de Montagut, Antoine Jean

Background: Born in 1763 into a noble Gascon family (1370), he joined as a soldier rising to cadet and then 2nd lieutenant in the Agenois regiment (January 1780).

American Service: He served at Yorktown and in the West Indies.

Post-American Career: He was promoted to lieutenant (June 1783). He resigned in July 1789 and emigrated. He served in Saint-Domingue as a colonel of colonial troops under British command (1795). He returned to France in 1801 and was *prefet* of the Gers on the Bourbon Restoration. He was a deputy from Pontoise. He died in 1815.

Source: Bod., 269.

Lameth, Alexandre Theodore Chevalier de

Background: He was born in Paris in 1760 into a noble
family from Picardy (1400), which received six *honneurs de
la cour*. He was named a second lieutenant in the Royal-
Champagne-cavalerie and then took his brother's captaincy
in the Royal-Cavalerie (November 1779).

American Service: He was sent to America to replace his
brother, Charles, who had been wounded at Yorktown, as
aide-de-camp to Rochambeau and then acted as a staff
officer.

Post-American Career: He was promoted to *mestre de
camp en second*. Dissatisfied with the career opportunities,
he and Edouard Dillon travelled to the Crimea to join the
Russian forces fighting there. No position was available. He
was an attached colonel to his brother Charles's cuirassiers
regiment. He belonged to the Society of Thirty and *la societe
des Amis des Noirs*—an abolitionist group—and then
colonel of the Hainaut Chasseurs (January 1789). He was
elected to the Estates General from Peronne at the behest of

Madame de Stael,[1] joining the Third Estate and later was active on several important committees in the National Assembly. He urged the abolition of noble privileges. He was elected president of the Assembly in November 1790.

He joined the Armée du nord as a *maréchal de camp* (1792) but refused to be Rochambeau's chief of staff. He was accused of treason and refused to pledge allegiance as required by the Legislative Assembly. He escaped with Lafayette and was a prisoner of the Austrians. He spent time in England and then in Hamburg, where he and his brothers ran a trading company. After returning to France, he served as *prefet* of the Basses-Alpes, Rhin et Moselle, Roer, and Po (April 1804–February 1809). He was named Lieutenant General honoraire (December 1814). He was elected deputy (1820–27). He died in 1829.

Notable Facts: He was the nephew of comte and maréchal de Broglie. His older brother, Augustin, was an army officer, rising to colonel who did not share the liberal ideas of his three surviving brothers. Brother Theodore was wounded at

---

[1]Madame de Stael was the daughter of Finance Minister Necker and was a lover of Alexandre Lameth. Bod., 2, 89–90.

Grenada and served in the Legislative Assembly from the Jura. He was forced to emigrate and fled to Switzerland. His liberal views were influenced by his tutor, l'abbe Massieu, who became a Montagnard deputy to the Convention.

Sources: Bod., 275–76; Scott, Dictionnairy, vol. 2, 542–43; Bod. 2, vol. 3, 89–94.

Lameth, Charles Malo Comte de

Background: He was born in 1752 into a noble family from Picardy (1400), receiving six *honneurs de la cour*. He was a 2nd lieutenant and then captain in the cavalry (April 1777).

American Service: He was aide-de-camp and staff officer to Rochambeau. He was grievously wounded at Yorktown and was awarded the order of Saint-Louis.

Post-American Career: He was named as *mestre de camp* (March 1788) and colonel of the Royal Cuirassiers. Elected to Estates General from Artois, he sat with the liberal faction. He dueled with the Duc de Castries over political issues and de Castries' Paris mansion was burned to the ground as a result. After the king's flight to Varenne, he advocated the renewal of the legislative oath and called for the arrest of Bouille and other royalist officers. He was elected president of the Assembly and worked to institute a workable constitutional monarchy. He condemned the storming of the Tuileries on August 10, 1792, and went into hiding. He was arrested and then released. He left for Hamburg, where he started a business with his brothers, and then moved to Basel. He returned to France in 1801 and was reintegrated into the army as a brigadier general and given command of Wurtzburg and then Santander. He was made an honorary lieutenant general (August 1814). He served as a deputy from Pontoise, taking his brother Alexander's seat. He died in 1832.

Notable Facts: He was the nephew of comte and maréchal de Broglie. His older brother, Augustin, was an army officer rising to colonel but did not share the liberal ideas of his three surviving brothers. Brother Theodore was wounded at Grenada. He was a member of the Jacobin Club.

Sources: Bod., 275–76; Six, vol. 2, 46; Scott, Dictionary, vol. 2, 543–44; Bod. 2, 95–98.

Langlois, Denis Jean Marquis du Bouchet

Background: Born in 1752 into a noble Norman family (1523), he was a student at Clamecy military school (1767). He served as an artillery and engineering officer, rising to captain in the Marche regiment (January 1779).

American Service: He volunteered for America with his brother-in-law Conway. He was made a major in the Continental Army following Saratoga, where he served with distinction. He went back to France in 1778 but returned as aide-de-camp to Rochambeau.

Post-American Career: He was promoted to lieutenant colonel (June 1783), serving on the general staff. He became adjutant general colonel (April 1791) and then was named to command the 21st infantry regiment. He refused to take the new oath which did not mention the king and emigrated, instead serving in Condé's army and being promoted to *maréchal de camp* (1797). He was garrison commander at Ypres and Breda. He was made an honorary lieutenant general (October 1816) and was created marquis that same year. He died in 1826.

Sources: Bod., 280; Lauberdiere, 192; Samuel F. Scott, *From Yorktown to Valmy: The Transformation of the French Army in the Age of Revolution* (Boulder, 1998), 157.

Laprun, Pierre

Background: Born in 1737, he served as a soldier in various militias (1756–57). He served in Germany (1757–62), including at the battles of Minden and Corbach. He became a lieutenant in Auxonne regiment (August 1778).

American Service: He served in America including at Yorktown.

Post-American Career: He was promoted to captain (June 1782). He served in l'Armée du Nord (1792–93) and as commander of artillery in l'Armée de la Moselle (February 1794). He was promoted to brigadier general (February 1794) and advanced to general de division (May 1794). He commanded large formations and military districts. He was relieved for being a royalist (December 1797), and he retired in 1799 and died in 1822.

Sources: Bod., 283; Six, vol. 2, 60.

La Roche-Fonteville, Pierre Paul Marquis de

Background: He was born in 1757 into a noble family from Armagnac (1387), receiving three *honneurs de la cour*. He was a 2nd lieutenant in the king's regiment (August 1772) and then captain in the Gatinais regiment (April 1778).

American Service: He served as a staff officer at Savannah.

Post-American Career: He was promoted to colonel (June 1780) and then *maréchal de camp* on retirement (March 1791). He served in the British Army in Saint-Domingue

(1793–98), returning to France in 1801. He was appointed lieutenant general (January 1823). He died in 1833.

Notable Facts: His son Cesar was made *maréchal de camp* in 1823.

Source: Bod., 283–84.

Laumoy, Jean Baptiste

Background: Born in 1750, he was a 2nd lieutenant at the Mezieres artillery school (March 1768) and captain (January 1777).

American Service: He joined the Continental Army as a lieutenant colonel in 1777 with three other engineering officers who had been given a two-year leave of absence from the French Army. He served as chief engineer in the Carolinas and was promoted to colonel. He was wounded at the attack at Stone Ferry and was taken prisoner at the siege of Charleston. He was promoted to brigadier general and returned to France in December 1782.

Post-American Career: During his stay in America he was appointed as a senior staff officer with the rank of lieutenant colonel. He was twice posted to the West Indies, including as deputy to Comte Viomenil in Martinique. He returned to France in 1790. He was promoted to colonel and was chief of staff to the 3rd division at Metz. He was advanced to *maréchal de camp* (August 1791) and served as chief of staff to Lafayette in l'Armée du Centre (April 1792). The taking of the Tuileries led him and Lafayette to desert. He spent several years in Philadelphia. He only returned to France in 1801 and was not re-employed due to the enmity of Bonaparte. He retired in 1811 and died in 1832.

Sources: Bod., 287–88; Six, vol. 2, 71; DBF, vol. 19, 1347; Bod. 2, 169–70.

Le Cat, Louis Charles Comte d'Hervilly

Background: Born in 1755 into a noble family from Picardie (1471), he was named a 2nd lieutenant in king's regiment (June 1770). He rose to captain in the Auxerrois regiment (March 1779).

American Service: He served at Savannah.

Post-American Career: He was promoted to colonel (June 1780), serving on the general staff, and then to *mestre de camp* (March 1788). He proposed to the king that troops be sent in to roust the Jacobins. He defended the Tuileries on August 10, 1792. He emigrated and then led a regiment at the Quiberon landing and was wounded. He died in 1795.

Source: Bod., 293.

Le Maire de Gimel, Jacques

Background: Born in 1749, he was a gendarme in 1764 but was put on half pay.

American Service: He volunteered for America in 1776 with the blessing of the court. He served in Virginia and was sent by the colony to obtain aid from France. He returned to America in 1779. He was taken prisoner three times and incarcerated in Canada, but he managed to escape. He rose to colonel of artillery in the Continental Army and oversaw the fortifications in New England. He was captured again in 1782 while trying to return to France.

Post-American Career: Unknown.

Source: Bod., 300.

Le Monnier, Rene Nicolas

Background: Born May 1741, he was a soldier in the Saintonge regiment (1758) rising to lieutenant in 1776.

American Service: He served with his regiment under Rochambeau.

Post-American Career: He was promoted to captain in 1789. He advanced rapidly during the Revolution, being named general de brigade (1793) and *general de division*

(1794). He was not able to take up his post as he had been badly wounded at the battle of Watzenau in October 1793. Retiring in 1795, he was admitted to the Invalides and died in 1819.

Sources: Bod., 302; Six, vol. 2,105–06.

Le Noir, Laurent François Marquis de Rouvray

Background: He was born in 1733 into a non-noble family but provided a certificate of nobility. He was named an ensign and then lieutenant (September 1760) in the La Sarre regiment. He served in Canada where he was wounded. He raised the *volontaires de Saint-Domingue* regiment at a cost of 120,000 livres as its colonel (April 1768). The regiment consisted of 156 white grenadiers and 547 black chasseurs.

American Service: He led his regiment at Savannah, where he did not distinguish himself.

Post-American Career: He returned to Saint-Domingue and was named brigadier (December 1781) and then *maréchal de camp* (March 1788). He was elected to the Estates General from Saint-Domingue but did not take up his seat although moving to France. He wrote a book trying to undermine the case against freeing the slaves. He returned to Saint-Domingue and later emigrated to Philadelphia where he died in 1798.

Source: Bod., 303; Bod. 2, 230–31.

Le Prestre, Jacques Anne Comte de Vauban

Background: Born in 1754 into a noble family (1550), he was a volunteer in the Cambressis regiment (1768). He became a cavalry lieutenant, rising to lieutenant colonel (May 1777). He was appointed *mestre de camp* (July 1780).

American Service: He was an aide-de-camp to Rochambeau at Yorktown and participated in the assault on redoubt no. 9.

Post-American Career: He served in two regiments and then went into Prussian service in April 1790. He resigned and joined the émigré army. In Russian service (1793), he took part in the Quiberon landing leading a detachment of Chouans.

He was arrested and imprisoned in the Temple on his return to France in 1801. He wrote a book on the Vendée campaign and was critical of the royalist leadership, which resulted in his being shunned by Louis XVIII. He died in 1816.

Notable Facts: He was a distant relative of Marshal Vauban. His grandfather was a lieutenant general and his father a brigadier. His two brothers were in the army.

Sources: Bod., 304–05; Lauberdiere, 116.

Lecrere, Jean Michel

Background: Born in 1759, he was a volunteer in the Auvergne and then Gatinais regiments (1776–78).

American Service: He served at Yorktown with his regiment (1777–83) and was badly wounded in the attack of October 15, 1781.

Post-American Career: He rose to captain and staff officer in l'Armée du nord. He was arrested and then released. He served in various armies and was promoted to adjudant general *chef de brigade* in June 1795. He then serves as an *sous-inspecteur* rising to chief inspector of the army of Portugal as a *general de division*. He retired in 1815 and died in 1847.

Source: Quintin, 217–18.

L'Eveille, Jean Pierre

Background: He was born in Saint-Domingue.

American Service: He served at Savannah as a volunteer with the *chasseurs volontaires de Saint-Domingue*.

Post-American Career: Having returned to Saint-Domingue, he commanded the 3rd colonial regiment. He was arrested and then released. He was named acting *general de brigade* in 1796 and named a district commander. He and commissioner Santhonax were expelled by Toussaint Louverture in August 1797 and returned to France. He was placed on the inactive list but recalled for the Leclerc expedition and died in Saint-Domingue in 1802.

Sources: Six, vol. 2, 117–18; Desmarais, *America's First Ally*, 201.

Liegard, François

Background: Born in 1745, he entered the *volontaires de la marine* as 2nd lieutenant (November 1778), serving on several ships under La Motte Picquet and Guichen and rising to lieutenant.

American Service: He served at Yorktown and the West Indies.

Post-American Career: He spent many years in Saint-Domingue (1783–92) but was relieved of his duties as hostile to the government. He returned to France and was promoted to captain (November 1793). Arrested for conspiracy, he was held in the Luxemburg Palace.

Reintegrated into the army, he was appointed brigadier general (March 1797) and commanded Marseille. Relieved after 18 Fructidor, he was reintegrated and served with l'Armée d'Italie and then the Neapolitan Army (1806–07). He commanded several cities in Italy. He was created baron d'Empire. He died in 1816.

Sources: Bod., 311–12; Six, vol. 2, 124.

Lomenie, François Alexandre Vicomte de

Background: He was born in 1758 into a Limousin family ennobled in 1552, which received six *honneurs de la cour*. He was named a 2nd lieutenant in the Artois-Cavalerie (August 1774). He was promoted to captain and then major (July 1779) after joining colonial troops. He transferred to the Lauzun Legion in 1780.

American Service: He served at Yorktown, returned to France and then came back to America in September 1782.

Post-American Career: Promoted to *mestre de camp* (March 1788), he rose to colonel of the Chasseurs de Champagne (September 1788). He was made *maréchal de camp* upon retirement (March 1791).

Notable Facts: He and his two brothers were guillotined in May 1794. They were the sons of a minister of state and nephews of finance minister Lomenie de Brienne.

Sources: Bod., 314–15; Bod. 2, 287.

Loppin, Claude Bernard Marquis de Monmort

Background: Born in 1752 into a noble family from Burgundy (1585), he was a musketeer (April 1772), 2nd lieutenant, and then captain (July 1776) in the Royal-Cravates regiment.

American Service: He served as aide-de-camp to his father-in-law, Baron de Viomenil, in America (1782–83).

Post-American Career: He was promoted to *mestre de camp* and then colonel (March 1788). He was imprisoned and later moved to England. He was named *maréchal de camp* (May 1817). He died in 1831.

Notable Fact: His son, Magloire, was a cavalry colonel.

Source: Bod., 315.

Lynch, Isidore

Background: Born in 1755, he enlisted in the Clare regiment of which his uncle was the colonel (June 1770), rising to captain (1778). He served in the West Indies with the Dillon regiment.

American Service: He served with his regiment at Grenada and Savannah, later acting as aide-de-camp to the Marquis de Chastellux, Rochambeau's deputy, and was at Yorktown. He served in the Gulf of Mexico under Baron de Viomenil.

Post-American Career: He was promoted to *mestre de camp* (January 1784) in the Walsh regiment and then *maréchal de camp* (February 1792). He served under Luckner and Kellerman and commanded the first line of infantry at Valmy. He was promoted to *general de division* (March 1793).

He was suspended and arrested along with Berthier and Champollon. He was reintegrated and then retired (1795) and subsequently brought back. He held various staff jobs until final retirement in February 1815. He died in 1838.

Sources: Bod., 319; Six, vol. 2, 136; Bod 2, 314–15.

MacDonald, Charles Edouard Comte de

Background: Born in May 1741 into a noble Scottish family (his godfather was Charles Edward Stuart), he joined the O'Gilvy regiment (1757) as a lieutenant in 1776. He transferred to the Foix regiment, rising to captain (1776).

American Service: He embarked in d'Estaing's squadron although his battalion had been designated to remain in France. He participated in the battles of Saint Lucia, Grenada, and Savannah, where his brother served in the British forces.

Post-American Career: He was promoted to *mestre de camp* in 1780 but could not obtain a posting at that rank. He retired in 1785. He was arrested, tried, and guillotined in 1794 as a spy for Prime Minister Pitt.

Source: Bod., 321.

MacMahon, Charles Laure Marquis d'Equilly

Background: Born in 1750 into an Irish noble family, he was a musketeer (1767) and captain in the Royal-dragoons (1770). He was appointed *mestre de camp* (1780) attached to the Irish brigade at the request of the king's aunts.

American Service: He sailed on *Aigle* in April 1782 and served as aide-de-camp to the Duc de Lauzun.

Post-American Career: He commanded the Dauphine regiment (1788), resigned in April 1791, and was promoted to *maréchal de camp* upon retirement. He emigrated and commanded a company of his regiment in the army of the

Princes. He returned to France. He was made a peer in 1827 and died in 1830.

Source: Bod., 319; Bod. 2, 320–21.

Mauduit du Plessis, Thomas Antoine Chevalier

Background: He travelled with two school friends, who died during the trip, to visit the battlefields of antiquity. He made it back to France with the assistance of the ambassador at Constantinople. He joined the artillery as an aspirant, rising to lieutenant (November 1774).

American Service: He obtained a commission as an artillery captain in the Continental Army. He served with distinction at Brandywine, Germantown, and Monmouth. He was promoted to lieutenant colonel. He went back to France with Lafayette to obtain further support for the Americans. Both returned to America and served in the Yorktown campaign.

Post-American Career: He was named a major in the Vosges battalion and later colonel of the Port-au-Prince regiment (March 1788). He was massacred by his troops in March 1791.

Sources: Bod., 34–35; Lauberdiere, 138; Schachtman, 312.

Mauroy, Charles Louis Vicomte de

Background: Born in 1734 to an Artois noble family (1333), he was a cadet, rising to lieutenant colonel (August 1772). He served as a member of the royal household.

American Service: He was hired by Silas Deane as a major general in the Continental Army but was not employed.

Post-American Career: He returned to France with d'Estaing's fleet. He was promoted to *maréchal de camp* (March 1791) for retirement.

Notable Facts: He was a known artist and poet.

Source: Bod., 336.

Mieszkosky, Jean Quirin

Background: Born in Poland in 1744, he served in the Polish cavalary. He was a volunteer rising to 2nd lieutenant (July 1776) in Legion de Conflans. He was named captain of hussards in the *volontaires etrangers de la ma*rine (November 1778), later the Lauzun Legion. He served in Senegal (1779) under Lauzun.

American Service: He served with the Lauzun Legion serving in America. He participated in the cavalry skirmish against Tarleton at Gloucester and Yorktown.

Post-American Career: He was promoted to squadron leader in Lauzun legion and then to lieutenant colonel 5th hussars (January 1791). He was named colonel and aide-de-camp to Biron—his former commanding officer in America in July 1792. He was promoted to *maréchal de camp* (September 1792). He beat Charette in the Vendée but lost the return engagement (1793). Suspended as a noble, he retired. He died in 1819.

Sources: Bod., 340; Six, vol. 2, 197–98; Bod. 2, 421–22.

Milfort, Jean Antoine

Background: Born in 1752, he served as a soldier in the Lorraine Regiment (1764–75).

American Service: He went to America, living among the Muscogee. He became grand chief of the Cree tribe. He was appointed commissioner to the indigenous tribes by the Spanish government in Louisiana.

Post-American Career: He was sent to France to negotiate the retrocession of that territory (1795). He was appointed brigadier general in the French Army (April 1796). He retired in 1801 to Vouziers, which he defended against the Prussian Army in the allied invasion of France in March 1814. He died in 1820.

Source: Six, vol. 2, 199; Six, vol. 1, 43.

Miollis, Sextius Alexander Vicomte de

Background: Born in 1759, he was named cadet and then 2nd lieutenant of the Soissonnais regiment (April 1779).

American Service: He served with Rochambeau in America and was badly wounded at Yorktown.

Post-American Career: He was promoted to captain in the Bearn regiment (September 1789) and then placed on half pay. Elected lieutenant colonel of a volunteer battalion, he served in the siege of Nice and in l'Armée d'Italie (September 1795–November 1800). He was named brigadier general (June 1795) and general de division (October 1799).

He was suspended for refusing to vote for Bonaparte as Life Consul and was recalled while serving in Holland and Italy. He was governor of Rome where he arrested Pope Pius VII. Sent to cut off Napoleon on his return from Elba, he joined him and served until September 1815 when he retired. He died in 1830.

Sources: Bod., 341–42; Six, vol. 2, 203–04.

Miranda, Francisco

Background: Born in Caracas in 1756 to a middle-class family from the Canary Islands, he joined the Spanish army serving in North Africa.

American Service: He distinguished himself at the siege of Pensacola.

Post-American Career: Fleeing from Havana, he spent several months in the United States in 1783, meeting Washington and Jefferson among others. He conspired for the liberation of what is now Venezuela. He wandered around Europe, finally setting in London. Attracted by the French Revolution, he used his military service in Spain and America to be appointed to brigadier general in the French Army (September 1792), serving at Valmy. He was advanced to lieutenant general (October 1792), serving in Northern France. He was arrested and acquitted (May 1793).

He was exiled from France, eventually leading a failed insurgency with Bolivar against the Spanish (August 1806). He tried again in 1811 and was part of the Constitutional Assembly after independence. He capitulated in July 1812 and was held in an old jail of the Inquisition's in Cadiz where he died in 1816.

Sources: Six, vol. 2, 204–05; Karen Racine, *Francisco Miranda: A Transatlantic Life in the Age of Revolution* (Lanham, MD, 2003), *passim.*; Jacques de Cazotte, *Miranda, 1750–1816: Histoire d'un seduxteur* (Paris, 2000), *passim.;* ERA, vol. 2, 554.

Monteuil, Joseph

Background: Born in 1726, he was a student, *garde marine,* and aspirant (January 1776).

American Service: He volunteered for America, where he served in the Continental Navy until 1784.

Post-American Career: He returned to France and was inactive. He defended the Tuileries on August 10, 1792, and then joined the National Guard to escape Paris. He was appointed a senior staff officer (August 1794). He joined the cavalry as a lieutenant, rising to colonel major in the *gardes du corps* and then to *maréchal de camp* (August 1814). He died in 1826.

Sources: La Jonquiere, 169; Bod., 346.

Montmorency Laval, Anne Alexandre Marquis and then Duc

Background: He was born in 1747 to one of the oldest noble families (955), which had received thirty *honneurs de la cour*. He was appointed as a musketeer (December 1762), cavalry captain (April 1765), and then colonel of Touraine and then the Bourbonnais regiments (June 1775).

American Service: He was wounded at Cape Henry aboard *Conquerant*. He commanded his regiment at Yorktown and was promoted to brigadier (December 1781).

Post-American Career: He was promoted to *maréchal de camp* (January 1784). He was made a duc in 1785. He was elected as a member of the Assembly of Notables and then emigrated in 1791. He served as colonel of the Montmorency regiment in British service (1794–95). He was appointed a lieutenant general in Russian service (1798) and then in the French Army on the Restoration (August 1814). He died in 1817.

Notable Facts: His father was a *maréchal de France*. His four sons served in the army, including Achille who died of wounds fighting in the émigré army. Pierre was a *maréchal de camp* and Eugene a lieutenant general.

Sources: Bod., 348; Lauberdiere, 179; Bod. 2, 482–84.

Morel, Louis Saint-Ange Chevalier de La Colombe

Background: Born in 1755 to a noble Auvergnat family (1390), his prewar career is unknown.

American Service: He volunteered for service in America with Lafayette in 1777 and was his aide-de-camp. He was promoted to captain of dragoons in 1780.

Post-American Career: He was chief of staff of the Paris National Guard (1789) and promoted to colonel of the 104th infantry regiment (1791). He served as Lafayette's aide-de-camp and was tasked with persuading the king to find refuge with Lafayette's army. He escaped with Lafayette in August 1792 and was held prisoner with him by the Austrians. He escaped and eventually returned to Philadelphia where he died in 1799.

Source: Bod., 349–50.

Motier du, Marie Joseph Marquis de Lafayette

Background: He was born in 1757 into a noble family of the Auvergne that could trace its ancestry to the thirteenth century and had received the *honneurs de la cour* twice. His father was an infantry colonel killed at Minden in 1759. He inherited a huge fortune which allowed him to marry into the Noailles, a leading court family at Versailles. He was appointed a musketeer at age fourteen and named a second lieutenant in the Noailles regiment in 1773, being promoted to captain the following year. He was not allowed to take up his captaincy until he reached the age of eighteen.

American Service: He volunteered for service in America and chartered a ship at his own expense. He arrived in America in 1777 and was appointed a major general. Given his youth and inexperience he was not given a command. Having shown his courage and having been wounded at Brandywine, he was placed in command of the Virginia division in December 1777. He fought at Monmouth. He returned to France on leave in January 1779 aboard the *Alliance*. He took part in military maneuvers in Northern France.

With the king's decision to send an expeditionary force, Lafayette was instructed to return to America to advise Washington of its arrival. He was put in charge of the light infantry and dispatched to Virginia to defeat Benedict Arnold in February 1781. He was at Yorktown.

Post-American Career: He returned to France after Yorktown and was named *maréchal de camp* as a reward for his service in America. He attended the Prussian military maneuvers in July 1785. He was a member of the Assemblee des Notables and served on its presiding body (1787). He was named brigadier in charge of a brigade in Roussillon (1788). He was cashiered for supporting the Breton nobility in its protest against the throne. He was elected to the Estates General in March 1789. He was made head of the new national guard formed in July 1789 after the fall of the Bastille. He was successively commanding general of the Centre and Nord armies.

He fled with twenty-one of his officers when he was accused of treason on August 19, 1792. He was held by the Austrians until September 1797. He was offered a seat in the senate and the ambassadorship to the United States by Bonaparte but refused both offers. He retired in 1802. After the Restoration he was elected deputy and then reelected in various constituencies until stepping down in 1831. In 1824–25 he made a triumphant visit to the United States with his son. He rallied to the Duc d'Orleans and welcomed him on July 31, 1830, to the Paris townhall. He was named general in chief of all French national guard units. He died there in 1834.

Sources: Bod., 167–68; Six, vol. 2, 27–30; Mike Duncan, *Hero of Two Worlds* (New York, 2021), *passim.*; Louis Gottschalk, *Lafayette Joins the American Army* (Chicago, 1937), *passim.*

Mottin de la Balme, Augustin

Background: He was born in 1736 to a noble family from the Dauphine (1372) which lost its status due to poverty. He was a gendarme in the Ecossaise company (February 1757), a captain (March 1765), and retired in 1773, after which he wrote several recognized works on riding and fencing.

American Service: He volunteered for America in February 1777 and was a lieutenant colonel in the Continental Army and was later promoted to colonel and inspector of cavalry. He resigned in October 1777, as Pulaski was named cavalry chief instead of him. He was massacred at Fort Miami (Fort Wayne, IN) in November 1780 leading a group of French-Canadians.

Post-American Service: None.

Source: Bod., 350–51.

Mullens, Thomas

Background: Born in 1738 in Ireland, he was a soldier in the Clare regiment (1756) and transferred to the Berwick regiment, where he rose to 2nd lieutenant (1770).

American Service: He served as a volunteer as aide-de-camp to general Borre in 1777. He was appointed major in the 3rd Pennsylvania and then as a staff officer to Conway. He was appointed as a major for his bravery at Germantown. He was promoted to lieutenant colonel for his conduct at Brandywine. He returned to France where he was promoted to lieutenant and then captain in the Berwick regiment. He returned to America with Rochambeau, leading a company of guides, and fought at Yorktown.

Post-American Career: He rose to captain in 1785 and retired in 1791. He joined the army of the Princes and died in 1793.

Source: Bod., 351–52.

Nadal, Antoine Xavier

Background: Born May 1733 into a noble family, he joined the artillery (1746), rising to lieutenant colonel (1780).

American Service: He commanded the artillery park under Rochambeau.

Post-American Career: He was promoted to colonel (1791). He emigrated in 1792 and served in Condé's army, commanding its artillery until 1801. He was promoted to *maréchal de camp* in 1794.

Source: Bod., 352.

Noailles, Louis Marie Vicomte de

Background: He was born in 1756 into a Limousin noble family that had served in the Crusades (1248) and received thirteen *honneurs de la cour*. He was a royal page and *garde du corps* in the *compagnie ecossaise* (December 1768). He served in the family cavalry regiment, which was disbanded. He rose to *mestre de camp* (April 1779) but was only twenty-three years old so could not take a command.

American Service: He volunteered for service with d'Estaing's fleet and led one of the four columns at the siege of Grenada. He fought at Savannah, although he had advised d'Estaing not to besiege the city. He went back to France but returned with Rochambeau and served as lieutenant colonel with the Soissonnais regiment at Yorktown. He helped prepare the acts of capitulation following the battle.

Post-American Career: On his return to France, he was named *mestre de camp* and served in cavalry units. Elected to the Estates General, he voted with the liberals. He was president of the military committee (February 1791). He was promoted to *maréchal de camp* (November 1791). Resigning in May 1792, he travelled to England and Philadelphia. He rejoined the army as brigadier general in Saint-Domingue (December 1802) and was mortally wounded boarding a British ship in January 1804.

Notable Facts: He was the eldest son of Maréchal de France, Philippe Duc de Mouchy who was guillotined in 1794. His father-in-law was the Duc of Ayen and Lafayette was his brother-in-law. His two sons were officers: Vicomte Alfred Louis died in Russia in November 1812. He was a Freemason and member of the Jacobins club.

Sources: Bod., 355–56; Lauberdiere, 23; Ketchum, 302; Six, vol. 2, 257; Quintin, 322; Selesky, vol. 2, 842; Bod. 2, 586–95.

O'Keefe, Patrice

Background: Born in 1740, he was a cadet in Dillon regiment (January 1760). He served in Germany (1760–61) and was promoted to lieutenant (July 1777).

American Service: He served at Savannah where he was wounded.

Post-American Career: Promoted to captain (February 1781), he served in France and Saint-Domingue. He was made a lieutenant colonel (September 1792). He served in l'Armée du Nord (1792-93). He was advanced to brigadier general (May 1795). He served in the Rhin-Moselle army and as military district commander. He was put on half pay but continued to serve in various capacities until retiring in August 1807. He died in 1809.

Sources: Bod., 360; Six, vol. 2, 264.

Olonne, Pierr François Comte de

Background: Born in 1757 to a noble family from Languedoc (1516), he was a 2nd lieutenant in Lorraine and then the Schomberg-Dragoons (November 1772), rising to cavalry captain (April 1778).

American Service: He served as aide-de-camp to Baron de Viomenil in America.

Post-American Career: He served on the general staff with rank of major (July 1788). He was promoted to lieutenant colonel (July 1789) and to colonel of the 47th infantry regiment (November 1791). He served on Lafayette's staff until he resigned in July 1792. He was named *maréchal de camp* (August 1814). He served in the army until January 1819 and died in 1831.

Notable Facts: He was related to the two de Viomenil generals through his mother. His grandfather was a *feldmarshal* in the Austrian Army.

Source: Bod., 361.

Olonne, Alexandre Paul Chevalier d'

Background: Born in 1758 into a noble family from Languedoc (1516), he was named a 2nd lieutenant in the Schomberg-Dragoons (December 1773).

American Service: He served as aide-de-camp to Baron de Viomenil in America.

Post-American Career: He was promoted to captain (February 1784) and resigned April 1791. He emigrated. He later served under Viomenil in Portugal rising to *maréchal general*. He was named *maréchal de camp* (August 1814) and *inspecteur general de la gendarmerie* (August 1816). He was made an honorary lieutenant general (March 1819). He died in 1822.

Notable Facts: He was related to the two de Viomenil generals through his mother. His grandfather was a *feldmarshal* in the Austrian Army.

Source: Bod., 360–61.

O'Moran, Jacques

Background: Born 1739 in Ireland to a noble family, he was sent to study at Tournai. He joined the Dillon regiment as a cadet (1752) serving in Germany. He rose to aide major (1769). He transferred to the 2nd chasseurs in 1776.

American Service: His battalion was shipped to America. He fought at the siege of Grenada and at Savannah where he was wounded. He was promoted to major.

Post-American Career: After recuperating from his wounds, he rejoined his regiment in the West Indies as *mestre de camp*. He was promoted to colonel (1791) and commanded the Berwick and then the Dillon regiments. He was made a *maréchal de camp* in February 1792 and acting lieutenant general in l'Armée du Nord in August of the same year. He held a number of commands in northern France. He was suspended and imprisoned. He was condemned to death along with generals Chancel and Davaine on March 4, 1794, and guillotined two days later.

Sources: Bod., 361–62; Six, vol. 2, 266; Bod. 2, 626–28.

O'Neill, Louis Alexandre

Background: Born 1729 in the Palatinate, he joined the *volontaires de Dauphine* and then Dillon regiment as 2nd lieutenant (1761). He was put on half pay in 1763 and joined the Polish forces as a captain in 1772.

American Service: He emigrated to America and was named colonel of the North Carolina Militia in 1781.

Post-American Career: He returned to France in 1787 and died shortly thereafter.

Source: Bod., 362.

Orillard de Villemanzy, Jacques-Pierre

Background: He was born in 1751 to a noble family from Amboise, and he trained to be a *commissaire de guerre* (1768–77). He served as *commissaire-inspecteur* to l'Armée des cotes de l'Ocean.

American Service: He was a *commissaire des guerres* in Rochambeau's corps throughout the campaign.

Post-American Career: He served in various posts in France. He was called to Paris to advise the war committee of the Constituent Assembly. He served as chief military judge in Strasbourg and then chief commissaire de l'Armée du rhin. Worried about the political climate and being arrested, he managed to get captured by the enemy. On being exchanged, he was chief commissaire in l'Armée d'Italie under Bonaparte. He was chief accountant of the army and then was promoted to *inspecteur general des revues* or *general de division* and assigned to l'Armée du Rhin until the end of 1801. As a peer of France, he voted for the death sentence during Marshal Ney's trial before that chamber. He died in 1830.

Notable Facts: While serving in Italy, he was persuaded by Dominique Larrey of the benefit of having campaign ambulances. He organized a competition to choose the best ambulance design and helped ensure that all army units were equipped with ambulances going forward. He was the first president of the *Caisse de Depots et Consignations* established in 1816 to regulate savings and pensions and act as France's sovereign wealth fund.

Sources: Bod., 362–63; Jean de Cilleuls, "L'Inspecteur Général Jacque de Villemanzy: Sénateur et Pair de France (1751–1830)," *Hist Sci Med.* 13, no. 4 (1979): 379–81.

Osmond, Marie Joseph Vicomte d'

Background: Born in 1756 in Saint-Domingue, he served in the militia (1771–73) and then became a second lieutenant in the Bourgogne regiment (1774). By 1779 he was a major in the Orleans-cavalerie stationed on the island.

American Service: He served at Grenada and then as aide-de-camp to Saint-Simon at Yorktown.

Post-American Career: Returning to France he was promoted to *mestre de camp* commanding the Neustrie regiment (1788) and then to *maréchal de camp* (1791) on retirement. He commanded a company of the Neustrie regiment in the army of the Princes and then was lieutenant colonel in the *uhlans britanniques* (1794-95). He then returned to Saint-Domingue, eventually coming back to France in 1801. He was promoted to lieutenant general in 1814 and served as inspector general in the 7th military division. He died in 1839.

Sources: Bod., 364; Bod. 2, 634–35.

Palys de Montrepot, Henry Dominique Chevalier de

Background: Born in 1722, he was named a cornet in the Royal-Piedmont regiment (April 1747). He served in

Flanders (1747–48), including at the siege of Maastricht. He was promoted to lieutenant and engineer (March 1755), serving in Germany (1760–62). He was advanced to captain of infantry (April 1763), then *ingenieur-en-chef* (March 1775) and major (January 1777).

American Service: He served at Yorktown under Rochambeau.

Post-American Career: He was promoted to lieutenant colonel and then colonel of engineers (April 1791). He served in l'Armée des Alpes (1792–93) and was promoted to brigadier general (March 1793). After various assignments, he was suspended in August 1793 and permitted to retire in October 1794. He died in 1803.

Sources: Bod., 366; Six, vol. 2, 283–84.

Patel, Philippe Joseph

Background: He joined as a soldier in the Touraine regiment (February 1759). He served in Hanover (1760–62) and rose to lieutenant (December 1779).

American Service: He served in America and the West Indies, including at Yorktown while with the fleet.

Post-American Career: He rose to lieutenant colonel (October 1792), designated to serve with the Martinique regiment but did not accept the assignment. He served with the 31st infantry in the Armée Armée de Sambre-et-Meuse (1794–97). He was promoted to brigadier general (February 1797), on half pay, and then retired in August 1803.

Sources: Bod., 369; Six, vol. 2, 294.

Penot Lombard de la Neuville, Louis PierreChevalier de

Background: Born in 1744, he was a lieutenant in the Paris militia (February 1750) and rose to major in the Laon regiment (January 1774).

American Service: He volunteered with his brother in October 1777 for service with the American forces. He was appointed inspector and then promoted to lieutenant colonel (May 1778). Made brigadier general (August 1778), he resigned as no appropriate role was found for him.

Post-American Career: He was promoted to lieutenant colonel (June 1780). He served at Cadiz and made several trips to Saint-Domingue. He retired in March 1791.

Sources: Bod., 371; WGAR, vol. 2, 245–46.

Pierre, Jean Ignace

Background: Born in 1740, he was a cannoneer (November 1759). He rose to sergeant and then garcon-major (September 1771) in La Fere regiment.

American Service: He volunteered with Coudray and was appointed as a captain in the Continental Army.

Post-American Career: On his way back to France, he was captured by the British. He was promoted to captain and then *chef de battalion* (August 1793). He served in l'Armée d'Italie and was promoted to brigadier general (November 1793). He commanded Colmar, Entrevaux, and then Toulon. Denounced, he was relieved of his duties. He retired in May 1796.

Sources: Bod., 373; Six, vol. 2, 312; Quintin, 259.

Poudenx, Henry François Vicomte de

Background: Born in 1747 into a noble Gascon family (1402), he was a student at cavalry school (January 1763). He served with several units, rising to *mestre de camp* (May 1774). He transferred to the Gatinais regiment which he commanded (1777–79). He was promoted to colonel, commanding the Touraine regiment (April 1780).

American Service: He commanded the Touraine regiment in Saint-Domingue and led his regiment at Yorktown.

Post-American Career: He was promoted to *maréchal de camp* (March 1788) but was not employed. Arrested during the Terror, he was released after fourteen months imprisoned. He died in 1814.

Source: Bod., 380.

Preudhomme de Borre, Philippe Hubert

Background: Born in 1717, he was a volunteer in the Champagne regiment (February 1740). He rose to captain (August 1744). On half pay in 1749, he was promoted to lieutenant colonel. (April 1757). He was on half pay again in 1762.

American Service: He volunteered and was named brigadier general in the Continental Army. He took part in the battle of Brandywine. He resigned due to the poor quality of troops.

Post-American Career: Promoted to brigadier in the French army (March 1780), he retired shortly thereafter.

Source: Bod., 381–82.

Prevost, Pierre Dominique

Background: Born in 1749, he was a child of the regiment of Bearn in which his father, a sergeant major, was killed at Crefeld (1758). He served in Germany (1757–62), rising through the ranks to become adjutant of the Agenais regiment (March 1776).

American Service: He served with his regiment in the fleet in the West Indies and at Yorktown.

Post-American Career: He rose to captain in the 16th infantry (February 1792). He was promoted to lieutenant colonel of artillery (October 1792) and served in l'Armée des Pyrenees-Orientale (1793–95). He was named acting brigadier general and commander of a military district (July 1795). He was confirmed as brigadier general (June 1795), serving in l'Armée du Nord. He was then on the inactive list (September 1801). He was recalled and was commandant of Cuneo when he died in 1807.

Source: Six, vol. 2, 332.

Quentin de Richebourg de Champcenetz, Louis Pierre

Background: He was born in 1754 into a noble family that settled in Brie (1534), he was named a 2nd lieutenant in the

Mestre de Camp-Dragons (November 1770) and promoted to *mestre de camp* (July 1779).

American Service: He arrived in America in September 1782 to serve as Baron de Viomenil's aide-de-camp.

Post-American Career: He served until promoted *maréchal de camp* on retirement (March 1791). He emigrated to England and returned to France after the Peace of Amiens. He was made honorary lieutenant general (June 1814).

Notable Facts: He was at the Tuileries, where his father was governor, when it was attacked on August 10, 1792, and hid in the apartments of the Duc d'Orleans' mistress. Upon the Restoration, he was named governor of the Tuileries. He died in 1822.

Source: Bod., 384.

Queyssat, Gabriel

Background: Born in 1743, he was named ensign in the grenadiers (June 1759). He rose to lieutenant (February 1763) but was put on the inactive list when his regiment was dissolved (1771). Recalled to active duty, he was promoted to captain (April 1773). He was then on the inactive list.

American Service: He was ordered to America to act as de Viomenil's aide-de-camp (April 1780). He traveled back and forth to France and was captured by the British at the entrance to the Chesapeake (February 1783).

Post-American Career: He was elected captain in the Paris National Guard (November 1789). Promoted to lieutenant colonel (August 1791), he served in l'Armée du Nord and then de Belgique (1791–93). He was promoted to brigadier general (May 1793) and then arrested and imprisoned in the Conciergerie (July 1793). He was acquitted and allowed to retire. He died in 1837.

Notable Facts: He was named chevalier de la legion d'honneur by Louis-Philippe in October 1830. His brother served in America and apparently died during the campaign.

Sources: Bod., 386; Six, vol. 2, 340.

Raffet, Nicolas

Background: Born in 1757, he was appointed a cadet in Guadeloupe (1772–76).

American Service: He served in the West Indies and was severely wounded at Savannah.

Post-American Career: He returned to France. He created a volunteer unit on July 13, 1789, and later commanded the

Saint-Roche battalion (August 1792). He was arrested and released the same day. He lost the election to become commander of the Paris National Guard to Hanriot (June 1783). He escaped and enlisted as a private. As a captain, he helped defend the Convention but was wounded.

He was commander of the Paris National Guard and later acting commander of Paris. He was promoted to brigadier general (August 1795). Relieved and then arrested, he escaped. He was reinstated by Berthier at the request of Mathieu Dumas in May 1802 and allowed to retire. He died in 1803.

Sources: Bod., 387–88; Six, vol. 2, 343.

Rey, Jean Andre

Background: Born in 1758, he was a volunteer in America.

American Service: He was named 2nd lieutenant in the Illinois regiment in 1777, rising to captain in 1780.

Post-American Career: He joined the Saint-Domingue national guard at the outset of the Revolution as a 2nd lieutenant but was arrested. Sent back to France he was captured on the way by the British. He returned to Saint-Domingue on various missions. He was promoted to adjudant general (1796) and to temporary *general de* *brigade* taking part in the Ireland expedition. Placed on the inactive list in 1804, he died in 1811.

Sources: Bod., 393; Six, vol. 2, 360.

Ricci, Gabriel Marie Vicomte de

Background: Born in 1744 into a Provencal noble family (1309) which had received two *honnuers de cour*. He was a page to the king (June 1772). He was appointed 2nd lieutenant in the Condé-Dragoons (December 1774), rising to captain (April 1779) in the Marine and then Bourbonnais regiments.

American Service: He sailed to America on the *Aigle* (September 1782) to be aide-de-camp to Baron de Viomenil.

Post-American career: He joined the general staff on his return to France. He was promoted to *mestre de camp* and then colonel (March 1788) attached to Dauphin regiment. Named adjutant general (August 1791), he became a *maréchal de camp* (January 1792). He served but then emigrated with Lafayette. He was a banker in Hamburg. He served in the army administration (1804–12). He was *préfet* of l'Orne and then Loiret. He died in 1832.

Sources: Bod., 395; Six, vol. 2, 367–68.

Rigaud, Jean Louis Vicomte de Vaudreuil

Background: He was born in 1763 to a noble family from Languedoc (1249) which had received seven *honneurs de cour*. He was a 2nd lieutenant in the King's regiment (July 1776) and captain in the Dauphin-Dragoons (June 1779).

American Service: He arrived in America in September 1782 and served as Chastellux's aide-de-camp.

Post-American Career: He was promoted to *mestre de camp* and then colonel (March 1788). He emigrated in 1789 with the Comte d'Artois and became his aide-de-camp. He was promoted to *maréchal de camp* (January 1797) and later to lieutenant general (September 1814). He died in 1816.

Notable Facts: His father, Jean, was a vice admiral, and his grandfather was lieutenant general des Armée Armées navales.

Source: Bod., 397–98.

Rigaud, Andre

Background: Born in 1761 in Saint-Domingue, he was a jeweler before entering military service in 1777 in the *chasseurs volontaires de Saint-Domingue*.

American Service: He served at Savannah where he was wounded.

Post-American Career: He served in Guadeloupe. He was promoted to lieutenant in 1790 and advanced to lieutenant colonel in 1793. As a result of his capture of Leogane and Tiburon he was promoted to brigadier general. He was betrayed by Toussaint Louverture who saw him as a competitor and fled to Saint Thomas but was captured by an American privateer on the way.

He was brought to France. He then was part of Leclerc's expedition to recapture Saint-Domingue but sent back to France where he was under house arrest. He eventually returned to Saint-Domingue in 1810 and died the next year.

Sources: Six, vol. 2, 371–72; Desmarais 1, 201.

Riquetti, Andre Boniface Chevalier and then Vicomte de Mirabeau

Background: He was born in 1754. He was a 2nd lieutenant in the Lorraine legion (November 1771). He was a Knight of Malta and spent time there before being sent back to France for poor conduct. He was made a captain (May 1778) and attached to first the Nivernais regiment and then the

Touraine regiment, which he joined in Saint-Domingue in January 1780.

American Service: He fought in the West Indies, distinguishing himself at St. Kitts and at Yorktown.

Post-American Career: He was promoted *mestre de camp* (March 1788), commanding the Touraine regiment. He was elected to the Estates General from Limousin, sitting with the ultraright. He fought or dueled with his own brother, among others. Sent to Perpignan to restore discipline in his regiment, he only aggravated the situation.

He left the regiment (June 1790). He emigrated and raised the Mirabeau Legion. He led a raid on the Jacobin Club and captured several of them. He died of a heart attack or possibly poisoning in 1792.

Notable Fact: He was a relative of Mirabeau, the politician, but a son of an army colonel which helped him more in his military career.

Source: Bod., 398.

Roche Fermoy, Mathias Alexis Chevalier de

Background: He was born in 1747 to a noble family of Spanish origin (recognized 1557)

American Service: He was named a brigadier general in the Continental Army (November 1776). In January 1778 he resigned having failed to gain promotion to major general.

Post-American Career: He returned to Saint-Domingue and was employed by Governor Bouille. He died c. 1792.

Sources: Bod., 400–01; WGAR, vol. 2, 265.

Bechet, Etienne Nicolas Chevalier de Rochefontaine

Background: Born in 1755, he was at the Mezieres engineering school but did not qualify.

American Service: He volunteered for America in 1777. He was wounded at Brandywine and fought at Monmouth. He was named captain in 1778 and served as aide-de-camp to Kalb. He fought at Yorktown and was promoted to major in 1783. Earlier he had been promoted to captain in the French Army.

Post-American Career: He returned to France in December 1783. He was named to the army staff (1784). He was appointed adjutant *chef de brigade* in Saint-Domingue (1792). He resigned and was employed as a civilian engineer with the US Army. He died in New York in 1814.

Source: Bod., 46.

Roqueplan de Lestrade, Claude Aimable baron de

Background: Born in 1729, he was a cadet in the Lyonnais regiment (1746), rising to captain (February 1757). He served in Germany (1761–62) and was promoted to lieutenant colonel in the Gatinais regiment (August 1777).

American Service: He served with his regiment at Yorktown where he distinguished himself and was promoted to brigadier (December 1781).

Post-American Career: He was promoted to *maréchal de camp* (March 1788). He served in the Armée du Midi and was made lieutenant general (July 1792). He was appointed to lead the forces to put down the Lyon insurrection, which he refused. He retired in October 1793, dying in 1819.

Sources: Bod., 404; Six, vol. 2, 112.

Rostaing, Juste Antoine Marquis de

Background: He was born in 1740 into a noble family from Forez (1498) which had received *honneurs de la cour* twice. He was a page to Louis XV (January 1756). He was appointed cornet, rising to captain in the Caraman-Dragoons (April 1765). He served in various units before becoming colonel of the Gatinais regiment (October 1777).

American Service: He commanded the Gatinais regiment in the West Indies and at Yorktown. His regiment took part in the assault on redoubt no. 9, which helped seal the fate of Cornwallis's forces.

Post-American Career: He was promoted to brigadier (December 1781) and to *maréchal de camp* (January 1784). He was elected to the Assemblée Nationale and served on its military committee. Promoted to lieutenant general in February 1792, he retired the following year. He died in 1826.

Source: Bod., 406.

Rouge, Antoine

Background: Born in 1763 in Saint-Domingue, he may have served as a lieutenant in the Hainaut regiment and later in the volunteers of Saint-Domingue.

American Service: He took part in the siege of Savannah as a volunteer with the Hainaut regiment.

Post-American Career: He resigned. He was lieutenant colonel of a volunteer unit in 1792 and promoted provisionally to *general de brigade,* which was later confirmed (1795). He served in the Pyrenees campaign (1793–95) and then resigned in 1796 to enter politics unsuccessfully. He commanded the rebels who wanted to take Toulouse. Having failed, he fled to Spain. He returned to France and was promoted to *maréchal de camp* in 1815. He died in 18321.

Sources: Bod., 407; Six, vol. 2, 395–96.

Rouvroy, Claude Baron de Saint-Simon

Background: He was born in 1752 into a noble family from Picardy (1334), which received nine *honneurs de la cour*. He was named a 2nd lieutenant in the Auvergne regiment (October 1770), later serving in the Gatinais and Touraine regiments. He was promoted to captain (April 1777).

American Service: He was aide-de-camp to his oldest brother, the Marquis de Saint-Simon and commanded a detachment of volunteers at Yorktown.

Post-American Career: He was promoted to *mestre de camp* (July 1782) and colonel (May 1788). He was later appointed commander of the 67th and then 50th infantry regiments, taking up neither appointment. He resigned due to the law on emigré relatives. He was employed as commander at Blay but put on the inactive list due to his conduct. He died in 1811.

Source: Bod., 409.

Rouvroy, Claude Henry Comte de Saint-Simon

Background: He was born in 1760 into a noble family from Picardy (1334), which received nine *honneurs de la cour*. He was named a 2nd lieutenant (1775) and then captain in the Touraine regiment.

American Service: He fought with his regiment at Yorktown. He was wounded aboard *Ville de Paris* at the battle of Saintes (1782).

Post–American Career: He was promoted to *mestre de camp* (1784) and colonel (1788) but was not attached to any regiment as he was residing in Spain. He returned to France and speculated in the purchase of nationalized property. He was imprisoned as a noble. He lost all his money and was supported by his former valet. He died in 1825.

Notable Fact: He was the author of the *New Christianism* and other works and unsuccessfully wooed Madame de Stael.

Source: Bod., 410–11.

Saint-Quentin, Claude Marie

Background: Born in 1739, he was a lieutenant in the Provence regiment (1756), rising to captain in 1758.

American Service: He served aboard ship and fought in several battles, including at Gloucester.

Post-American Career: He was promoted to lieutenant colonel and then colonel in the 56th infantry regiment (1791). He was promoted to *maréchal de camp* and wounded in the retreat from Aachen. He was put on the inactive list as a noble. He died in 1832.

Sources: Bod., 415; Six, vol. 2, 416–17.

Segon de Sederon, Marie Blaise Chevalier de

Background: Born in 1758, he may have served in the Martinique regiment under his uncle, but records are unclear.

American Service: He volunteered for America and fought at Brandywine, Germantown, and Valley Forge. He was a captain in Pulaski's Legion (1778). He served at Savannah and was taken prisoner at Charleston. He was promoted to major in the Continental Army in 1783 after being exchanged and resigned that November.

Post-American Career: He joined the Dutch Army, rising to lieutenant colonel after passing into Russian service (1788–90), He returned to France and served in his same grade in the infantry. He was promoted to acting *general de* *brigade* by Dumouriez in 1792 but deserted with him the following April. He was given the title of general major and a pension by the Austrians but not employed. He returned to France in 1810 and died in 1832.

Sources: Bod., 421–22; Six, vol. 2, 443.

Segur, Louis Philippe Comte de

Background: He was born in 1753 into a noble Limousin family (1453) which received nine *honneurs de la cour*. He was named a 2nd lieutenant and then captain in the cavalry (March 1772) and was later promoted to *mestre de camp* (October 1776) of the Orleans and then Soissonnais regiments.

American Service: He landed in America in September 1782 as a replacement officer aboard *Glorieux*, taking over as lieutenant colonel of the Soissonais regiment from his nephew, the vicomte de Noailles.

Post-American Career: He was France's ambassador to Russia (1784–89). On his return to France, he joined the liberal noble faction. He was promoted *to maréchal de camp* on retirement in March 1791. He served as ambassador to the Papal States but was not received by the Pope. He was sent on an unsuccessful mission to dissuade Prussia from going to war with France.

He remained in France during the Terror. Elected Depute to the Corps Legislatif (1801), he was appointed counselor of state (1802) and grand master of ceremonies (1805). He was senator and count of the Empire (1813). He died in 1830.

Notable Facts: He was the eldest son of Maréchal de France and Minister of War Philippe de Segur. His son Philippe was aide-de-camp to Napoleon and achieved the rank of lieutenant general in 1831. He was a prolific author of prose (including his memoirs), poetry, and dramatic works and a member of the Académie Francaise.

Sources: Bod., 423; Lauberdiere, 234; Gerard Shelley, *The Memoirs and Anecdotes of the Count de Segur* (New York, 1928, hereafter cited at Segur; Scott, FYTV, 97; Schachtman, 313.

Sheldon, Dominique

Background: He was born in 1757 into a noble Warwickshire family. He was named a cadet in the Dillon regiment (October 1770). He was promoted to captain in the regiment (February 1778) and then to colonel of infantry (September 1779).

American Service: He served in the hussars of the Lauzun Legion, including at Yorktown.

Post-American Career: He served in Corsica and was promoted to *maréchal de camp* (January 1792). He was aide-de-camp to Marshal Luckner (June 1791). He served in l'Armée du Rhin under Kellerman and was promoted to lieutenant general (September 1792). He later served in l'Armée d'Italie and was suspended in September 1793 and retired in December 1794. He was recalled on the recommendation of Talleyrand and served as commander of Perpignan until he died of epilepsy in 1801.

Notable Facts: His ancestor, Dominique, served as lieutenant general, and another, François, was a brigadier and colonel in the Dillon regiment. François served in America and later emigrated.

Sources: Bod., 426–27; Six, vol. 2, 454.

Sibaud, Jacques François

Background: Born in 1753, he was a gendarme in 1774. He then joined the Nassau-Siegen legion as a 2nd lieutenant in 1779. He volunteered for the Lauzun Legion in 1780.

American Service: He served with his unit under Rochambeau.

Post-American Career: He was put on half pay in 1783. He was a captain of volunteers, rising to colonel (1792). He was promoted to acting *general de brigade* (1793). On half pay twice, he returned to active duty and served until 1803.

Sources: Bod., 428; Six, vol. 2, 454–55.

Silvestre de Valfort, Louis

Background: He was born in 1727 and enlisted as a soldier in the Aunis regiment (November 1753). He rose to captain in that regiment in April 1771.

American Service: He travelled with Lafayette and obtained a commission as lieutenant colonel in the Continental Army. He rose to brigadier despite having served little due to health issues.

Post-American Career: He returned to France in 1778 and was promoted to lieutenant colonel in June 1779. He was director of studies for the military academies. He was appointed *maréchal de camp* on retirement in March 1791. He died in 1808.

Notable Facts: He was a brigade chief at the Invalides to which he was admitted in December 1795.

Source: Bod., 430.

Stack de Crotto, Edouard

Background: He was born into an Irish gentry family and appointed a cadet in the Walsh regiment (November 1770), rising to lieutenant (March 1777).

American Service: He served as a volunteer on the *Bonhomme Richard* under John Paul Jones and was involved in the fight with the *Serapis*. He then rejoined his regiment in the West Indies and fought in several engagements under Guichen. He was wrecked twice and made prisoner of the British. He was promoted captain (December 1779). He returned to France and served with his regiment. He returned to America with Vicomte Rochambeau as aide-de-camp to the Comte de Viomenil.

Post-American Career: He was promoted to lieutenant colonel in the 87th infantry but did not join up with his unit, emigrating instead. He served in l'Armée des Princes (1792) and then joined the Irish brigade in British service and served in Jamaica. He was promoted to colonel (1801) and then brigadier general (1803) in the British Army. He returned to France after the Peace of Amiens. He was apparently promoted in the British Army to major general (1808) and then lieutenant general (1813). He died in 1833.

Notable Facts: Four of his uncles served in the French Army, and two of them were killed at Fontenoy.

Source: Bod., 434.

Stedingk, Curt Bogislas Baron de

Background: Born in 1747 into a noble Swedish family (thirteenth century), he served as an officer in the Swedish Army (1759). He joined the French Army as a 2nd lieutenant, rising to captain (April 1771) in the Royal-Suedois regiment. He was in Sweden from 1773 to 1778. He was promoted to colonel (March 1779).

American Service: He commanded one of the divisions at Savannah in 1779 under d'Estaing and was wounded there.

Post-American Career: He was promoted *mestre de camp* in the Alsace regiment (April 1780). He received the *honneurs de la cour* (1783) and was appointed commander of the Royal-Suedois regiment (March 1784). He left France and became Swedish deputy army commander in Finland during the war against Russia. Appointed major general (1790), he was sent as ambassador to Russia until 1808.

Promoted to lieutenant general (1799), he participated in the war against Russia in 1808. He also took part in the coup forcing Gustav IV to abdicate. He returned to Russia as ambassador (1808–11) and was appointed field marshal (1811). He was involved in the campaigns against France and successfully commanded the Swedish forces at the Battle of Leipzig (1813) and served briefly as Swedish ambassador to France.

Source: Bod., 436.

Talleyrand-Perigord, Boson Jacques Comte de

Background: He was born in 1764 into a noble family from Perigord (1166). His family received sixteen *honneurs de la cour*. He was a student at a military academy and then 2nd lieutenant in the Dauphin-Dragoons (April 1780).

American Service: He sailed to America as a replacement officer, arriving in September 1782. He was on Baron de Viomenil's staff and then joined the Soissonnais regiment to see active service.

Post-American Career: He was promoted to captain (May 1783), *mestre de camp,* and then colonel in the Bourbon-Dragoons (1788). He was elected deputy to the Estates General but did not take his seat. He emigrated and served as aide-de-camp to the Comte de Provence and later as lieutenant colonel in the Périgord regiment.

Notable Fact: His father served as a lieutenant general. His oldest brother, Maurice was the former bishop of Autun and foreign minister of France under Napoleon and the Restoration. His sister-in-law was guillotined. His son was minister to Florence and then Copenhagen.

Sources: Bod., 438; Scott, FYTV, 97; Tulard, 834–35.

Tarle, Jean Josse

Background: Born to a noble family in 1739, he began in naval administration (1758). He switched to the army and was named an ensign in the Alsace regiment, rising to captain (November 1770) in Bouillon regiment.

American Service: He served as intendant and lieutenant colonel to Rochambeau. He was promoted to colonel (June 1783).

Post-American Career: He was inactive on his return to France. He was named adjutant general colonel in March 1793. Refusing the appointment, he was retired as *maréchal de camp* on the same day. He died in 1813.

Source: Bod., 440.

Tenet de Lauberdiere, Germain Felix

Background: He was born in 1749 into a noble family from Astarac (1602), volunteering in the Auvergne regiment (May 1772) and rising to captain (September 1778).

American Service: He may have served with the Gatinais regiment at Yorktown.

Post-American Career: He was promoted to captain (July 1784) and to lieutenant colonel in 12th infantry regiment (February 1792). Colonel of the 30th infantry regiment (October 1792). He was promoted to brigadier general and then to *general de division* (June 1793). He served in the Armée du Nord and Moselle, he was wounded at Arlon in 1793 and ceased active service. He died in 1799.

Sources: Bod., 443; Six, vol. 2, 70.

Ternant, Jean Chevalier then Comte de

Background: Born in 1751, he was an engineering student (1772).

American Service: He volunteered for America and served as a staff officer under von Steuben. He fought at Monmouth (1778) and was promoted to lieutenant colonel and inspector of the Southern Department. He was taken prisoner at

Charleston and exchanged in 1782. He was promoted to colonel in the Armand Legion when the latter was made a brigadier general. He was discharged in November 1783.

Post-American Career: He returned to France in 1783 and served as a colonel in the Dutch Army (1785). He was colonel of the Royal-Liegois regiment (1788-91). Named French ambassador to the United States (August 1791), he was later relieved by the Directory. He eventually returned to France where he died in 1823.

Notable Fact: The Independence National Park has a portrait of him by Charles Wilson Peale.

Source: Bod., 443.

Terrasse de Tessonnet, Jacques Marie

Background: Born in 1755, he entered the Lyonnais regiment in 1770 and become a 2nd lieutenant (April 1773) and a lieutenant in the Maine regiment (July 1779).

American Service: He was embarked on the *Marseillais* and served at the siege of Gloucester.

Post–American Career: He was promoted to captain (September 1786). He was involved in the plot to deliver Lyon to the Royalist cause. Arrested, he was imprisoned until September 1791. He served on several missions on behalf of the princes in Lyon and Franche-Comte, as well as in the émigré army (1797–1801). He was promoted to *maréchal de camp* (August 1814) and died the following year.

Source: Bod., 444.

Thevet de Lessert, Jean

Background: Born in 1737, he was a lieutenant in the Aunis regiment (September 1747) and then in the Vaubecourt regiment. He was wounded at Hastembeck and promoted to captain (August 1764).

American Service: He was ordered to go to America as a colonel in the Continental Army in November 1776 but was never employed.

Post-American Career: He was promoted to lieutenant colonel (May 1788) and then to colonel (February 1792) of the 72nd infantry regiment. He was named *maréchal de camp* (March 1792) and served in l'Armée du Rhin. He was suspended in November 1793 but allowed to retire in July 1795. He died in 1822.

Sources: Bod., 444–45; Six, vol. 2, 493.

Thibault de Menonville, Louis Antoine Comte de

Background: Born in 1738 into a family of English origins who settled in Lorraine (1659), he was named a lieutenant in the Chartres-Infanterie (October 1754). He was later promoted to captain and then major in the Touraine regiment (September 1775).

American Service: He was offered the rank of colonel in the Continental Army but was not employed. He served at Yorktown as first deputy adjutant general.

Post-American Career: He was promoted to lieutenant colonel in the Hainaut regiment (April 1784). He retired in April 1788. He died in 1816.

Notable Facts: His younger brother, François rose to *maréchal de camp* and was a deputy to the Estates General. François did not serve in America.

Source: Bod., 445–46.

Tourville, Charles Bertin

Background: Born in 1740, he volunteered in the *grenadiers de France* (June 1755) and was promoted to 2nd Lieutenant (December 1755). He served in Germany (1757–62) and rose to major in the Gatinais regiment (April 1776).

American Service: He served in the West Indies and in North America. He was awarded the Order of Cincinnati.

Post-American Career: He was promoted to lieutenant colonel then colonel (July 1791). He served in l'Armée du Nord and was promoted to *maréchal de camp* (July 1792). Promoted to general de division (March 1793), he was suspended and then recalled. Named commander of the Belgian division based in Brussels (May 1795). He was suspended again and retired in April 1796. He died in 1809.

Source: Six, vol. 2, 506.

Tronson de Coudray, Philippe Charles

Background: Born in 1738, he was appointed lieutenant of artillery (August 1760), captain, and then *chef de brigade* (September 1786). He was a leading artillery officer and instructed the Duc d'Artois and Duc de Chartres (Later King Louis-Philippe). He did a national inventory of all weapons that were outdated or surplus to requirements and many of these ended up in America. He was also tasked with sending the Americans artillery manuals.

American Service: He was engaged by Silas Deane as a major general to lead the artillery and engineering components of the Continental Army. Due to jealousy on the part of senior American officers, he only served as Inspector General of Ordnance. He drowned crossing the Schuylkill River in 1777.

Post-American Career: None.

Notable Facts: He was considered France's leading artilleryman, having written *"l'ordre profond et l'ordre mince consideres par rapport aux effets d'artillerie."* Translated as the effects of artillery fire on various tactical formations.

Sources: Bod., 453; WGAR, vol. 2, 243–45; Selesky, vol. 2, 1166; Schachtman, 56.

Vallou de Villeneuve, Adrien Michel

Background: Born in 1752, he was an engineer in 1772, being promoted to lieutenant in the Guadeloupe regiment (1775).

American Service: He served at Savannah and was promoted to captain on the field for his actions.

Post-American Career: He returned to Guadeloupe. He went to France in 1795 and was named a battalion commander by General Hoche. He was made commander of the 2nd Legion of Francs for the Ireland expedition. He later became chief of staff to General Desfourneaux (1797). After being a prisoner of the British, he was released in Lisbon. He joined l'Armée d'Italie under Deshesme in 1800. He was made adjutant general in 1800 and posted to Milan. He retired in 1803, dying in 1827.

Source: Quintin, 63.

Verger de Barreaux, Pierre François

Background: He was born in 1755, he enlisted as a soldier in the Vivarais regiment (1773–74). He was named a 2nd lieutenant in the Saint-Domingue militia (1775–77) and then in the *chasseurs volontaires de Saint-Domingue*.

American Service: He served as a volunteer on *le Vaillant* in d'Estaing's fleet. With the chasseurs he served in the West Indies and was wounded at Savannah.

Post-American Career: He left active service until the Revolution when he was made captain of a volunteer battalion (March 1793). He was named adjutant chef de brigade (June 1795), serving in l'Armée Armée de l'Interieur and then of Sambre-et-Meuse.

He had administrative responsibilities (1797–1806) and served in the Grande Armée Armée (1807–09) during which time he was badly wounded at Leopoldstadt. He was promoted to brigadier general in June 1809. He was placed on the inactive list but recalled during the Hundred Days He retired in October 1815 and died in 1829.

Sources: Bod., 461; Six, vol. 2, 541.

Verger, Jean Baptiste

Background: Born in 1762 to a family ennobled by Charles VI, he was a cadet in the Royal Deux-Ponts (February 1780) and promoted to 2nd lieutenant (April 1780).

American Service: He and his regiment were part of Rochambeau's army.

Post-American Career: He was promoted to lieutenant (May 1786). He resigned and emigrated to serve as aide-de-camp to Baron Guillaume des Deux-Ponts, his former commanding officer. He entered Prussian and then Bavarian service. He served as Bavarian ambassador first to Switzerland and then Wurttemberg. He was named major general (1808) and lieutenant general (1822). He died in 1851.

Sources: Bod., 460–61; Ketchum, 305.

Vienne, Louis Pierre Marquis de

Background: Born in 1746 into a noble family (1670), he was named a lieutenant in the Clermont-Cavalerie (July 1754), which was commanded by his father (later a lieutenant general). He was promoted to captain (October 1757).

American Service: He resigned from his unit to go to America where he was named a lieutenant colonel in the Continental Army (1778). With the arrival of d'Estaing, he returned to French service in a staff role.

Post-American Career: He returned to France for health reasons in May 1779. He emigrated, returning to France in 1802. He was promoted to colonel and then honorary *maréchal de camp* (May 1825). He may have died in 1829.

Source: Bod., 466.

Vienot de Vaublanc, Jean Baptiste

Background: Born in 1765, he joined the *chasseurs volontaires de Saint-Domingue* as a lieutenant in March 1779.

American Service: He took part in the siege of Savannah with his unit.

Post-American Career: He returned to France and resigned in 1789. He was a gendarmerie captain in 1791 and was later named as a staff officer in various armies. He was suspended for moderation but reinstated within three months. He retired for health reasons but was recalled as an *inspecteur des revues* in 1800. He was chief inspector or *general de division* in Spain and eventually for the Grande Armée in Russia. He died in 1812 near Kaliningrad.

Sources: Bod., 466–67; Quintin, 306–07.

Vigoureux, Jean Baptiste Comte Duplessis

Background: He was born in 1735. He was named 2nd lieutenant in the Ile-de-France battalion (January 1752). He advanced to major (May 1759) and fought in the Persian Gulf where he was wounded. He was a major general commanding the troops at Batavia (May 1761). Promoted to Lieutenant Colonel (November 1771), he commanded at Mahe (Seychelles) in March 1778 and taken prisoner the next year. He was named Governor of Saint Vincent (May 1780) and later returned to France.

American Service: His service in America is unknown, but he apparently was awarded the order of Cincinnati.

Post-American Career: He was promoted to brigadier (January 1784) and then to *maréchal de camp* (September 1788). He served in the West Indies and was recalled to France (May 1795). He was promoted to general de division (May 1796) and served in l'Armée d'Interieur and was then put on inactive list. He was recalled in December 1799 and then commanded a demi-brigade. He was created a count in December 1814. He died in 1825.

Notable Facts: He was a commander of the Legion of Honor (1804) and grand cross of Saint Louis (1822).

Source: Six, vol. 2, 553.

Vimeur, Jean Baptiste Marquis and later Comte de Rochambeau

Background: He was born in 1725 into a noble family from Vendome (1477). He was named a cavalry cornet (May 1742). He served in Bavaria and then on the Rhine (1743–45). He was promoted to captain (July 1743) and served as aide-de-camp to the Duc d'Orleans and then the Comte de Clermont in l'Armée Armée des Flandres. He was at the battle of Rocroix and advanced to colonel (March 1747). He was badly wounded at Lawfeld leading his regiment in a charge, later serving at Maastricht and Minorca. He was promoted to colonel as a result.

He was appointed acting major general (1758) and colonel commanding the Auvergne regiment (1759). He was promoted to maréchal de camp (February 1761) in recognition for his role at Clostercamp where one of his adversaries was Cornwallis. He was named inspector general of infantry, responsible for training and tactics.

American Service: He was named commander of French expeditionary force (1780) and transported to Newport in d'Estaing's fleet. He commanded the French forces at Yorktown and remained in command until January 1783. He was rewarded with the order of Saint Esprit, which ranked higher than that of Saint Louis.

Post-American Career: He commanded the armies of Alsace and the Nord (1788–92). Promoted to *maréchal de France* (December 1791) as the last of 295 *marechaux* created under the Ancien Regime. He was arrested and then released. He died in 1807.

Notable Facts: He was a recipient of the grand cross of Saint Louis, as well as grand officier de la legion d'honneur. He, his father, and his son were all governors of Vendôme. His mother was governess to the children of the Duc d'Orleans. He was a Freemason.

Sources: Bod., 470; Lauberdiere, 77; Ketchum, 303; Six, vol. 2, 378; Selesky, vol. 2, 995–96; Ebel, 40, 123–24; ERA, vol. 2, 697–98; Schachtman, 313.

Vimeur, Donatien Joseph Vicomte and later Comte de Rochambeau

Background: He was born in 1755 into a noble family from Vendôme (1477). He was named lieutenant of artillery (August 1769). And promoted to aide-major and then deputy colonel (January 1779) of the Bourbonnais regiment.

American Service: He embarked for America with his father, serving as adjutant general at Yorktown but also seeing some fighting while attacking Pigeon Hill. He was named *mestre de camp* in the Saintonge regiment (November 1782).

Post-American Career: He returned to France with his regiment in June 1783 and commanded the Royal-Auvergne (July 1783). He was promoted to *maréchal de camp* (June 1791) and served in l'Armée du Nord. He resigned and was named governor of the Windward Islands (his appointment was not recognized at first). He repulsed a British attack on Martinique but was eventually taken prisoner.

He returned to France in 1797. He was named *general de division* (January 1800) and served in l'Armée d'Italie. He commanded a division in Leclerc's expedition to Saint-Domingue (October 1801). Replacing Leclerc, he capitulated and was taken prisoner. Inactive for two years, he was appointed to command the 4th division under Lauriston (January 1813). He was wounded at Eichberg and fought at Bautzen and Siebenecken. Commanding a division, he was mortally wounded during the battle of Leipzig in 1813.

Sources: Bod., 470; Lauberdiere, 77; Ketchum, 303; Six, vol. 2, 378–79; Selesky, vol. 2, 994.

Wisch, Jean Christophe

Background: Born in 1739, he was named a lieutenant in the Deux-Ponts regiment (March 1758) when a 4th battalion was raised for France to fight in Germany (1758–62). He fought at Wolfenbüttel and was wounded at Bergen. He was promoted to captain of grenadiers (April 1780).

American Service: He served with his regiment in America, including at Yorktown (1780–83).

Post-American Career: He was promoted to lieutenant colonel (July 1791) of his regiment which had become the 99th infantry and became its colonel in 1792. He served in the Armées du nord and Belgique under O'Moran and then as colonel (October 1792). He was wounded at Aachen and was promoted to *maréchal de camp* (March 1793) and commander of Philipeville. He was made a *general de division* (May 1793) in the Ardennes army. He was named commander of the 2nd military division by Kilmaine. He was encouraged to retire because of his age and many wounds, which he did in August 1794, and moved to Holstein. He died in 1808.

Sources: Bod, 473–74; Six, vol. 2, 573–74.

Wuibert de Mezieres, Antoine Felix

Background: Born in 1741, he moved to Saint-Domingue in 1763 and worked as a surveyor under his godfather, who was serving as director general of fortifications there. Mezieres moved to America in 1773.

American Service: He joined the Continental Army as a lieutenant colonel in June 1776 and took part in the battle of Fort Washington, where he was taken prisoner and taken to England.

Exchanged and back in France, John Paul Jones appointed him a marine lieutenant on *Bonhomme Richard.* He was captured again aboard USS *Alliance* and once again imprisoned in England. He was exchanged and landed in Saint-Domingue. He sailed for America on the *Confederacy,* which was also captured in April 1781. He was imprisoned in New York before arriving in Philadelphia in November 1781. Chief engineer du Portail recommended Wuibert as his successor when he returned to France. He was discharged in November 1783.

Post-American Career: He retired in November 1783 and moved back to Saint-Domingue. He finally returned to Philadelphia.

Source: Larrie D. Ferreiro, "Antoine Felix Wuibert: The 'Forest Gump' of the American Revolution," Journal of the American Revolution (April 19, 2018), allthingsliberty.com, hereafter cited as Ferreiro.

Chapter 6: The Cutting Room Floor

Abbadie de Saint-Germain, Chevalier de

Background: He was a *garde de vaisseau* in 1756.

American Service: He commanded *Seduisant* (1779–80) and served aboard *Marseillais* (1780).

Post-American Career: He was promoted to *capitaine de vaisseau* in 1782. He was first officer on *Pluton* in the fight against HMS *Leander* in February 1783.

Source: La Jonquiere, 19.

Alban, Jean Joseph

Background: Born in May 1741 in Saint-Domingue, he enlisted in the Saint-Domingue militia in 1762and rose to captain in the *chasseurs volontaires de Saint-Domingue* in March 1779.

American Service: He took part in the Savannah expedition with his unit and later in the siege of Pensacola.

Post-American Career: He returned to Saint-Domingue, where he continued his career. He rose to *chef de brigade* in 1795 and was commander of 106th infantry regiment. He commanded Fort-de-France from September 1797 until the

French withdrawal from Saint-Domingue. He returned to France where he died in March 1816.

Source: Bod., 15.

Ambroise de Genton, Jean Louis Chevalier de Villefranche

Background: Born in 1747, he wanted to be an engineer but there was no space for him. He joined the Royal-dragoons as a 2nd lieutenant (1772).

American Service: He was a volunteer with Coudray in February 1777, having been given a commission as a captain of engineers (December 1776). He was promoted to major and then lieutenant colonel (1783).

Post-American Career: He returned to France in November 1783. He died in 1784.

Notable Facts: He prepared the first set of plans for West Point. His brother, Louis, rose to captain in the Saintonge regiment and served with Rochambeau in America. He emigrated, serving in his regiment and died of wounds in 1794.

Source: Bod, 216.

Anselme de Saint Victor, François d'

Background: He was born April 1745 to a noble Florentine family that had settled in the Comtat Venaissin; he was an ensign in the Soissonnais regiment, then lieutenant and captain (April 1779).

American Service: He served in Rochambeau's corps.

Post-American Career: He was promoted to major in Bourbonnais regiment (April 1784) and eventually to colonel (September 1789) in the Bretagne regiment. He resigned in August 1792 and emigrated. He died in 1821.

Source: Bod., 21–22.

Balazer, François Antoine

Background: Born in 1750, he joined the Navarre regiment as a soldier in 1774, later transferring to Armagnac regiment (1776).

American Service: He served with his regiment at Savannah and at the sieges of Tobago and St. Kitts.

Post-American Career: He returned to France in June 1783. He progressed to the rank of *chef de brigade* in 1795. He served in various armies and retired in 1803, dying in 1806.

Source: Quintin, 84–85.

Barrier, Louis Charles

Background: Born into a bourgeois family in Dreux, he served as a gendarme (June 1764) and was promoted to lieutenant (May 1776).

American Service: He was provost marshal in Rochambeau corps (December 1781).

Post-American Career: He was appointed provost marshal of Franche-Comté (August 1784) and was later named colonel, commanding 16th gendarmerie division. He was placed on half pay (August 1792).

Source: Bod., 37–38.

Basquiat, François Leonard

Background: He was born in 1747–50 to a noble family of Spanish origin (recognized 1557). He was a volunteer in the Navarre regiment (March 1768). He was appointed 2nd lieutenant in the Auvergne regiment (May 1772) and then to the Gatinais regiment.

American Service: He may have served at Yorktown with the Gatinais regiment.

Post-American Career: He rose to colonel (March 1793) and then was suspended (October 1793).

Source: Bod., 38–39.

Baudoin, Louis Gabriel

Background: Born in the 1740s, he was a volunteer in the Fisher regiment (1753). He rose to captain in the Camp-Drago0ns (January 1773). He was placed on half pay (June 1776).

American Service: He joined the Lauzun Legion and served with it in America. He left America in 1780.

Post-American Career: He was appointed Lieutenant du Roi (deputy governor) of Fort-Dauphin and then promoted to colonel (July 1782).

Source: Bod. 39–40.

Beaumanoir, Julien François Vicomte de

Background: He was a *garde de marine* in 1756. He served aboard *Actif* at Ouessant where he was wounded.

American Service: He served aboard *Inconstant* (1778–80) and then aboard *Hector* at the Chesapeake and later Saintes, when he took over command after the captain was killed.

Post-American Career: He was promoted to *capitaine de vaisseau* in 1782.

Source: La Jonquiere, 33.

Beaurepaire, Amedee Bernard Comte de

Background: Born in 1739, he was a *garde de marine* in 1756.

American Service: He served aboard *Guerrier* under d'Estaing and then aboard *Sagittaire* (1780) and *Marseillais* at the Chesapeake and later Saintes.

Post-American Career: He was promoted to *capitaine de vaisseau* in 1782. He died on Elba in 1794.

Source: La Jonquiere, 33.

Bechet de la Rochefontaine, Etienne Nicolas

Background: Born July 1755, he was a student at Mezieres but could not join the engineer's corps due to lack of positions.

American Service: He joined the Continental Army as a captain of engineers in 1777, rising to major.

Post-American Career: He was promoted to captain in the French army in 1783 and joined the army general staff the following year. He was transferred to Saint-Domingue in 1791 as adjutant general *chef de brigade*. He left for the United States in 1792 and became a temporary engineer in the American Army working on the fortifications in New England. He died in 1814.

Source: Bod., 46.

Beffroy, Louis Henry

Background: Born in 1745 into a noble family from Champagne (1422), he was a student at a military academy (July 1756), cornet in Royal-Dragoons (June 1761), capitain in the *volontaires etrangers de la marine* (November 1778). This became the Lauzun Legion.

American Service: He served in America in Lauzun Legion.

Post-American Career: He rose to colonel of the 12th Dragoons (February 1792), later resigning. He did not emigrate.

Source: Bod., 47.

Belleville l'Etendard

Background: He was a *garde de marine* in 1741. He was promoted to *capitaine de vaisseau* in 1772.

American Service: He served aboard Palmier (1778) and Bretagne. He was Chabert's flag captain aboard *Saint-Esprit* at the Chesapeake.

Post-American Career: Unknown.

Source: La Jonquiere, 35.

Berthier

Background: Born in 1739, he joined the Cosne battalion as a gunner in 1758. He served in Germany (1758–62). He transferred to the Auxonne regiment in 1765 rising to third lieutenant.

American Service: He served in America (1780–83).

Post-American Career: He rose to *chef de battalion* in 1794 and was at the siege of Maastricht. He was soon promoted to *chef de brigade*. He was transferred to Cherbourg. He retired in 1801 and died the following year.

Sources: Bod., 54–55; Quintin, 96–97.

Bire, Pierre Chevalier de

Background: Born in 1741, he was a *garde de marine* in 1756.

American Service: He served aboard *Duc de Bourgogne* and *Auguste* under Grasse and then Vaudreil and was present at all the engagements, including at the Chesapeake and the Saintes, where he was wounded. He was promoted to *capitaine de vaisseau* in 1782.

Post-American Career: Unknown.

Source: La Jonquiere, 37.

Blois de la Calande, Jean Joseph

Background: Born in 1760, he entered the navy as an aspirant in 1776. He served at Ouessant as an *enseigne de vaisseau*.

American Service: He served in d'Estaing squadron at Grenada, Savannah, and St. Vincent.

Post-American Career: He rose to *capitaine de vaisseau* in 1815 and died in 1852.

Notable Facts: He was active in preserving Breton archaeological artifacts as well as Breton literature.

Source: La Jonquiere, 39.

Boades Lebrun de Joseph

Background: He was a *garde de marine* in 1748 and was promoted to *capitaine de vaisseau* in 1777.

American Service: He commanded *Magicienne* (1778) and then *Reflechi*. He served under Monteil at Pensacola and died of wounds suffered at the Chesapeake.

Source: La Jonquiere, 40.

Bordenave, Jean Ignace de

Background: Born December 1742 to a noble family (mid1600s), he was named an ensign in the Auvergne regiment (December 1761), rising to captain (August 1777).

American Service: He served at Yorktown with the Gatinais regiment for which action he was awarded the *croix de Saint Louis*.

Post-American Career: He was promoted to colonel of the 50th infantry regiment (July 1791). He was removed by his soldiers from command "despite his bravery" because he was a noble officer. He retired in February 1794 and died in 1808.

Source: Bod., 71–72.

Botderu, Nicolas Chevalier de

Background: Born in 1732, he was a *garde de marine* in 1748 and was promoted to *capitaine de vaisseau* in 1777. He commanded *l'Eveille* at Ouessant.

American Service: He was first officer on *Intrepide* and was taken prisoner (1780). As the captain of *Actionnaire*, he led one of the columns at Pensacola in 1782.

Post-American Career: He was promoted to brigadier and died in 1802.

Source: La Jonquiere, 42.

Bourayne, Joseph Baron de

Background: Born in 1768, he was a volunteer in 1781.

American Service: Serving aboard *Auguste*, he participated in the battles of the Chesapeake, St. Kitts, and Saintes.

Post-American Career: He went into the merchant navy. He spent three years in the Far East (1788–91) and was promoted to *capitaine de vaisseau* in 1803. He fought in the Indian Ocean, capturing several ships including HMS *Laurel* (1808). He was chief of staff at Brest (1814) and then interim *prefet maritime*, dying in 1817.

Sources: La Jonquiere, 45; Taillemite, 65.

Buzelet, Charles Adrien

Background: Born August 1733 to a noble family from Maine, he was a supernumerary in the artillery (February 1747). He rose to captain (January 1763).

American Service: He served with Rochambeau in America.

Post-American Career: He was promoted to lieutenant colonel (August 1788) and colonel (August 1791), commanding the artillery at Le Havre. He was suspended in August 1793. He died in 1814.

Source: Bod., 82.

Cambray-Digny, Louis Antoine Chevalier de

Background: Born June 1751 in Florence to a noble family from Picardy (1530), he was an *aspirant d'artillerie* (1770) and put on half pay (1774).

American Service: He joined the Continental Army as a lieutenant colonel in 1777 and was taken prisoner at Savannah. He was promoted to colonel after being exchanged (May 1783).

Post-American Career: Upon return to France, he retired. He died in 1822.

Source: Bod., 87.

Carcaradec de Villegusio, Charles Louis de

Background: Born in 1741, he was a *garde de marine* in 1756.

American Service: He served aboard *Nymphe* (1778), *Bretagne* (1779), and *Magnanime*, the latter at the Chesapeake and Saintes where he was wounded.

Post-American Career: He was promoted to *capitaine de vaisseau* in 1782. He died in 1802.

Source: La Jonquiere, 55.

Carne Carnavalet, Louis Marie Comte de

Background: Born in 1755, he was a *garde de marine* (1762). He served in various ships under Grasse and Orvilliers.

American Service: Serving on the *Dauphin Royal*, he took part in the siege of Savannah.

Post-American Career: He served in the West Indies and then under La Motte Picquet on *Invincible* against Howe. He was promoted to *capitaine de vaisseau* (1814). He died in 1827.

Notable Facts: He was *sous-prefet* of Brest. His brother, Louis, also served as a naval officer in the West Indies and was wounded at the attack on Grenada.

Source: La Jonquiere, 56.

Cars, Jacques Vicomte de

Background: He was born in 1738, he became a *garde de marine* in 1754, rising to *capitaine de vaisseau* in 1777.

American Service: Commanding *Prudente* under d'Estaing, his ship was defeated and taken by three British men of war. He commanded *Glorieux* under Grasse, taking the *Loyalist,* and then was killed at the Saintes.

Source: La Jonquiere, 56.

Castellan, Pierre Julien Chevalier de

Background: Born in 1733, he was a *garde de marine* 1748, rising to *capitaine de vaisseau* 1779. He was first officer aboard *Triton* (1778–79) at Ouessant. He served aboard *Languedoc* and *Auguste*.

American Service: He was flag captain to Bougainville at the Chesapeake and Saintes.

Post-American Career: He served aboard *Conquerant*. He was promoted brigadier in 1785 and died in 1812.

Source: La Jonquiere, 57.

Casteras de Seignan, François Marquis de

Background: Born into a noble family of Spanish origin (1531), he became a musketeer (July 1772) and later captain in the Agenois regiment (August 1770).

American Service: He served at Savannah as senior staff officer and was promoted to colonel (June 1780).

Post-American Career: Upon returning to France, he retired and served as *sous-prefe*t of Saint-Gironde.

Source: Bod., 92.

Causse, Joseph

Background: Born in 1738, he joined the navy as a sailor in 1745, rising to first mate in 1766.

American Service: He was aboard *Fantasque* in d'Estaing's squadron and took part in the Rhode Island actions in August 1778.

Post-American Career: He served on *Hector* and then *Zele* under Suffren and took part in the la Praya battle and subsequent actions in the Indian Ocean. He was promoted to *capitaine de vaisseau* 3rd class in 1793 and commanded la *Bellette, Centaure,* and *Infante.* He was promoted to *capitaine de vaisseau* 1st class in 1795 and commanded *Orient* (1796–97) and *Guerrier* (1797–98). He served under Brueys in the Egyptian expedition but was left at Malta. When Malta capitulated to the British, he was made a prisoner. He returned to France in 1800 and immediately retired. He died in 1809.

Source: Quintin, 349–50.

Chabannes, Jacques Gilbert Comte de la Palice

Background: He was born August 1760 into a noble family from the Angoumois (1395) which received five *honneurs de la cour.* He was a volunteer in the Ezterhazy and then Chartres-Dragono regiment (July 1777), where he was promoted to lieutenant (1776).

American Service: He served as aide-de-camp to Rochambeau and as a staff officer.

Post-American Career: He was promoted *mestre de camp* in the Saintonge regiment in 1783 and then in the Deux-Ponts, where he became colonel in 1788. He died in 1789 in Saint-Domingue.

Notable Facts: His brother was aide-de-camp to Baron de Viomenil in the American campaign, and his two nephews rose to brigadier general.

Sources: Bod., 96; Lauberdiere, 249.

Chabot, Marie Esprit Armand

Background: Born in 1749, he was a *garde de marine* (1766).

American Service: He served on *Pluton, Neptune* (1779), *Bourgogne,* and *Neptune* again (1781). Serving aboard *Neptune* under Ternay, he was recommended by Barras for the *croix de Saint-Louis* for his brave conduct in two actions.

Post-American Career: He was promoted to *capitaine de vaisseau* (1785) and died in 1818.

Source: La Jonquiere, 60.

Champmartin, Pierre Joseph Comte Sanson de

Background: Born in 1735, he was a *garde de marine* (1751).

American Service: He served on *Tonnant* under d'Estaing and then as first officer on *le Marseillais* under de Grasse at the Cheasapeake, where he was wounded. He was promoted to *capitaine de vaisseau* (1780).

Post-American Career: He commanded *le Duc de Bourgogne* at the Saintes, where he was wounded. In 1783 he commanded *Bourgogne* when it foundered with the losses of over 150 officers and men. He retired in 1784.

Source: La Jonquiere, 62.

Chaffault de Chaon, Charles Julien Comte de

Background: Born in 1736, he was a *garde de marine* (1751) and was promoted to *capitaine de vaisseau* (1777). He was wounded aboard *Saint Michel* at Ouessant.

American Service: He served as Vaudreuil's flag captain aboard *le Fendant* (1778–81).

Post-American Career: Unknown. He died in 1817.

Notable Facts: His brother Louis Charles rose to lieutenant general des Armées navales. He commanded the advanced division at Ouessant aboard *La Couronne* and was wounded.

Source: La Jonquiere, 60.

Chavagnac, Frederic Joseph Chevalier de

Background: Born in 1749, he was a *garde de marine* in 1764. He distinguished himself aboard *Juno* in the capture of HMS *Fox* (1778).

American Service: He served aboard *Artesien* (1779) in d'Estaing's squadron, *Annibal* (1780), *Saint Michel,* and *Argonaute* (1781). He later served aboard *Bien-Aime* (1782) and then *Invincible* (1783). He was promoted to *capitaine de vaisseau* in 1792.

Post-American Career: Unknown. He died in 1812.

Notable Facts: His younger brother, Gilbert, was a naval officer rising to *capitaine de vaisseau.* He did not serve in America but on the Africa station.

Source: La Jonquiere, 64.

Cibon, Jean Baptiste de

Background: Born in 1740, he was a *garde de marine* in 1755, advancing to capitaine de vaisseau in 1780. He served aboard *Robuste* at Ouessant under Guichen.

American Service: He served aboard *Ville de Paris* under de Grasse and was taken prisoner at the Saintes.

Post-American Career: Unknown.

Source: La Jonquiere, 67.

Cipieres, Jean Bruno Chevalier de

Background: Born in 1734, he was a *garde de marine* in 1754, advancing to *capitaine de vaisseau* in 1779.

American Service: He served aboard *Provence* (1778–79) under d'Estaing and then aboard *Aurore* (1780). He commanded *Precieuse* (1782–83).

Post-American Career: He was promoted to *chef de division* in 1786 and died in 1804.

Source: La Jonquiere, 68.

Clavel, Pierre Antoine Comte de

Background: Born in 1734, he was a a *garde de marine* (1750), rising to *capitaine de vaisseau* in 1777.

American Service: He commanded *Scipion* at the Chesapeake.

Post-American Career: He was promoted brigadier in 1781 and died in 1797.

Source: La Jonquiere, 69.

Clonard, Robert Chevalier de

Background: Born in 1731, he was a *garde de marine* in 1767. He was aboard *Saint-Esprit* at Ouessant.

American Service: While commanding *Pilote* he was attacked by three British ships, wounded, and taken prisoner. In command of *Comte d'Artois* he was faced with the same situation and result. He served on *Glorieux*, which sank.

Post-American Career: He commanded *Guyane* (1783) and was promoted *capitaine de vaisseau* in 1786 posthumously, having perished in the La Perouse expedition.

Notable Facts: His brother Thomas was killed aboard *Languedoc* during the siege of Saint Lucia.

Source: La Jonquiere, 69.

Costebelle, Pierre Alexandre Chevalier de

Background: Born in 1750, he was a *garde de marine* in 1766.

American Service: He served aboard *Languedoc* (1778–79) under d'Estaing and then aboard *Amazone, Sybille,* and

Bretagne (1781). He commanded *Naiade* on which he was wounded and then *Bellone* (1782–83) under Suffren.

Post-American Career: He was *capitaine de vaisseau* in 1784 and died in 1791.

Source: La Jonquiere, 74.

Cramazel Kerhue, Joseph Chevalier de

Background: Born in 1738, he was a *garde de marine* in 1756. He served aboard *Sphinx* and *l'Indien* under Orvilliers,

American Service: He served aboard *Glorieux* at the Chesapeake. He took command when his captain was killed at Saintes.

Post-American Career: He was promoted to *capitaine de vaisseau* in 1782. He commanded *Cleopatre* (1782) and then *Hardi* (1783–84) in Suffren's squadron in the Indian Ocean.

Source: La Jonquiere, 118.

Dalons, Sebastien-Joseph

Background: Born in 1752, he joined the naval artillery at Toulon in 1763. He rose through the ranks to sergeant (1776).

American Service: He served aboard *Marseillais* (1778–79) and was at Savannah.

Post-American Career: Rising to captain, he served at Toulon until it was taken by the British in September 1793. He was then posted to Corsica. He was commander of the port of Marseille (November 1794) and was promoted to adjutant general *chef de brigade* in 1795. He served in l'Armée d'Italie until 1800. He was retired on disability in 1803 and died in 1829.

Source: Quintin, 136.

Darodes de Choisy, Joseph

Background: Born in 1740, he was an aspirant in the artillery (1760), rising to captain in the Strasbourg regiment (1772). He moved to the West Indies for personal reasons.

American Service: He joined the Continental Army in 1778 and then served in Saint-Domingue (1780–83).

Post-American Career: He commanded a company of Metz artillery in Saint-Domingue. He was promoted to lieutenant colonel and then *chef de brigade* (1793). He retired in 1801, dying in 1804.

Source: Bod., 128.

Desbordes, Charles Etienne

Background: Born in 1736 into a noble family from Bresse (1562), he was a lieutenant in the Dijon militia (January 1755). He advanced to captain in the Touraine regiment (July 1769).

American Service: He served with his regiment at Yorktown.

Post-American Career: He was promoted to major in the Cambressis regiment (June 1782) and to colonel (November 1791). He resisted the royalist attempt to take Perpignan. He then retired (November 1792).

Source: Bod., 136–37.

Deslon de Moneril, Charles Georges

Background: Born in 1747, he was an engineering student and a 2nd lieutenant (January 1777). He was a captain of volunteers and transferred to the Lauzun Legion as a staff officer (April 1780).

American Service: He served in the Lauzun Legion in America, rising to captain.

Post-American Service: He was promoted to *chef d'escadron* (July 1789).

Notable Facts: He led a detachment of hussars, covering the king's flight to Varennes, and then went to Varennes to rescue the king, who through his indecision was arrested and returned to Paris.

Source: Bod., 142.

Drouhot, Jacques

Background: Born in 1741, he was a lieutenant in the local militia (1756) and then in the LaMarck regiment. He resigned in 1759 and rejoined the army nearly twenty years later. He was a captain in what became the Lauzun Legion in July 1779.

American Service: He served with the legion in America and returned to France after Yorktown.

Post-American Career: He continued to serve in the Lauzun hussars. He was then promoted to lieutenant colonel in the 5th Hussars in 1791 and colonel of the 6th *chasseurs a cheval* (1793). He was suspended and then imprisoned for having been an agent of Dumouriez. He was released but never recalled to active duty, retiring in 1797.

Notable Facts: His son, also named Jacques, served in the Lauzun Legion, rising to colonel but may not have been in America. He served until 1813.

Source: Bod., 152.

Dubois-Martin, François Augustin

Background: Born in 1742, he joined the navy and then entered the merchant marine. He was a lieutenant in Port-au-Prince regiment (November 1773).

American Service: While in France on regimental business, he was persuaded by Lafayette to volunteer for America. Dubois-Martin arranged for himself, Lafayette, and fourteen others to travel to America. They landed in South Carolina in June 1777. Congress did not grant him a commission, so he returned to Saint Domingue.

Post-American Career: He rejoined his regiment and retired two years later to take care of his family's plantations. He was ruined by the Black revolt and went to Baltimore in January 1803. He died in 1825.

Source: Bod., 330.

Dupleix de Cadignan, Jean Baptiste

Background: Born in 1738 into noble Gascon family (1667), he was named a lieutenant (April 1754) in the Bourgogne regiment, rising to captain (December 1756). He was promoted to lieutenant colonel in the Agenais regiment (April 1777).

American Service: He served as colonel of his regiment at Yorktown and in the West Indies.

Post-American Career: He retired July 1785 and died in 1824.

Notable Facts: His four brothers served in the army.

Source: Bod., 171.

Dupuy, Pierre Pascal Chevalier

Background: He was born in 1738 into a noble family. He was named a lieutenant in Royal Comtois regiment (July 1757). He was on half pay in 1763. He was recalled as a lieutenant and advanced to captain in various colonial units, including le Cap (May 1775).

American Service: He served at the siege of Savannah as part of a detachment from the Cap regiment.

Post-American Career: He retired in January 1787 but was recalled and advanced to colonel of the 110th regiment (formerly Port-au-Prince). He was removed as a noble but back in the army in October 1795.

Source: Bod., 175.

Esmery de Boisloge, Henry Chevalier de

Background: Born in 1736 to a Norman noble family (1669), he was a volunteer at the Metz artillery school (October 1749), rising to captain (July 1766).

American Service: He served with the Auxonne regiment under Rochambeau in America.

Post-American Career: He was promoted to major and then *chef de brigade* (July 1784). He died in 1791.

Source: Bod., 186.

Fabry, Charles Jean Chevalier de

Background: He was a *garde de marine* in 1775.

American Service: He served aboard *Destin* (1778), *Hero* (1779–81), and *Auguste* (1781–82). He served at the Chesapeake.

Post-American Career: He was promoted to *capitaine de vaisseau* in 1792.

Source: La Jonquiere, 90.

Failly, Alexandre François Chevalier de

Background: He was a *garde de marine* (1778), and he served on *Saint-Michel* in Orvilliers' squadron.

American Service: He served on the *Dauphin Royal* (1778–80) and was at Savannah.

Post-American Career: He served on *Lion* and then *Zodiaque* at Cadiz (1783). He was promoted to *lieutenant de vaisseau* (1786) and *capitaine de vaisseau* (1814).

Source: La Jonquiere, 90.

Ferrand, Pierre

Background: Born in 1744, he joined the navy in 1756 and became an *officier auxillaire* (1779).

American Service: He served on *Vaillant* (1778–79) under d'Estaing and was wounded at Savannah. He was with de Grasse on *Marseillais* (1780–81), *Pluton,* and *Couronne* (1781–83).

Post-American Career: He was promoted to *capitaine de flute* (1784) and *capitaine de vaisseau* (1793).

Notable Facts: He served in eighteen campaigns and was wounded several times.

Source: La Jonquiere, 91.

Framond, Auguste Charles Chevalier de Framond de Grezes

Background: Born in 1739, he was a *garde de marine* (1754).

American Service: He served as a lieutenant on *Cesar* in the Rhode Island operations. He was promoted to *capitaine de vaisseau* in July 1779 and take part in the siege of Savannah aboard *Cesar*. He was first officer on *Magnifique* (1781).

Post-American Career: He was promoted to brigadier in 1785 and died in 1790.

Notable Facts: His brother Georges also served in the navy under de Grasse.

Source: La Jonquiere, 95.

Froger, Louis Chevalier d'Eguille

Background: Born in 1750, he was a *garde de marine* in 1764.

American Service: He served aboard *Fendant* under Vaudreuil. He was chief staff officer in Vaudreuil's squadron off the New England coast on *Triomphant* in 1782. Commanding *Nereide*, he took a portion of the French troops to India.

Post-American Career: He was promoted to *capitaine de vaisseau* in 1786 and killed during the Quiberon expedition in 1795.

Notable Facts: His father commanded at Rochefort and was promoted to lieutenant general in 1766.

Source: La Jonquiere, 96.

Furstenwoerder, Charles Leopold Baron de

Background: Born in 1741 into a noble family in the Duchy of Deux-Ponts, he served as a volunteer in the Deux-Ponts regiment, rising to captain (February 1768).

American Service: He and his regiment were with Rochambeau, including at Yorktown.

Post-American Career: He transferred to the Royal-Suedois regiment where he rose to colonel (July 1781) and retired in December 1792.

Source: Bod., 206.

Galaup, François

Background: Born in 1739 into a noble family (1550), he was an artillery cadet. He transferred to the marine regiment rising to captain (1760) and was placed on inactive duty in 1763. He was re-employed in 1768 and later was assigned to the Auxerrois regiment.

American Service: He participated in the battles of Grenada, Savannah, and Dominica.

Post-American Career: He was promoted to major (1780), rising to colonel (1791). He emigrated and served in various units, including at the siege of Maastricht until 1809. He was last sighted in Malta in 1816.

Source: Bod., 207–08.

Galbert, Gaspard Vicomte de

Background: Born in 1752, he was a *garde de marine* (1766).

American Service: He served with Orvilliers on l'Artesien and then with La Motte Picquet. He took part in the taking of Grenada and siege of Savannah.

Post-American Career: He was with Guichen's fleet (1782–83) serving on the *Dauphin Royal* and *Lion*. He was promoted to *capitaine de vaisseau* (1792). He died in 1807.

Notable Facts: He was the member of the Constituent Assembly from Guadeloupe.

Source: La Jonquiere, 98.

Gantes, Jean François Seigneur de Roque

Background: He was a *garde de marine* in 1746 and promoted to *capitaine de vaisseau* in 1772.

American Service: He was first officer on *Zele* (1778–79) under d'Estaing.

Post-American Career: Unknown.

Source: La Jonquiere, 99.

Garavaque, Joseph

Background: Born in 1728, he was a student naval engineer and then engineer (1764). He then attended the Mezieres engineering school and became a 2nd lieutenant. He served at several bases around France (1764–78).

American Service: He served as a captain at Yorktown.

Post-American Career: He returned to France serving in several posts and was promoted to lieutenant colonel (1791). He served in l'Armée du nord and was tasked with reviewing the defenses of several bases by General Kilmaine. He was promoted to *chef de brigade* in 1793 and served as director of fortifications in Cambrai, Embrun, and Toulon. He retired in 1800 and died shortly thereafter.

Source: Quintin, 167.

Geant des Mottes, Jean Louis

Background: Born in 1756, he was a military inspector (1776).

American Service: He volunteered in America in 1778 with Lafayette. He was at Yorktown.

Post-American Career: In 1784 he killed someone in a duel and was condemned to be hanged. He did not serve until the Revolution when he was an aide-de-camp to Lafayette. He was promoted to lieutenant colonel and then adjutant colonel (July 1792). He was wounded at Longwy and died three days later.

Source: Bod., 215.

Gimel, Paul

Background: Born in 1752, he was a gendarme and then joined the artillery in 1767 rising to lieutenant (1770). **American Service:** He commanded the Metz artillery detachment at Pensacola. **Post-American Career:** On his return to France, he was promoted to captain in 1784. He resigned in 1791 and then emigrated and served in the Army of the Princes. He took part in the defense of Maastricht in 1793. He served in Holland (1794–95) and then moved to Hamburg. He died in 1807. **Source:** Bod., 219.

Gouyon de Varaouault, Joseph Charles

Background: Born in 1746, he was a *garde de marine* in 1764. **American Service:** He served aboard *Glorieux* and *Indien* (1779) under Orvilliers. He served on Caton (1780–82) under de Grasse. He was wounded at the Chesapeake and considered one of the best officers in the navy according to his captain Framond.

Post-American Career: He was promoted *capitaine de vaisseau* in 1792 and died in 1820.

Source: La Jonquiere, 103.

Gouzillon, Charles Comte de Kermeno et Kermorvan

Background: Born in 1740, he was a *garde de marine* in 1754.

American Service: He served aboard *Saint Esprit* (1780), *Fendant, Bretagne,* and *Ardent* under Ternay and Grasse. He was promoted to *capitaine de vaisseau* in 1780 and was wounded and taken prisoner at the Saintes.

Post-American Career: He died in 1786.

Notable Facts: His brother Andre also served in the navy in America and was promoted to *chef de division* in 1786. He was killed during the Quiberon expedition (1795).

Source: La Jonquiere, 104.

Grouchet de Soquence, Pierre Comte de

Background: Born in 1736 into a noble family (1464), he was a page to the Duchesse du Maine in 1747. He served as a volunteer in the campaigns of 1747–48. He was an officer in the La Fere artillery regiment (1756) and a cornet in the

Carabiniers (1756). He served in Germany (1757–63) and was wounded at Krefeld. He resigned to look after his mother's financial affairs in Saint-Domingue. He joined the local militia.

American Service: He may have served at Savannah, where he was wounded, and at Pensacola under Galvez. He was named *colonel a la suite* for the abortive Jamaica expedition in 1782.

Post-American Career: He returned to France for health reasons and served as *lieutenant des marechaux de France* (1785). He led a national guard unit to protect the Chateau de Saint-Germain-en-Laye. He participated in the defense of the Tuilleries on August 10, 1792. He was admitted to the Invalides and died in 1816.

Source: Bod., 231–32.

Le Joille, Louis Jean

Background: Born in 1759, he joined the merchant marine sailing in his father's ship.

American Service: He served on *Vengeance* in the American fleet. He was at the battle of La Playa.

Post-American Career: He commanded *Degranbourg* in Suffren's squadron (1780–83). He was promoted to *capitaine de vaisseau* (1795) and to *chef de division* (1798). He commanded *Genereux* in the Egyptian expedition and escaped after Aboukir taking HMS *Leander* off Corfu. He died in combat at Brindisi in 1799.

Sources: La Jonquiere, 141; Taillemite, 323.

Kergariou de Roscouet, Pierre Joseph Marquis de Kergariou

Background: He commanded *Danae* at Ouessant and then *Medee* in Guichen's squadron.

American Service: He served on *l'Engageante,* which brought the funds to pay for Barras's squadron and Rochambeau's corps to Boston in September 1781.

Post-American Career: He was promoted to *chef de division* in 1786. He was shot and killed during the Quiberon expedition in 1795 along with his younger brother Theobald.

Source: La Jonquiere, 116.

La Borde de Pecomme, Jean François

Background: He was born in 1743 to a noble family whose antecedents are unclear. He was an ensign, rising to captain (August 1775) in the Auvergne regiment.

American Service: He served with the Gatinais regiment at Yorktown.

Post-American Career: He was promoted to major, rising to colonel (March 1793). He was forced out due to his noble origins. He may have died in 1793.

Notable Facts: Two of his brothers were in the army, including Hyacinthe who also served at Yorktown in the Gatinais regiment.

Source: Bod., 261.

La Palisse, Pierre Felix de

Background: Born in 1735, he volunteered for the navy in 1778.

American Service: He served aboard several ships, including at Yorktown, and participated in two battles aboard *l'Aigle* (1782) and *Guadeloupe* (1782).

Post-American Career: He was promoted to *capitaine de vaisseau* in 1794. He died in 1826.

Source: La Jonquiere, 131.

Laserre, Louis Henry

Background: Born in 1757, he joined the Port-au-Prince regiment as a soldier in 1777.

American Service: He served as a sergeant with his regiment at Savannah. On board *Hannibal*, he was wounded.

Post-American Career: He retired in 1785. He joined the Paris National Guard as a 2nd lieutenant and served as secretary of a pension committee at the Constituent Assembly. He was named *commissaire de guerre* in several military divisions but retired in June 1795. He was brought back a year later. He served in the West Indies, including as commander of St. Eustatius where he was wounded during a British attack in 1800.

He returned to Paris and was then assigned as commander of Senegal as a *chef de brigade*. His tenure was controversial, and he was later investigated for his conduct. He commanded a column under Kellermann against Hessian forces in 1806 and then two regiments in Germany. He was assigned to Spain where he commanded several posts and served eventually as *sous-inspecteur des revues* and died in Portugal in 1809.

Source: Quintin, 214–15.

Mouchet-Battefort, Gabriel Marquis de Laubespin

Background: He was a *garde de marine* in 1751 and *capitaine de vaisseau* in 1777.

American Service: He was first officer on *Protecteur* in d'Estaing's squadron and participated in the operations off Newport and at the siege of Savannah. He served on *Invicible* (1781).

Post-American Career: He commanded *l'Indien* (1781–82) in the combined Franco-Spanish fleet based at Cadiz in 1780.

Source: La Jonquiere, 135.

Lombard, Louis Andre Chevalier de

Background: He was a *garde de marine* (1751), rising to *capitaine de vaisseau* (1777). He commanded *Terpsicorde* in Orvilliers's squadron (1778).

American Service: He commanded Provence (1780–82) under Ternay and at the battle of Cape Henry in March 1781. He later commanded *Marseillais* (1782–83) under de Grasse.

Post-American Career: Unknown.

Sources: La Jonquiere, 151; Desmarais, 139.

Longueville, Jacques Dominique, Chevalier de

Background: He was a *garde de marine* (1741), rising to *capitaine de vaisseau* (1772).

American Service: He was flag captain aboard *Robuste* (1778) under Grasse. They joined d'Estaing's squadron in the West Indies. He took part in the siege of Savannah.

Post-American Career: He retired in 1784 and died in 1785.

Source: La Jonquiere, 152.

Martelli de Chautard, Joseph Jacques

Background: Born in 1734, he was a *garde de marine* in 1734 and promoted to *capitaine de vaisseau* in 1777. He commanded *Pleiade* in 1778 and then *Experiment,* in which he took part in the capture of Tobago under Bouille.

American Service: He joined Grasse's squadron on *Experiment* and served at the Chesapeake. He was part of the convoy bringing Saint-Simon's troops back to Saint-Domingue. He commanded *Palmier* at the Saintes.

Post-American Career: He commanded the Saint-Domingue naval station. He died in 1810.

Source: La Jonquiere, 160.

Martinegg-Gineste, Joseph Jules

Background: Born in 1739, he became a *garde de marine* in 1755, rising to *capitaine de vaisseau* in 1779.

American Service: He served aboard *Guerrier* (1778–79) commanded by Bougainville at Newport and Grenada and was first officer at Savannah, where he was wounded. He then commanded *Boudeuse* (1781–82).

Post-American Career: He died in Cartagena in 1794.

Source: La Jonquiere, 160.

Martraire, Charles

Background: Born in 1741, he was a volunteer gunner in 1757 and participated in the Hannover campaign (1758–61), including the battle of Minden where he was taken prisoner. He rose to 3rd lieutenant in the Auxonne regiment.

American Service: He served with Rochambeau (1780–83) and took part in the siege of Yorktown.

Post-American Career: He remained in the army and was promoted to *chef de battalion* and then *de brigade,* serving against the Spanish. He was then assigned to l'Armée d'italie in 1797 where he was commander of Mantua. He was relieved because of his age and retired in 1801. He died in 1812.

Sources: Bod., 332; Quintin, 230.

Merlet, Joseph

Background: Born in 1756, he joined the merchant navy in 1774; he was enrolled in the navy at the outset of the War of Independence.

American Service: He served as second pilot on *Northumberland* and then held the same position on *Hardi* and *la Couronne*.

Post-American Career: He was aboard *Robuste* at the siege of Gibraltar (1782). He rejoined the merchant navy as captain of *Pointe-a-Pitre* (1783–85), Baron de Halde (1786–91), and *Bonne Mere* (1791–92). He rejoined the navy, rising to *capitaine de vaisseau* in 1794. He served in the West Indies as commander of several islands. In December 1796 he was attacked by four British ships but managed to fend them off. He returned to France for health reasons but was captured.

Source: Quintin, 405.

Mondion de Sassey, François Joseph

Background: Born May 1737 into a noble family (1425), he was a lieutenant in the Foix regiment, rising to captain (1762).

American Service: With his regiment, he participated in the battles of Grenada and Savannah.

Post-American Career: He was promoted to major in the Conti regiment in 1780 and then advanced to colonel (1791). He retired in 1792 and died in 1827.

Source: Bod., 343.

Pontgibaud More de, Charles Albert

Background: Born in 1758 to a noble family from Gevaudan (1529), he ended up in debtor's prison—from which he escaped—held under a *letter de cachet*.

American Service: He volunteered for America and was named a major in the Continental Army, serving as Lafayette's aide-de-camp. He returned with Lafayette to France when he was on a mission to obtain more financial and military support in 1779. He was appointed captain in the King's Dragoons (June 1779), and he accompanied Lafayette back to America and served at Yorktown.

Post-American Career: He returned to France in November 1783. He was reformed. He was offered a position in the Paris National Guard by Lafayette but refused and emigrated with his brother. He died in 1837.

Source: Bod., 348–49.

Mories de Castellet, Pierre de Cheylan Comte de

Background: He was a *garde de marine* (1755), rising to *capitaine de vaisseau* in 1762 and *chef d'escadre* in 1778.

American Service: He commanded *Hector* in d'Estaing's squadron and participated in the Rhode Island and Savannah campaigns.

Post-American Career: He died in 1794.

Source: La Jonquiere, 171.

Pitot, François Marie

Background: Born in 1767, he joined the navy as a volunteer on *le Conquerant* in Ternay's squadron which brought Rochambeau's corps to Newport.

American Service: He served at the Chesapeake and Saintes.

Post-American Career: He served in the merchant marine (1783–88) and rejoined the navy as a volunteer. He progressed to *enseigne de vaisseau* and acted as interim commander of *le Republicain* (1792). He commanded *Nymphe* which was wrecked. Commanding *Renommee* he was named *capitaine de vaisseau* 2nd class in 1796. He commanded several ships in the West Indies and was captured by HMS *Seine* off Puerto Rico. Exchanged in 1801, he was briefly on the inactive list. He was recalled to service by Bruix and commanded one of the gunnery divisions. He lost the use of his right hand and was forced to retire in 1803. He died in 1816.

Source: Quintin, 417–18.

Prez de Crassier, Louis Aimable

Background: Born in 1730, he entered the Swiss regiment of Wittner (1747), rising to 2nd lieutenant. He joined the Deux-Ponts regiment, rising to captain in 1758 and then major (1780).

American Service. He served with his regiment in America.

Post-American Career: He was promoted to lieutenant colonel and then colonel (1791). He died the same year.

Source: Bod., 382.

Puget de Bras, Louis Chevalier de

Background: Born in 1740, he was a *garde de marine* (1755).

American Service: He was first officer on *Chimere* (1778) and then served on *Zele* and *Ville de Paris* (1781) under d'Estaing. He commanded *Renommee* (1780), *Nereide* (1781), and *Pluton* (1782) under Vaudreuil. He was promoted to *capitaine de vaisseau* in 1781.

Post-American Career: He commanded *Hercule* in the combined Franco-Spanish fleet at Cadiz. He died in 1808.

Source: La Jonquiere, 186.

Postscript

Les 'Americains': The Opportunity of War

The sixty years of war between 1756 and 1815, with brief interludes, provided opportunities for soldiers and sailors to have meteoric careers. It was like the period from 1914 to 1945 which formed many exceptional officers in various armies and navies, e.g., Marshall, Montgomery, and Rommel.

For the French army of this period, the commander of the forces in America, the Comte de Rochambeau,[1] was promoted to *maréchal de France* at the outset of the French Revolution. Rochambeau's career spanned the battles of Minden and Clostercamp, where Cornwallis was an opponent, until 1792 when he retired. Rochambeau's son, who served at Yorktown, died of wounds incurred leading his division at the battle of Leipzig in 1813. His own son won an immediate Legion of Honor for bravery as aide-de-camp to Marshal Murat at Friedland.

---

[1]Arnold Whitridge, *Rochambeau America's Neglected Founding Father* (New York, 1965). Hereafter cited as Whitridge

One of Rochambeau's staff officers at Yorktown, Berthier,[2] became a marshal under Napoleon and served as his major general on most campaigns as well as Minister of War.[3] Despite not being a front-line soldier, he helped lead the assault across the bridge at Lodi and was instrumental in rallying the French forces at Wagram.[4]

Marshal Jourdan served as a soldier at Savannah and then resigned from the army and entered civilian life.[5] He joined the national guard at the outbreak of the Revolution and then proved Napoleon right when he allegedly said that each soldier carries a marshal's baton in his knapsack.

An émigré, Joseph Hyacinthe du Houx, Vicomte de Viomenil was promoted to Marshal of France upon the restoration of the monarchy in 1816. He had previously served as a lieutenant general in the Russian army and in Portugal. His older brother, Antoine Baron de Viomenil was

---

[2]Frederic Hulot, *Le Maréchal Berthier* (Paris 2007). Hereafter cited as Hulot I.

[3]Edouard Ebel, ed., *Les Ministres de la Guerre, 1792–1870: Histoire et Dictionnaire* (Rennes 2018), 125–234. Hereafter cited as Ebel.

[4]Frederic Hulot, *Le Maréchal Berthier* (Paris, 2007), 54. Hereafter cited as Hulot.

[5]Frederic Hulot, *Le Maréchal Jourdan* (Paris, 2010). Hereafter cited as Hulot II.

second in command to Rochambeau in America and died of wounds incurred defending the Tuileries on August 10, 1792. Two other Viomenils who served in America reached general rank.

Several 'Americains' served as French Ministers of War. Duportail was instrumental in reorganizing the army at the beginning of the Revolution. Aubert du Bayet served,[6] as well as Berthier. Mathieu Dumas was Minister of War in Naples[7] and headed the conscription directorate in the war ministry in 1811 in preparation for the Russian campaign.[8]

Military life was international, and officers could serve in different armies and navies. The Forbach brothers, who in turn commanded the Deux-Ponts regiment and served at Yorktown, went on to become lieutenant generals in the Bavarian Army. Jean Verger also rose to lieutenant general in Bavarian service and acted as Bavarian ambassador to Switzerland and Wurttemberg. Count Fersen was Marshal of the Palace in Sweden,[9] and Baron Stedingk,

---

[6]Ebel, 71–73.
[7]Ebel, 253.
[8]Ebel, 150.
[9]H. Arnold Barton, *Count Axel Fersen: Aristocrat in the Age of Revolution* (Woodbridge, CT, 1975).

who had risen to *maréchal de camp* before the Revolution, was promoted to lieutenant general and then to marshal in the Swedish Army. Stack de Crotto, who was Irish born and had served in the Walsh regiment, emigrated and rose to lieutenant general in the British Army.

The Comte de Langeron rose to lieutenant general in Russian service after emigrating in 1790. He unsuccessfully commanded the left flank at Austerlitz and was temporarily disgraced as a result. From 1806 to 1811 he served in the Moldavian Army against the Turks. He was recalled to Russia and commanded the 1st corps at Berezina. He helped develop the city of Odessa while Governor of New Russia.[10]

On the naval side, American veterans Brueys and Villeneuve, respectively commanded the French fleets at Aboukir and Trafalgar. Count d'Estaing was promoted to admiral in 1792 but refused the appointment.[11] Truguet was made an admiral on the Restoration and given a marshal's

---

[10]Alexander Mikaberidze, *The Russian Officer Corps in the Revolutionary and Napoleonic Wars 1792–1815* (New York, 2005), 218–20.
[11]I had the privilege to hear former President Giscard d'Estaing speak about his ancestor at an annual dinner of the French branch of the Sons of the American Revolution at the Luxemburg Palace in Paris some years ago.

baton. A fourth position of vice admiral was created by Louis XVI to recognize Suffren's successes in the Indian Ocean in 1784.

Several 'Americains' served as Minister of the Navy in France and in Russia (the Marquis de Traversay). Decres served continuously from 1801 until 1815. Truguet, Pleville, and Bruix were navy ministers,[12] and Chayla served as assistant minister. Bougainville refused both appointment to naval minister and promotion to vice admiral. Nauckoff rose to admiral and head of the Swedish Navy, and Lowenhorn became an admiral in the Danish Navy. Both had volunteered to serve with the French Navy during the war and had been given permission to do so by their respective governments. An émigré, Capellis, was a rear admiral in the Russian Navy and served as commander of Kronstadt. Another émigré, Chastellet, served as a rear admiral in the Portuguese Navy.

Some of the officers were active in politics during the Revolution and after. I am consciously omitting Lafayette, as his role both in politics and the army has been

---

[12]Georges Six, *Les Generaux de la Revolution et de l'Empire* (Paris, 1947), 276. Hereafter cited as Six.

well covered.[13] Eleven former 'Americains' served in the Etats Generaux out of 278 representatives of the Second Estate.[14] Several 'Americains' served in the Constituent Assembly. [15] De Noailles introduced the motion to abolish feudal privileges on August 4, 1789.[16] Six officers served in the Legislative Assembly.[17] Alexander and Theodore Lameth were prominent members of the Jacobin Club and later the Feuillants. Mathieu Dumas returned from exile and was elected to the *Conseil de Cinq Cents*.[18] He later served as a deputy under the Restoration and then under the July Monarchy, as did Lafayette and Charles Lameth.

Several 'Americains' served in senior government positions under the Empire, including as *prefets* and sous-

---

[13]Brancier & Villiers, *La Fayette: Rever la Gloire* (Saint-Rémy-en-l'Eau, 2013); Mike Duncan, *Hero of Two Worlds* (New York, 2021); and Louis Gottschalk, *Lafayette joins the American Army* (Chicago, 1937).

[14]Bod. 2, 384–85. They were all colonels or generals and 70 percent of them voted "liberal."

[15]Bod. 2, 383.

[16]Bod. 2, 391.

[17]Bod. 2, 397–99. As the nobles' influence was reduced, only one 'Americain' served in the Convention and two in the Constitutional Convention.

[18]Bod. 2, 400.

prefets,[19] the government's representative in each department. Others served on the *conseil d'état, corps legislative,* and in the Senate or in the chamber of peers after the Restoration. De Segur was elected a Member of the Academie Française.[20]

Further afield, Francisco Miranda, who served at Pensacola and then in the French revolutionary armies, led an abortive uprising to secure independence from Spain for what is now Venezuela.[21]

Two "Americains"—Theobald Dillon and Admiral Bougainville—received the highest accolade given by the French Republic: burial in the Pantheon.

---

[19]Each of France's 100 departments had a *prefet* at its head who reported to the Ministry of the Interior in Paris. Depending on the size and importance of the department, it would contain *sous-prefectures* headed by a *sous-prefet.*
[20]Six I, 277.
[21]Karen Racine, *Francisco de Miranda: A Transatlantic Life in the Age of Revolution* (Lanham, MD, 2003); and Jacques de Cazotte, *Miranda (1750–1816): Histoire d'un Seducteur* (Paris, 2000).

Appendix I

Foreign Financial Contribution to the American War of Independence (in 1775 USD terms)

Type	Donor	1776	1777	1778–79	1780	1781	1782–83	Total	Total (French)
Cash	France	$212,766	$0	$0	$2,229,283	$0	$0	$2,442,049	$2,442,049
Cash	Spain	$1,461,702	$2,282,979	$0	$0	$255,319	$0	$4,000,000	
Cash	Netherlands	$0	$0	$0	$0	$0	$0	$0	
Total Cash		$1,674,468	$2,282,979	$0	$2,229,283	$255,319	$0	$6,442,049	
Loans	France		$1,276,596		$1,702,128	$1,276,596	$1,276,596	$5,531,915	$5,531,915
Loans	Spain			$6,349,206		$1,923,077	$0	$8,272,283	
Loans	Netherlands					$1,000,000	$0	$1,000,000	
Loans	Various					$211,528	$638,298	$849,826	
Total Loans		$0	$1,276,596	$6,349,206	$1,702,128	$4,411,201	$1,914,894	$15,654,024	
Total Cash and Loans		$1,674,468	$3,559,574	$6,349,206	$3,931,411	$4,666,520	$1,919,894	$22,096,073	
Fleet Costs[1]	France	$0	$0	$3,059,043	$775,532	$2,558,617	$0	$6,393,191	$6,393,191
Army Costs[2]	France	$0	$0	$0	$622,340	$1,244,681	$1,348,404	$3,215,426	$3,215,426
Supplies	France	$1,500,000	$0	$0	$0	$0	$0	$1,500,000	$1,500,000
Supplies	Spain	$0	$79,787	$0	$751,513	$0	$0	$831,300	
Total Military Costs		$1,500,000	$79,787	$3,059,043	$2,149,385	$3,803,298	$1,348,404	$11,939,917	$11,108,191
Total Costs[3]		$3,174,468	$3,639,362	$9,408,249	$6,080,796	$8,469,818	$3,263,298	$45,975,907[4]	$19,082,581[4]

[1] Operating costs only, as it is hard to ascribe a portion of capital costs for ships that were not specifically commissioned to support the Americans.

[2] Costs of Rochambeau's army at 75 livres per soldier per month.

[3] These are net of borrowing costs, which Wenger estimated at 7 percent per annum for a ten-year loan.

[4] In 2010 dollars: $1,301,989,919.06 and $540,398,867.86 respectively.

Bibliography

Abel, Jonathan. *Father of Napoleon's Grand Armée.* Norman: University of Oklahoma Press, 2016.

Acomb, Evelyn. *The Revolutionary Journal of Baron Ludwig von Closen.* Chapel Hill: University of North Carolina Press, 1958.

Adler, Ken. *Engineering the Revolution: Arms and Enlightenment in France, 1763–1815.* Princeton: Princeton University Press, 1997.

Allen, Rodney. *Threshold of Terror: The Last Hours of the French Monarchy.* Stroud, UK: Sutton Publishing, 1999.

Atkinson, Rick. *The British are Coming: The War for America, Lexington to Princeton.* New York: Henry Holt, 1019.

Balch, Thomas. *Les Français en Amerique pendant la guerre de l'independence des États-Unis, 1777–1783.* N.p.: FB Editions (reprint), 1872/2015.

Balteau, J. *et al. Dictionnaire de Biographie Française.* 19 volumes. Paris: Letouzey et Ane, 1933–.

Barton, H. Arnold. *Count Hans Axel Fersen: Aristrocrat in the Age of Revolution*. Boston: Twayne Publishers, 1975.

Bicheno, Hugh. *"Redcoats and Rebels": The American Revolutionary War*. London: Harper Collins, 2004.

Blancpain, François. *La colonie Française de Saint-Domingue de l'esclavage a l'independence*. Paris: Karthala, 2002.

Blaufarb, Rafe. *The French Army, 1750–1820: Careers, Talent, Merit*. Manchester: Manchester University Press, 2002.

_____. *Interpreting the Ancient Regime: David Bien*. Manchester: Manchester University Press, 2014.

Boatner III, Mark M. *Encyclopedia of the American Revolution*. New York: McKay, 1966.

Bodinier, Gilbert. *Dictionnaire des officiers de l'armée royale qui ont combatus pendant la guerre d'indpendence: 1776–1783*. 5th Edition. Paris: SN Memoires, 2010.

_____. *Dictionnaire des Officiers Genereaux de l'armée Royale, 1688–1762*. 4 volumes. Paris: Archives and Culture, 2014–2023.

_____. *La France de la Revolution et les Étas-Unis d'Amerique*. Paris: Foundation Singer-Polignac, 1994.

_____. *Les Officiers de l'Armée Royale combattants de la guerre d'independence des Étas-Unis: De Yorktown à l'an II*. Vincennes: Ministere de l'armée de terre, 1983.

_____. *Les Officiers du Consulat et de l'Empire*. Paris: Editions Soteca, 2014.

Bonin, Pierre. *Construire l'Armée Française*. Volume 2. Brepols, 2006.

Boucheron, Patrick. *France in the World: A New Global History*. New York: Other Press, 2019.

Boulaire, Alain. *La Marine Française de la Royale aux missions d'aujourdhui*. Paris: Palantines, 2011.

Brancion et Villiers. *La Fayette: Rever la gloire*. Éditions Monelle Hayot, 2013.

Brands, H.W. *Our First Civil War: Patriots and Loyalists in the American Revolution*. New York: Anchor Books, 2022.

Cazotte, Jacques. *Miranda, 1750–1816: Histoire d'un seducteur*. Paris: Perrin, 2000.

Chaline, Olivier. *L'amiral de Grasse et l'independence Americaine*. Paris: Université Paris La Sorbonne, 2023.

_____. *Les Marines de la Guerre d'independence americaine*. Paris: Université Paris La Sorbonne, 2013.

Chandler, David. *Napoleon's Marshals*. New York: Macmillan, 1987.

Chartrand, René. *Émigré and Foreign Troops in British Service*. Oxford: Osprey, 1999.

_____. *The French Army in the American War of Independence*. Oxford: Osprey, 1991.

_____. *Napoleonic Wars: Napoleon's Army*. London: Brassey's, 2000.

_____. *The Spanish Army in North America, 1700–1793*. Oxford: Osprey, 1987.

Cilleuls, Jean de. "L'Inspecteur Général Jacque de Villemanzy: Sénateur et Pair de France (1751–1830)." *Hist Sci Med.* 13, no. 4 (1979): 379–81.

Clauw, Fabien. *Capitaine de Bonaparte*. Paris: Paulsen, 2020.

_____. *Trafalgar la Sanglande*. Paris: Paulsen, 2021.

Cole, Hubert. *Christofre: King of Haiti*. London: Eyre & Spottiswood, 1967.

Contenson, Ludovic. *La Societé des Cincinnati de France et la guerre d'amerique (1778–1783)*. Paris: August Picard, 1934.

Dawson, Warrington. "Les 2112 Français morts aux Étas-Unis de 1777 a 1783 combattant pour l'independence americaine." *Journal de la societé des americainistes* 28, no. 1 (1936):

Desmarais, Norman. *America's First Ally: France in the Revolutionary War*. Philadelphia: Casemate, 2019.

_____. *The Road to Yorktown by L-F du Pont d'Aubevoye, comte de Lauberdiere*. El Dorado Hills, CA: Savas Beatie, 2021.

Dolin, Eric Jay. *Rebels at Sea: Privateering in the American Revolution*. New York: WW Norton, 2022.

Doyle, William. *Origins of the French Revolution*. Oxford: Oxford University Press, 1999.

_____. *The Oxford Handbook of the Ancient Regime*. Oxford: Oxford University Press, 2012.

Drevillon, Herve. *Guerres et Armées Napoleoniennes: Nouveaux Regards*. Paris: Nouveau Monde, 2013.

_____. *Histoire Militaire de la France: des Merovingiens au Second Empire*. Paris: Perrin, 2018.

Dull, Jonathan. *The Age of the Ship of the Line: The British and French Navies, 1650–1815*. Omaha: University of Nebraska Press, 2009.

_____. *The French Navy and American Independence*. Princeton: Princeton University Press, 1975.

Duncan, Mike. *Hero of Two Worlds*. New York: Public Affairs, 2021.

Dunn-Pattison, R.P. *Napoleon's Marshals*. EP Publishing, 1977.

Ebel, Edouard. *Les Ministres de la Guerre: 1792–1870*. Rennes: Presses Universitaires de Rennes, 2018.

Elting, John R. *The Battles of Saratoga*. NJ: Philip Freneau Press, 1977.

_____. *Swords around a Throne: Napoleon's Grande Armée*. New York: De Capo Press, 1997.

Epstein, Robert. *Napoleon's Last Victory and the Emergence of Modern War*. Lawrence, KS: University Press Kansas, 1994.

Esdaile, Charles. *The Peninsular War*. New York: Penguin, 2002.

Expedition Particularie. https://expeditionparticuliere.com/

Ferling, John. *Winning Independence*. Bloomsbury Publishing, 2021.

Larrie D. Ferreiro, "Antoine Felix Wuibert: The 'Forest Gump' of the American Revolution," Journal of the American Revolution (April 19, 2018), allthingsliberty.com, hereafter cited as Ferreiro.

_____. *Brothers in Arms: The American Revolution and the Men of France and Spain.* New York: Vintage Press, 2016.

Ford, Franklin. *Robe and Sword: The Regrouping of the French Aristocracy after Louis XIV.* Cambridge, MA: Harvard University Press, 1953.

Furet, François. *A Critical Dictionary of the French Revolution.* Cambridge, MA: Harvard University Press, 1988.

_____. *Revolutionary France, 1770–1880.* Blackwell, 1998 (reprint).

Gardiner, Asa Bird. *The Institutions of the Society of The Cincinnati.* 4th Edition.Order of Cincinnatti, 1905.

Garray and Carnes. *American National Biography.* New York: Oxford University Press, 1999.

Garrigus, John. *Before Haiti: Race and Citizenship in French Saint-Domingue*. New York: Palgrave Macmillan, 2006.

Gilet, Jean-Claude. *La Marine Imperiale: Le Grand Reve de Napoleon*. Paris: Bernard Giovanageli, 2010.

_____. *La part d'ombre des marechaux de Napoleon*. Paris: Bernard Giovangeli Editeur, 2012.

Gilje, Paul. *Encyclopedia of Revolutionary America*. 3 volumes. New York: Facts on File, 2010.

Girard, Philippe. *Toussaint Louverture*. New York: Basic Books, 2016.

Gottschalk, Louis. *Lafayette joins the American Army*. Chicago: University of Chicago Press, 1937.

Greene, Jerome. *The Guns of Independence: The Siege of Yorktown, 1781*. El Dorado Hills, CA: Savas Beatie, 2013.

Griswold, Rufus. *Washington and the Generals of the American Revolution*. Volume 1. Philadelphia: Carey & Hart, 1847.

Hannah-Jones, Nikole. *The 1619 Project*. New York: One World, 2021.

Holton, Woody. *Liberty is Sweet: The Hidden History of the American Revolution*. New York: Simon & Schuster, 2021.

Horne, Alistair. *Friend or Foe: An Anglo-Saxon History of France*. London: Weinfeld 7 Nicholson, 2004.

Howarth, Stephen. *To Shining Sea: A History of the United States Navy*. New York: Random House, 1991.

Hulot, Frederic. *Le Maréchal Berthier*. Paris: Pygmalion, 2007.

_____. *Le Maréchal Jourdan*. Paris: Pygmalion, 2010.

Humble, Richard. *Napoleon's Admirals*. Philadelphia: Casemate, 2019.

_____. *Napoleon's Peninsular Marshals*. London: Macdonald, 1973.

Jenkins, E.H. *A History of the French Navy*. London: Macdonald & Co., 1973.

Jofrin, Laurent. *Le Cadavre du Palais Royal*. Paris: Buchet Chastel, 2022.

Jones, Colin. *The Fall of Robespierre: 24 Hours in Revolutionary Paris*. Oxford: Oxford University Press, 20021.

_____. *The Great Nation*. New York: Penguin Books, 2002.

de la Jonquiere, Christian. *Les Marins Français sous Louix XVI guerre independenc Americaine*. Issy-les-Moulineaux: Muller, 1996.

_____. *Officiers de Marine aux Cincinnati*. Toulouse: Editions de Poliphile, 1988.

Keegan, John. *Warpaths: Travels of a Military Historian in North America*. London: Hodder and Stoughton, 1995.

Kennett, Lee. *The French Forces in America, 1780–83*. Westport, CT: Greenwood Press, 1977.

Ketchum, Richard M. *Victory at Yorktown: The Campaign that Won the Revolution*. New York: Henry Holt, 2004.

Knight, Roger. *Convoys: The British Struggle Against Napoleonic Europe and America.* New Haven: Yale University Press, 2022.

Lanier, Clement. "Les negres d'Haiti dans la guerre d'independence americaine." *Genese: Journal genealogique et historiqu Port-au-prince Haiti* 51 (1933).

Larrabee, Harold. *Decision at the Chesapeake.* Philip Freneau Press, 1964.

Le Bozec, Christine. *Barras.* Paris: Perrin, 2016.

Le Pottier, Serge. *Duportail ou le Genie de George Washington.* Paris: Economica, 2011.

Lengel, Edward. *The 10 Key Campaigns of the American Revolution.* Washington, D.C.: Regnery Publishing, 2020.

Lentz, Thierry. *Les Mythes de la Grande Armée.* Paris: Perrin, 2022.

Lepore, Jill. *These Truths: A History of the United States.* New York: WW Norton, 2019.

Lewis, Charles Lee. *Admiral de Grasse and American Independence*. Grenwood Press (repreing), 1980.

"Louis XVI's l'Incompris." *Figaro Magazine*, no. 24539–40 (Jul. 23).

Lyons, Renee Critcher. *Foreign-Born American Patriots: Sixteen Volunteer Leader in the Revolutionary War*. Jefferson, NC: McFarland & Co., 2014.

Maas, John. *The Road to Yorktown: Jefferson, Lafayette and the British Invasion of Virginia*. Charleston, SC: History Press, 2015.

Mahan, Alfred Thayer. *The Influence of Sea Power upon History (1660–1783)*. Digireads, 2020.

Martin, Jean-Clement. *Nouvelle Histoire de la Revolution Française*. Paris: Tempus, 2019.

Martin, Scott. *Savannah 1779: The British Turn South*. Oxford: Osprey, 2017.

McBurney, Christian. *The Rhode Island Campaign*. Westholme: Yardley, 2011.

Mention, Louis. *L'armée de l'ancien regime*. Legare Street Press (reprint), 2022.

Metcalf, Bryce. *Original Members and the Other Offficiers Eligible to the Society of Cincinnati*. Shenandoah Publishing, 1938.

Mikaberidze, Alexander. *The Napoleonic Wars: A Global History*. Oxford: Oxford University Press, 2020.

_____. *The Russian Officer Corps in the Revolutionary and Napoleonic Wars, 1792–1815*. New York: Savas Beattie, 2005.

Ministere des Affaires Etrangeres. *Les Combattants Français de la Guerre Americaine, 1778–1783*. 1903.

Montagnon, Pierre. *Histoire de l'Armée Française: Des Milices Royales a l'Armée de Metier*. Paris: Pygmalion, 1993.

Morrissey, Brendan. *Yorktown 1781: The World Turned Upside Down*. Oxford: Osprey, 2008.

Nagourney, Eric. "Six Facts to Remember on the Repartations Owed by Haiti to France." *The New York Times* (May 22, 2022).

Nicolson, Adam. *Seize the Fire: Heroism, Duty and the Battle of Trafalgar*. New York: Harper Collins, 2005.

Noel, Erik. *Les Beauharnais: Une Fortune Antillaise, 1756–96*. Paris: Droz, 2002.

Nogaret, Guy Chaussinand. *The French Nobility in the Eighteenth Century*. Cambridge: Cambridge University Press, 1985.

O'Brien, Patrick. *Joseph Banks: A Life*. London: Harvill Press, 1997.

Perkins, James. *France in the American Revolution*. New York: Burt Franklin, 1970.

Petitfils, Jean-Christian. *Louis XVI*. Paris: Tempus (Perrin), 2021.

Philbrick, Nathaniel. *In the Hurricane's Eye: The Genius of George Washington and the Victory at Yorktown*. New York: Penguin Books, 2018.

Phipps, Ramsay. *The Armies of the First French Republic.* Greenwood Press, 1980.

Pigeard, Alain. *L'Armée de Napoleon: Organization et Vie Quotidienne.* Paris: Tallandier, 2000.

_____. *Dictionnaire de la Grande Armée.* Paris: Tallandier, 2002.

Pigeard, Andre. *Historie de la Grande Armée, 1805–1815.* Paris: La Bisquine, 2015.

Pocock, Tom. *Horatio Nelson.* London: Pimlico, 1994.

Quintero Sarava, Gonzalo. *Bernardo de Galvez: Spanish Hero of the American Revolution.* Chapel Hill: University of North Carolina Press, 2018.

Quintin, Bernard and Danielle Quintin. *Dictionnaire de Chefs de Brigade...Premier Consul.* Paris: SPM, 2012.

_____. *Dictionnaire de Colonels de Napoleon.* Paris: SPM, 1996.

Racine, Karen. *Francisco Miranda: A Transatlantic Life in the Age of Revolution.* Scholarly Resources, 2003.

Robb, Graham. *France: An Adventure in History*. London: Picador, 2022.

_____. *Parisians: An Adventure in the History of Paris*. London: Picador, 2010.

Rodger, N.A.M. *The Command of the Ocean: A Naval History of Britain*. London: Allen Lane, 2002.

Rummage, Everett. *Age of Napoleon: The Podcast*.

Schactman, Tom. *How the French Saved America*. New York: St. Martin's Press, 2017.

Schama, Simon. *Citizens: A Chronicle of the French Revolution*. New York: Alfred A. Knopf, 1989.

Schiff, Stacy. *A Great Improvisation: Franklin, France and the Birth of America*. New York: Henry Holt, 2005.

Scott, Samuel F. *Dictionary of the French Revolution*. Volume 1. Greenwood Press, 1985.

_____. *From Yorktown to Valmy: The Transformation of the French Army in an Age of Revolution*. Boulder: Colorado University Press, 1998.

Selesky, Harold. *Encyclopedia of the American Revolution.* 2 volumes. New York: Charles Scribner, 2006.

Shea, J.G. *The Operations of the French Fleet under the Count de Grasse, 1781–1782.* New York: De Capo Press, 1971.

Shelley, Gerard. *The Memoirs and Anecdotes of the Count de Segur.* New York: Charles Scribner, 1928.

Six, George. *Dictionnaire de Biographie des Generaux et Amiraux Français de la Revolution et l'Empire.* Volumes 1 and 2. Paris: Librairie Historique et Nobilaire, 1934.

_____. *Les Generaux de la Revolution et l'Empire.* Paris: Bordas, 1947.

Smith, Digby. *An Illustrated Encyclopedia of Uniforms of the American War of Independence.* Seattle, WA: Lorenz Books, 2021.

_____. *Napoleon's Regiments: Battle Histoies of the Regiments of the French Army, 1792–1815.* London: Greenhill Books, 2000.

Smith, Jay M. *The French Nobility in the Eighteenth Century*. College Station, PA: Penn State University Press, 2006.

_____. *Nobility Reimagined: The Patriotic Nation in Eighteenth-Century France*. Ithaca, NY: Cornell University Press, 2005.

Soboul, Albert. *Dictionnaire Historique de la Revolution Française*. Paris: Presses Universitaires de France, 1789.

Stephenson, Alex. *Napoleonic Quarterly: The Podcast*.

Steward, T.G. *Blank Santo Domingo Legion saved the patriot army at the siege of Svannah*. American Negro Academy, 1899. Project Gutenberg (reprint), 2010.

Susane, Louis. *Histoire de l'Ancienne Infanterie Française*. Volume 4. London: Forgotten Books (reprint), 2018.

Swan, Julian. *The Crisis of the Monarchy: France from the Old Regime to Revolution*. London: British Academy, 2013.

Symonds, Craig. *A Battlefield Atlas of the American Revolution*. El Dorado Hills, CA: Sava Beatie, 2018.

Taafe, Stephen. *Washington's Revolutionary War Generals*. Norman: University of Oklahoma Press, 2019.

Taillemite, Etienne. *Bougainville*. Paris: Perrin, 2011.

_____. *Dictionnaire des Marins Français*. 2nd edition. Paris: Tallandier, 2002.

_____. *L'Histoire Ignorée de la Marine Française*. Paris: Perrin, 1988.

_____. *Louis XVI, ou le navigateur immobile*. Paris: Payot, 2002.

Terraine, John. *Trafalgar*. London: Wordsworth Editions, 1976.

Toll, Ian. *Six Frigates: The Epic History of the Founding of the U.S. Navy*. New York: WW Norton, 2008.

Tozzi, Christopher. *Nationalizing France's Army: Foreign, Black and Jewish Troops in the French Military, 1715–1831*. Charlottesville: University of Virginia Press, 2016.

Tuchman, Barbara. *The First Salute: A View of the American Revolution*. New York: Knopf, 1988.

Tulard, Jean. *Dictionnarie Napoleon*. Paris: Fayard, 1989.

_____. *Napoleon et quarante million de sujets*. Paris: Tallendier, 2014.

Van Crefeld, Martin. *Supplying War: Logistics from Wallenstein to Patton*. Cambridge: Cambridge University Press, 1979.

Wenger, William. *The Key to American Independence: Quantifying Foreign Assistance to the American Revolution*. Amazon, 2018.

Whitridge, Arnold. *Rochambeau: America's Neglected Founding Father*. New York: Macmillan Co., 1965.

Willis, Sam. *The Struggle for Sea Power: a naval history of the American Revolution*. New York: Norton, 2015.

Wood, W.J. *Battles of the Revolutionary War*. Chapel Hill: Algonquin Books, 1990.

Index

A

Aboukir Bay, battle of...66, 67, 99, 103, 110, 118, 123, 173, 200, 411, 426
Aboville
  Augstin-Gabriel............ 203
  François-Marie, comte d'9, 202
  Julien, general............... 202
Ache de Serquigny............... 81
Albert de Rions 81, 100
Albert de Saint-Hippolyte . 82
Amblimont........................... 83
Andigne 204
Andrault
  Louis, marquis de
    Langeron............. 40, 204
Angely 39, 207
Anselme 207
Anselme de la Gardette ... 206
Apchon........*See* Saint-Germain
Arlande de Salton.............. 208
Armée du Nord.58, 61, 73, 74, 202, 218, 246, 254, 256, 274, 283, 289, 300, 326, 328, 336, 338, 358, 362, 370
  Arros d'..................................84
  Arrot......................................246
Attel de Luttange............... 211
Aubert du Bayet........ 211, 425
Audibert de Ramatuelle 85
Austerlitz, battle of.....40, 205, 266, 426

B

Bacqua 86

Barazer de Kermorvan..... 213
Barney.................................86
Barras 16, 45, 87, 88, 102, 120, 137, 157, 184, 390, 412
Barre.................................89
Baville.................................213
Beaumarchais 18, 54, 268
Beaumont d'Antichamp...214
Beauvoir de Chastellux 232
Bedout..............................64, 90
Belley 24, 215, 216
Berezina, battle of....205, 426
Berthier
  Louis Alexandre, Prince
    de Neuchatel and
    Wagram ... 61, 217, 242, 266, 280, 288, 310, 339, 424, 425
Besse 24, 25, 220, 221
Bethisy............................. 4, 221
Beville............................222
Beville de Pont: 223
Binet de Marcognet..........223
Biron......................*See* Gontaut
Blanchard 9, 225
Bodinier......vii, 3, 5, 34, 76, 78
Bonaparte........... *See* Napoleon
Borda................... 91, 108, 130
Bougainville........ 92, 143, 388, 416, 427, 429
Boulainvilliers 93
Boyvin de la Martiniere ...225
Brach.................................94
Brentano 226
Bressoles.............................227
Breugnon 94
Briqueville...........................95

Broglie 222, 227, 265, 296, 298

Brueys 65, 67, 97, 99, 103, 110, 118, 160, 197, 200, 389, 426

Bruix 96, 97, 120, 154, 420, 427

Bruyeres 99

Buchold 229

C

Caffarelli 100

Cambis 101

Canada . 3, 21, 22, 31, 88, 120, 156, 159, 194, 250, 303, 304

Capellis 42, 102, 427

Caribbean ..... iii, 14, 19, 22, 23, 41, 54, 58, 72, 120, 211, 215

Casabianca 99, 103

Castellane Majastres 104

Casteras de Seignan
    Raphael 229

Chabannes
    Jean Frederic, marquis de
        la Palice 230

Chabert 105, 109, 381

Champagny 106

Champion de Cice 107

Chandeon de la Valette 231

Chapuis de Tourville 231

Charité, Charles Comte de
    107

Charleston, siege of .... iv, 48, 108, 112, 262, 268, 301, 349, 359

Chastenet de Puysegur 108

Chaussegros
    François, comte de Lery
        233
    Martin Benoit 108

Chayla 109, 427

Cherisey 110

Choin de Montchoisy 234

Choisy 7
    Claude Gabriel, marquis
        de 235
    Duc de 7

Cillart 111, 198

Cillart de Villeneuve . 111, *See* Cillart

Clark 236

Closen de Haydenbourg .. 236

Cocherel 238

Coetnempren 111

Coigny 238

Colbert 113

Collot 239

Consulate .... v, 53, 77, 279

Continental Army 3, 10, 46, 47, 53, 55, 57, 141, 213, 233, 240, 251, 262, 263, 264, 268, 272, 274, 281, 282, 285, 291, 299, 301, 303, 312, 313, 322, 334, 335, 344, 349, 353, 360, 361, 362, 366, 372, 379, 385, 397, 419

Continental Navy 20, 70, 86, 143, 317

Conway 75, 240, 299, 323

Coriolis d'Espinousse 114

Coueret de Secqueville 114

Couturier 115

Croizet 116

Cromot de Bourg 241

Crublier d'Opterre 241

Custine de Sarrebeck 242

D

d'Estaing 4, 12, 13, 18, 23, 54, 63, 84, 85, 88, 91, 92, 94, 99, 100, 101, 104, 105, 109, 115, 116, 123, 125, 127, 130, 131,

133, 135, 140, 141, 151, 158,
159, 161, 163, 166, 169, 173,
174, 175, 177, 179, 182, 183,
186, 191, 193, 196, 198, 275,
280, 292, 311, 313, 324, 355,
364, 366, 369, 379, 382, 387,
389, 391, 392, 393, 395, 403,
406, 414, 415, 420, 421, 426
Dallemagne............... 243
Dalmas de Pracontal......... 244
Damas d'Antigny 245
Dampierre............................ 116
Dardenne............................. 246
Daurier 247
Deane, Silas 20, 46, 49, 157,
291, 313, 362
Decres........ 117, 136, 181, 427
Delmas................................. 248
Delmotte 119
Denis de la Ronde 249
Des Hayes de La Radiere 251
Desandrouins 9, 250
Desbordes 250
Destouches..15, 102, 120, 138
Deux-Ponts 8, 10, 37, 45, 237,
270, 277, 278, 291, 365, 371,
390, 405, 421, 425
Devrigny 251
Dezoteux de Cormatin 252
Digonet................................. 253
Dillon
    Arthur................... 4, 73, 253
    Barthelemy 75
    Edouard.......................... 295
    François Theobald Comte
    de................................. 254
    François Theobald, comte
    de................................. 74
    Guillaume 75

Regiment.4, 10, 37, 73, 75,
229, 254, 256, 310,
325, 328, 329, 351, 352
Theobald Chevalier........73,
256, 429
Dillon,
    Robert Guillaume 255
Directory 64, 89, 236, 359
Dorre..................................122
Du Buyssonc des Aix..........264
du Houx.................*See* Viomenil
Du Lau d'Allemans.............261
du Portail.... *See* Duportail, *See*
Duportail
Dumas....... 265, 339, 425, 428
Duportail.....20, 46, 47, 48, 49,
50, 53, 425
Durand.................................267
Duval...................................267

E

Egypt67, 93, 97, 99, 118, 197,
218, 273
Emeriau de Beauverger...123
Empire .. 29, 53, 77, 192, 203,
219, 224, 226, 234, 237, 247,
273, 289, 290, 308, 351, 428,
438
Enfant.......................48, 79, 268
Ervoil 269
Esebeck...................................270
Estaing ....*See* d'Estaing
Estates General .. 73, 106, 141,
145, 228, 230, 238, 242, 254,
283, 293, 295, 297, 304, 321,
325, 343, 356, 361
Ethis de Corny 9, 271
Eustace..................................272

F

Felix d'Olliere.......................272

Fersen, Axel, count.44, 45, 46, 270, 273, 425

Flanders 49, 202, 217, 235, 332

Fleuriot de Langle 126

Fleury 46, 48, 49

Fontanges 275

Fontbonne 276

Forbach des Deux-Ponts
  Christian, comte and
    marquise de..............277
  Guillaume Philippe,
    vicomte and comte.278

Franklin, Benjamin 46, 47, 57, 208

French Revolution...28, 35, 41, 76, 316, 423

G

Galaup
  Jean Fraçois, comte de
    Laperouse 127

Ganteaume..64, 136, 150, 162

Gau de Voves 279

Gaultier de Kerveguen......280

Gauthier de Murnan..........281

Gimat de Soubadere..........282

Glandevez de Castellet 128

Goullet de la Tour..............284

Gouvion...................47, 48, 285

Granchain de Semervile...129

Gras...130

Grasse... 15, 16, 45, 55, 61, 72, 82, 83, 84, 98, 104, 105, 107, 117, 121, 123, 129, 130, 131, 133, 138, 141, 142, 148, 153, 155, 158, 165, 166, 168, 176, 177, 184, 188, 190, 194, 195, 382, 386, 387, 391, 393, 403, 404, 409, 415, 416

Grasse du Bar ....See Grasse

Grasse-Limermont 132

Great Britain......20, 31, 52, 54, 58, 170

Grenier de Cauville...........286

Grimouart.............................133

Guerin de la Chaise...........286

Guichen..14, 16, 83, 107, 114, 128, 130, 136, 147, 153, 155, 158, 163, 167, 186, 188, 194, 307, 354, 393, 406, 411

H

Haiti.........See Saint-Domingue

Hamilton, Alexander ..57, 236

honneurs de la cour 35, 73, 80, 124, 214, 221, 227, 230, 232, 236, 242, 253, 256, 257, 258, 260, 261, 275, 282, 293, 295, 297, 300, 308, 318, 319, 324, 345, 347, 348, 350, 355, 356, 389

Houx de Viomenil ....*See* Viomenil

Huon de Kermadec...........134

I

Infernet 135

J

Jemappes, battle of... 123, 288

Jennings de Kilmaine.75, 287

Jourdan......232, 288, 290, 424

K

Kalb 18, 20, 53, 264, 291, 344

Kergariou-Locmaria 136

L

l'Armée d'Italie218, 243, 248, 276, 280, 288, 292, 308, 315, 330, 334, 352, 364, 371, 396

L'Eveille............................25, 306
L'Hermite.............................. 148
La Barre................................. 292
La Clocheterie...................... 137
La Croix........................ 104, 292
La Galissoniere.................... 138
La Jonquiere.....................77, 78
La Laune de Saint Didier. 139
La Motte Picquet....... 116, 139, 168, 387, 406
La Poype 140
La Roche Kerandraon....... 141
La Roche-Fonteville 300
Lafargue 142
Lafayette...........*See* Motier, *See* Motier
Lafitte ....*See* Lafitte de Montagut
Lafitte de Montagut........... 294
Lameth
    Alexandre Theodore, chevalier de ... 293, 295, 296, 428
    Charles Malo, comte de 297, 428
Landais 143
Langeron..............*See* Andrault
Langlois 240, 298
Laprun 299
Latouche-Treville 124, 127, 144, 155
Lauberdiere .... *See* Tenet de Lauberdiere
Laumoy 47, 301
Lauzun Legion.........iv, 7, 8, 74, 102, 247, 251, 254, 255, 283, 287, 308, 313, 352, 378, 380, 398, 399
Lavilleon de la Villevalio. 142
Le Begue de Germiny 147
Le Cat..................................... 302

Le Gardeur de Tilly............ 146
Le Maire de Gimel 303
Le Monnier........................... 303
Le Noir 304
Le Prestre 305
Le Saige.................................. 147
Leclerc ... 26, 27, 62, 217, 307, 342, 371
Lecrere................................... 306
Liegard................................... 307
Lodi, battle of ...218, 243, 424
Lomenie.................................. 308
Loppin 309
Louis XIV 51
Louis XV 51, 255, 345
Louis XVI.... iv, 20, 41, 46, 50, 51, 52, 55, 74, 82, 128, 157, 167, 210, 224, 225, 251, 265, 285, 291, 427, 445, 447, 452
Louis XVIII65, 152, 230, 266, 305
Lowenhorn 150, 427
Lucas,.. 151
Lynch 75, 309

M

MacCarthy de Marteigue.152
MacDonald 310
MacMahon.............................311
Maistral.................................. 154
Maitz 156
Marigny.................................. 157
Martel..................................... 158
Martin........ 117, 119, 159, 200
Mauduit du Plessis............. 312
Mauroy.................................... 313
Medine 153
Medine d'Isambert.............. 160
Mezieres...........*See* Wuibert de Mezieres
Mieszkosky............................. 313

Milfort...........314
Minden, battle of55, 238, 300, 320, 417, 423
Miollis...............315
Miranda..........56, 58, 316, 429
Missiessy...............161
Monier..................164
Montcabrier.................163
Montclair..................164
Monteil..7, 165, 167, 180, 383
Monteuil 317
Montmorency............. 42, 318
Morel...............319
Motier...............319
Mottin de la Balme...........322
Mullens..............75, 323

N

Nadal...............323
Napoleon 27, 30, 61, 73, 99, 136, 145, 152, 189, 200, 203, 219, 248, 254, 258, 266, 267, 268, 276, 279, 294, 315, 351, 357, 424, 441, 448
Nauckhoff..................... 43, 166
Netherlands 40, 246, 260
Noailles, Louis Marie, vicomte de ...4, 223, 261, 264, 320, 324, 350, 428

O

O'Keefe 75, 325
O'Moran.............328, 372
O'Neill 75, 329
Olonne
   Alexandre Paul, chevalier d' 327
   Pierre François, comte de 326
Orillard de Villemanzy 329
Osmond..............331

P

Palys de Montrepot........... 331
Parscau du Plessix............. 167
Patel.................... 332
Penot Lombard de la Neuville 333
Pensacola, siege of..... iv, 7, 11, 24, 26, 57, 69, 71, 147, 165, 166, 167, 180, 316, 374, 383, 384, 408, 410, 429
Pierre 333
Pitray....................... 168
Pleville Le Pelley .64, 97, 168, 192
Ponteves-Gien 171
Poudenx 334
Preudhomme de Borre.... 335
Prevost 336
Prevost de Sansac....... 41, 188
Pulaski Legion 49

Q

Quentin de Richebourg de Champcenetz 336
Quesne..................... 172
Queyssat 337

R

Racord.................... 172
Raffet.................... 338
Raimondis 173, 174
Renaud d' Aleins............... 174
Restoration......42, 43, 75, 113, 124, 142, 161, 163, 181, 203, 204, 224, 239, 245, 246, 248, 256, 258, 266, 279, 294, 318, 321, 337, 357, 426, 428, 429
Revolution...............See French Revolution
Rey............................. 339

Ricci 340
Richery 175
Rigaud
   Andre 26, 341
   Jean Louis, vicomte de
     Vaudreuil 341
   Louis Philippe, marquis de
     Vaudreuil 193
   Louis, comte de Vaudreuil
     .... 24, 27, 176
Riquetti 342
Robespierre 61, 63, 93, 192
Rochambeau
   Donatien Marie 62, 370
   Jean Baptiste Vimeur,
   marquis and comte de
   .5, 7, 8, 9, 10, 14, 16, 27,
   40, 44, 45, 50, 55, 60,
   61, 62, 107, 119, 127,
   129, 130, 131, 137,
   154, 157, 184, 185,
   193, 194, 202, 206,
   207, 209, 214, 217,
   218, 222, 223, 225,
   227, 229, 230, 232,
   234, 237, 238, 239,
   241, 244, 245, 246,
   247, 249, 250, 253,
   255,257, 260, 261, 265,
   269, 270, 271, 272,
   273, 277, 278, 279,
   283, 284, 293, 295,
   296, 297, 299, 303,
   305, 310, 315, 323,
   324, 329, 332, 353,
   354, 357, 365, 368,
   375, 376, 377, 385,
   390, 401, 405, 412,
   417, 420, 423, 424, 425
Roche Fermoy 343
Rochefontaine 344

Roqueplan de Lestrade 345
Rossel, ... 176
Rostaing 345
Rouge 346
Rouvroy
   Claude Henry, comte de
     Saint--Simon 348
   Claude, baron de Saint-
     Simon 347
Ruffo 177
Russia.40, 41, 42, 43, 57, 102,
205, 206, 208, 325, 350, 355,
356, 367, 426, 427

S

Sainneville 178
Saint-Domingue.. 4, 21, 22, 23,
24, 25, 26, 27, 62, 90, 96, 98,
102, 120, 122, 124, 134, 138,
145, 146, 149, 154, 180, 187,
190, 195, 215, 216, 217, 220,
238, 247, 248, 261, 262, 276,
280, 294, 300, 304, 305, 306,
307, 325, 326, 331, 333, 334,
339, 341, 342, 343, 344, 346,
364, 366, 371, 372, 373, 374,
375, 380, 390, 397, 410, 416,
434
Saint-Germain
   Chevalier d'Apchon 47, 84,
     262, 410
Saint-Quentin 348
Saint-Simon .... *See* Rouvroy,
Claude, baron de, *See*
Rouvroy, Claude Henry,
comte de
Sambucy de Luzenson 178
Santhonax 25, 26, 220, 307
Saqui des Tourres 179
Segon de Sederon 349
Segur 33, 350, 351, 429

Sercey............................149, 180
Seven Years' War....iii, 31, 68, 82, 178, 185, 294
Sheldon............................ 75, 351
Sibaud..............................352
Silvestre de Valfort............353
Six..............................77, 78
George 234, 246, 345, 347, 350, 360
Society of Cincinnati............ See Society of Cincinnatus
Society of Cincinnatus........61, 265
Soulange..............................182
Stack de Crotto..........354, 426
Stedingk............ 4, 43, 355, 425
Suffren .15, 16, 100, 122, 128, 141, 175, 182, 187, 389, 395, 396, 411, 427
Sweden..44, 46, 273, 355, 425

T

Talleyrand-Perigord..........356
Tanouarn..............................184
Tarle..............................9, 357
Tenet de Lauberdiere........358
Ternant..............................358
Ternay.... 14, 15, 88, 102, 111, 119, 120, 127, 129, 138, 147, 148, 160, 184, 198, 390, 409, 415, 420
Terrasse de Tessonnet.....359
Thevet de Lessert..............360
Thibault de Menonville....361
Thierry.........See Thierry de La Prevalaye
Thierry de La Prevalaye ..185
Thomassin............................186
Thy..............................187
Toulon, siege of12, 63, 67, 82, 83, 97, 99, 109, 117, 124,

125, 132, 133, 145, 158, 159, 160, 162, 163, 172, 173, 178, 190, 191, 192, 193, 196, 197, 199, 200, 242, 243, 244, 292, 334, 396, 407
Tourville.............................. 361
Trafalgar, battle of.......67, 136, 145, 152, 154, 155, 170, 201, 426
Traversay..........See Prevost de Sansac
Trogoff de Kerlessy........... 189
Tromelin.............................. 190
Tronson de Coudray....20, 48, 362
Truguet...63, 64, 98, 149, 162, 173, 191, 199, 426, 427
Tuffin.............................. 209
Tuileries... 257, 298, 302, 317, 337, 425

V

Vallongue.............................. 193
Vallou de Villeneuve......... 363
Vaudreuil....See Rigaud, Louis, comte de Vaudreuil, See Rigaud, Louis Philippe, marquis de Vaudreuil
Vaugirard de Rosnay........ 194
Vence.............................. 195
Verdun de la Crenne......... 197
Verger............................ 365, 425
Verger de Barreaux........... 364
Vienne.............................. 366
Vienot de Vaublanc........... 366
Vigoureux.............................. 367
Villeneuve.... 65, 66, 118, 136, 154, 155, 162, 199, 200, 201, 426
Vimeur..........See Rochambeau Viomenil

Antoine Chales, Baron du
.... 6, 257, 406, 424
Antoine Louis Chevalier
.... 43, 259
Charles Gabriel.............. 258
Joseph Hyacinthe,
marquis du 42, 260,
424
volontaires de Saint
Dominique 4

W

Wagram, battle of 266, 424
War of Independence.... iii, v, 3,
34, 39, 50, 63, 76, 77, 79,
125, 150, 166, 180, 275, 417
Washington
George........... 237, 240, 285
Washington, George......45, 48,
57, 89, 130, 269, 293, 316,
320
Waterloo, battle of....... 80, 224
Wisch....................................... 371

Wuibert de Mezieres.......... 372

Y

Yorktown, battle of.iii, iv, 5, 6,
7, 10, 11, 15, 16, 45, 48, 50,
55, 57, 60, 62, 73, 74, 75, 88,
90, 107, 111, 121, 129, 147,
157, 167, 184, 199, 202, 210,
211, 214, 215, 222, 223, 227,
231, 232, 235, 237, 241, 242,
247, 248, 250, 253, 254, 256,
260, 261, 263, 267, 272, 274,
276, 277, 278, 281, 282, 283,
284, 285, 286, 293, 294, 295,
297, 299, 300, 305, 306, 307,
308, 310, 312, 313, 315, 318,
320, 321, 323, 324, 331, 332,
334, 336, 343, 344, 345, 346,
347, 348, 352, 358, 361, 369,
370, 371, 377, 383, 397, 399,
400, 405, 407, 408, 412, 413,
417, 419, 423, 424, 425